English Historical Pragmatics

D1610658

Edinburgh Textbooks on the English Language – Advanced

General Editor
Heinz Giegerich, Professor of English Linguistics, University of Edinburgh

Editorial Board
Laurie Bauer (University of Wellington)
Olga Fischer (University of Amsterdam)
Rochelle Lieber (University of New Hampshire)
Norman Macleod (University of Edinburgh)
Donka Minkova (UCLA)
Edgar W. Schneider (University of Regensburg)
Katie Wales (University of Leeds)
Anthony Warner (University of York)

English Historical Pragmatics

Andreas H. Jucker and Irma Taavitsainen

EDINBURGH
University Press

© Andreas H. Jucker and Irma Taavitsainen, 2013

Edinburgh University Press Ltd
22 George Square, Edinburgh EH8 9LF

www.euppublishing.com

Typeset in 10.5/12 Janson by
Servis Filmsetting Ltd, Stockport, Cheshire,
and printed and bound in Great Britain by
CPI Group (UK) Ltd, Croydon CR0 4YY

A CIP record for this book is available from the British Library

ISBN 978 0 7486 4469 8 (hardback)
ISBN 978 0 7486 4468 1 (paperback)
ISBN 978 0 7486 4470 4 (webready PDF)
ISBN 978 0 7486 7789 4 (epub)

Contents

Figures and tables

To readers

This textbook is designed to introduce one of the most versatile fields in the historical study of English at present. It is intended for advanced undergraduates, graduate students, and students pursuing their doctoral studies, and it will also serve more advanced researchers by giving an update of the present state of scholarship in the field. It is hoped that the book will broaden its readers' views on current topics and inspire novel approaches and applications. The book presumes some familiarity with pragmatics and the history of English but all the necessary concepts are carefully introduced in the text. All pre-1500 texts are presented with a translation. The relevant examples in this book are mostly drawn from the history of the English language, which makes this book particularly suitable for use in English departments, but researchers in other languages will also profit from the ideas presented in it. The topic of this book is clearly more specialised than a general introduction to the history of English or a course book on pragmatics. Historical pragmatics has often been placed at the intersection between pragmatics and historical linguistics, but the area is, in fact, broader as its edges overlap with other neighbouring disciplines like (historical) sociolinguistics and stylistics. It is often at the interfaces where exciting new developments take place, and in our view this is the case with historical pragmatics.

Historical pragmatics studies language use in its social, cultural and above all historical context. It investigates patterns of language use in earlier periods and examines how such patterns changed over time. As such it adopts a broad and largely Continental European approach to pragmatics, which includes the social and cultural context of language use in its study of utterance interpretation. Historical pragmatics was launched in 1995 with a scholarly research volume *Historical Pragmatics: Pragmatic Developments in the History of English* (Jucker (ed.) 1995), and it has become a well-established field in its own right with a journal of its own, the *Journal of Historical Pragmatics* (2000–) and a comprehensive handbook volume, *Historical Pragmatics* (Jucker and Taavitsainen (eds)

2010). Now the first textbook has been completed. Our knowledge of communicative patterns in earlier times and their developments is still somewhat patchy, and there is room for further research. This textbook tries to strike a balance between an overview of what is already known in these fields, an outline of what is still controversial and an invitation to pursue independent research projects to extend our knowledge further. We believe that a textbook for advanced students should not present a field of study as a set of established facts, but as a range of research interests and questions, and a set of tools to tackle these questions. Thus all chapters of this textbook focus on different aspects of approaching historical data from a pragmatic perspective and give guidelines on how to pursue the topics further. In this way, we want to encourage and inspire new developments in the field.

The first three chapters are introductory. They introduce the issues and methodological considerations that inform the case studies of the later chapters. The second chapter is devoted more specifically to the data problems and to the available sources, and the third chapter to the methodologies in historical pragmatics. Chapters 4 to 6 are devoted to small units, such as discourse markers, interjections, terms of address and speech acts. Chapter 7 extends the view to different forms of politeness from Old English to Present-day English. Chapter 8 discusses a range of pragmatic explanations that have been offered as accounts for different types of language change. Chapters 9 to 11 open up the perspective to genres and text types, to the dissemination of knowledge in scientific and medical discourse, and to the development of news discourse from the early newspapers in the early seventeenth century to the Internet newspapers of the early twenty-first century. The final chapter is devoted to pragmatic issues at the interface between language and literature, which is still a fairly little charted but increasingly important area of research. It deals with narrative patterns in fairy tales and other story-telling situations and conventions. Each chapter finishes with study questions and suggestions for further reading.

We started working on this textbook by drafting the outline and chapter topics in August 2010 as a response to the invitation by Edinburgh University Press. We shared the workload evenly, produced the preliminary drafts and worked them out to their present form jointly. We have carried the work out at the Universities of Zurich and Helsinki, and we would like to thank the Departments of English and Modern Languages (respectively) for the facilities for research. We are grateful for the Research Unit for Variation, Contacts and Change at the University of Helsinki for its support in the last phase of the preparation of this book.

We discussed suitable texts to serve as examples with our colleagues, and we would like to thank Maria Salenius for pointing out John Donne's marriage sermon, Mark Shackleton for suggesting the fairy tale, and Minna Palander-Collin for a letter text which we have used in one of the exercises, and 'Ashley' deserves to be thanked as well for trusting her private messages to us. In addition to our home institutions, King's College, Cambridge deserves a special word of thanks for providing access to additional electronic resources relied on in this book.

We have tried out a draft version of this textbook with our students in Zurich and Helsinki, and we are grateful to them for their comments which helped us improve the readability and usability of this book. We are grateful to Daniela Landert for her constructive and insightful criticism of the pre-final version of the book, and to Mark Shackleton for his careful reading and polishing the manuscript for publication.

Over the years that we have been working in this field, we have had the pleasure of discussing the pertinent issues, methodologies and data, and various research topics dealt with in this book with our various colleagues with similar interests. They are too numerous to be mentioned here, but many of them are listed in the references, and we would like to extend our thanks to all of them for their inspiration. Finally, our home teams deserve a special word of thanks for their patience and support.

1 Historical pragmatics: Communicative patterns of the past

1.1 Introduction

In 1618, Sir Walter Raleigh (1552–1618), an English courtier, explorer, writer and favourite of Elizabeth I, was imprisoned and tried for treason under James I, and finally beheaded. During his trial the following exchange between him and the Attorney took place:

> 1. *Raleigh.* I do not hear yet, that you have spoken one word against me; here is no Treason of mine done: If my Lord *Cobham* be a Traitor, what is that to me?
>
> *Attorney.* All that he did was by thy Instigation, thou Viper; for I *thou* thee, thou Traitor. (*Helsinki Corpus.* E2 XX TRI RALEIGH I, 208)

The Attorney addresses Sir Walter Raleigh with *thou* rather than *you* as would have been expected in the formality of the courtroom, and he comments on his own usage, which indicates both that there was a choice between *you* and *thou* and that choosing *thou* was unexpected and needed a justification. It appears that the choice of pronoun was even more insulting in this context than the name-calling with the terms *Viper* and *Traitor.* This may seem surprising because only three hundred years earlier, *thou* was the only pronoun of address that could be used to a single addressee. By the time of Geoffrey Chaucer, at the end of the fourteenth century, both pronouns could be used for a single addressee, but the patterns of usage were still very different than at the time of William Shakespeare and Sir Walter Raleigh. In order to understand the precise impact of such usages, we need to know a great deal about patterns of language use in the past and how such patterns developed in the course of time. And this – together with a large range of similar questions – is the subject matter of historical pragmatics.

Historical pragmatics as a field of study combines pragmatics and historical linguistics. Pragmatics can be defined very simply as the study of language use. It studies language not as an abstract entity but as a means of communication that is being used by people interacting in specific situations, with specific intentions and goals and within specific contexts. Historical linguistics is interested in the ways in which language changes. Traditionally, historical studies have focused on the language system, on the sounds of language, on the structure of words and sentences and on the meanings of individual words. The two fields of pragmatics and of historical linguistics, therefore, seem to be difficult to reconcile. For the past, we do not have access to spoken material, we cannot ask native speakers, and we cannot carry out communicative experiments, and thus some of the preferred methodologies in the tool kit of today's pragmaticists are not available for the historical pragmaticists. However, over the last two decades both fields have changed quite considerably. Pragmaticists and historical linguists have extended their range of tools as well as their range of research interests. The pragmaticists have come to accept a broader range of data, including written data, as genuinely interesting objects of investigation, and the historical linguists developed an interest in patterns of language use. And the combination of expertise of both specialists has led to this new and exciting field of study: the study of patterns of language use in the past and the way in which these patterns change over time.

In the next section we are going to give an overview of the scope of pragmatics and how that applies to historical pragmatics.

1.2 The scope of pragmatics

In comparison to historical linguistics, pragmatics is still a relatively young field of inquiry. The first major textbooks appeared in the late 1970s and in the 1980s. This is also the time of the first international conferences in the field and the start of the publication of the *Journal of Pragmatics* (1977). As pointed out above, pragmatics can be defined in a preliminary way as the study of how people use language. Since the early days of pragmatics, however, definitions of the term 'pragmatics' have been controversial. It seems that pragmaticists themselves do not agree on what should be included in the field and what should not.

Even in the early textbooks two more or less distinct ways of drawing the boundaries around the academic field of pragmatics have established themselves. Huang (2007: 4) refers to these fields as Anglo-American pragmatics versus Continental European pragmatics, while Chapman (2011: 5) in another recent textbook of pragmatics suggests the terms 'theoretical pragmatics' and 'social pragmatics'. Huang's terms reflect the fact that theoretical pragmatics is generally favoured by scholars with an Anglo-American background, while Continental European scholars generally work within a social pragmatics framework. The term 'social pragmatics' indicates a crucial element of its scope. As a field of study it includes information about the social context in which language is used, about the speakers, their relationships to one another, and so on. It traces its history to the work of anthropologists and sociologists. The social pragmaticists regularly rely on actual data, preferably rich data in the sense that a lot of contextual information about the conversationalists and the context in which the interaction takes place is available. 'Theoretical pragmatics', on the other hand, lacks this social dimension. It traces its history to work in the philosophy of language. In many cases it relies on data invented by the scholar. Theoretical pragmaticists may, for instance, reflect on what it means to ask a question, to make a promise or to issue a request. Or they may be interested in the general ways in which people manage to read between the lines of utterances they hear and figure out implicit meanings.

The distinction is, of course, not watertight, but as a rough generalisation it works surprisingly well. This is particularly clear when one considers textbooks and handbooks. The choice of topics that they include and the definitions of pragmatics that they provide generally reflect Huang's terminological distinction. Handbooks and textbooks in the field of theoretical pragmatics generally focus on the core areas of pragmatics. They include the study of how people use language to perform actions, how they are able to interpret not only what their interlocutors say explicitly, but also implicit meanings and how certain linguistic elements refer to the context of language use. Similar books in social pragmatics are more likely to also include chapters on politeness, on pragmatics in educational contexts or in literature, or on language use in relation to social class, gender or regional origin of the speakers.

The field of historical pragmatics tends to adopt the broader view of social pragmatics. The historical and cultural context in which language is being used is important for our understanding of the patterns of language use. But Traugott (2004: 538) defines historical pragmatics in the theoretical or Anglo-American context as a 'usage-based approach to language change'. Pragmatics itself, according to Traugott, focuses on 'non-literal meaning that arises in language use' (2004: 539). In the context of such definitions, historical pragmatics endeavours to provide pragmatic explanations for patterns of language change. Language changes because people use it in novel ways. They shift their pronunciations, they use old words to cover new meanings, they invent new words on the basis of material borrowed from other languages, they reinterpret old structural patterns in new ways and so on. Moreover, they always do this while using language to communicate with their interlocutors. Historical pragmatics focuses on this communicative context of language change and tries to find patterns of communication that help to explain such changes on various levels of language description.

Taavitsainen and Fitzmaurice (2007: 13) adopt the broader social pragmatics or Continental European point of view when they state that 'historical pragmatics focuses on language use in past contexts and examines how meaning is made. It is an empirical branch of linguistic study, with focus on authentic language use of the past'. Jucker (2008a), likewise, adopts a broad view of pragmatics when he defines historical pragmatics as follows:

> In a broader sense adopting the more European conceptualization of pragmatics, historical pragmatics can be defined as a field of study that wants to understand the patterns of intentional human interaction (as determined by the conditions of society) of earlier periods, the historical developments of these patterns, and the general principles underlying such developments. (Jucker 2008a: 895)

This broad definition sketches out three more or less distinct subfields of historical pragmatics. The first of these investigates the communicative patterns of earlier periods and explicitly sets them in their social context. To pick up the example of the address terms at the beginning of this chapter, this branch of historical pragmatics investigates the social conditions of the use of address terms at a particular point in time. What kind of speakers used *thou* to address what kinds of addressee? And who used the pronoun *you* for the same purpose? And what was the effect of changing from one pronoun to the other in a particular social context, for example in the context of a trial at the Old Bailey? Such questions often require an interdisciplinary approach that includes not just linguistic expertise but also historical, social and cultural expertise.

The second subfield studies the development of communicative patterns. In the first instance, it would compare the use of the two pronouns of address across two different periods, for example in the works of Geoffrey Chaucer at the end of the fourteenth century and in the works of William Shakespeare at the turn of the sixteenth and seventeenth centuries. In a second step, such studies would try to complement our knowledge of the usage patterns in Chaucer's and Shakespeare's works by adding other types of data from the relevant periods to obtain a more comprehensive picture of the time of Chaucer and Shakespeare. They would then try to find additional points on the time line in order to fill in the two-hundred-year gap between Chaucer and Shakespeare and to get information about earlier and later patterns. The use of the pronoun *ye/you* for a single addressee had started in the thirteenth century and therefore already had a considerable history by the time of Chaucer. By the time of Shakespeare there are already some signs of erosion. For Chaucer it was clear that in subject position the pronoun was *ye*, in non-subject position it was *you*. Shakespeare's use, on the other hand, is often inconsistent. Both forms can appear both in subject and in non-subject position. The pronoun *thou*, moreover, could be used as an insult, as in the trial of Sir Walter Raleigh. Indeed, one hundred years after Shakespeare, the normal pronoun of address for single addressees was almost universally *you*. The inclusion of additional data points would thus turn a contrastive analysis of an earlier and a later period into an increasingly diachronic study of step-by-step developments.

The third subfield sketched out by the definition given above consists of the study of the pragmatic principles underlying language change in general, and as such it asks for the communicative principles that lead to certain changes. The first and the second subfield of historical pragmatics are clearly part of social pragmatics. They are challenging because of the broad and interdisciplinary scope of expertise that is required for a serious study. The third field is a more clearly linguistic endeavour within the confines of theoretical pragmatics. Our knowledge in this field is still severely limited. Some principles have been claimed to be strong enough to allow predictions of particular paths of development, or at least strong enough to allow predictions of what kinds of development are not possible or very unlikely. However, scholars have regularly been quick to come up with counter examples. Pragmatic principles of language change, therefore, are today usually proposed as general tendencies and not as predictive principles. We will take up this discussion in Chapter 8, when we introduce pragmatic principles that have been proposed under the label of grammaticalisation, subjectivisation and pragmaticalisation. In the other chapters we adopt the broader social pragmatics approach to historical pragmatics.

1.3 Recent paradigm changes in pragmatics and in historical linguistics

The success story of historical pragmatics over the last fifteen to twenty years must be seen in the context of several paradigm shifts that have radically altered the nature of linguistics (see Traugott 2008: 207–10 for a more comprehensive list).

1.3.1 From core areas to sociolinguistics and pragmatics

The first paradigm shift concerns the shift from core areas of linguistic investigation, i.e. phonetics, phonology, morphology, syntax and semantics to areas such as sociolinguistics and pragmatics. 'What was marginal in the 1970's has come to be of central interest, above all pragmatics' (Traugott 2008: 207). Hesitations, repetitions, interjections, discourse markers and so on are no longer seen as irrelevant deviations. On the contrary, they have come to be recognised as highly regular and systematic. Sociolinguistics and pragmatics established themselves as important branches of linguistics, and within a relatively short period of time some scholars no longer saw these fields as branches of linguistics, but as linguistics in general. For sociolinguists, linguistic investigations always have to consider the social context of the speakers, and therefore, linguistics properly understood is always sociolinguistics. Likewise for pragmaticists, linguistics properly understood is always linguistics from a pragmatic perspective because language cannot be studied adequately unless the context of use is taken into consideration.

1.3.2 From homogeneity to heterogeneity

The second shift is the shift from homogeneity to heterogeneity. Linguists from the 1970s were interested in a coherent and homogeneous language system. They ignored idiosyncrasies as irrelevant deviations that must be ignored for the sake of workable generalisations. But in the course of time, scholars became more and more interested in these 'irrelevant deviations'. Language is not homogeneous but heterogenous, and the variability of language became the focus of attention. This shift had far-reaching implications also for the kind of data that can be used for linguistic investigations. A scholar who searches for the generalisations of a largely homogeneous language system necessarily concentrates on data that reflects this system in an undiluted and undefiled way. Chomsky was very explicit about his interest in a language system free of irrelevant corruptions. Such a system could only be accessed through the intuition of a competent native speaker. This intuition in his opinion is free from the vagaries of speech production which potentially involve lack of concentration, distraction, tiredness and other irrelevancies. With a shift to precisely these vagaries and to heterogeneity the range of acceptable data increased drastically. In fact, all traces of communicative behaviour became interesting and relevant, but none of them can be taken – without further investigation – to reveal the system of language as a whole. Specific data – first and foremost – reveals the usage patterns in this type of data and in similar types of data. The differences between different instantiations of language are no longer annoying disturbances in the data but are instead the focus of the pragmaticist's interest.

1.3.3 From internalised to externalised language

Concomitant with the shift from homogeneous to heterogeneous language descriptions there was a shift from internalised language to externalised language. In the 1960s and 1970s of the last century, linguists were interested in the native speaker's competence, that is to say their internalised language system, the homogeneous language system in their brain. Actual language use, externalised language, was of little interest in itself because it only offered an imperfect reflection of the internalised system. Externalised language was seen as affected by irrelevant errors due to interruptions, digressions, insufficient concentration, exhaustion and so on. But in the 1970s and 1980s, linguists turned their attention to the investigation of externalised language, and they found it to be highly regular. Externalised language was generally understood as spoken language, which was transcribed to make it available for inspection and close scrutiny.

1.3.4 From introspection to empirical investigation

As a result of this shift in interest, introspection, which had been seen as the most reliable tool for the investigation of the internalised language system, was no longer acceptable. Externalised language was seen as defective in two ways. It contained irrelevant errors that were not part of the language system and – perhaps even more seriously – it never contained all the possible sentences of a language. The language system allows for an infinite number of possible sentences, while a text as a collection of sentences can only contain a limited and necessarily finite number of sentences. With the shift from internalised language to externalised language as an object of study, the investigation turned from introspection to empirical investigation. Some scholars influenced by anthropological and ethnomethodological studies focused on detailed transcriptions of very brief extracts from naturally occurring conversations, while other scholars started to compile and use increasingly larger and larger corpora. In the 1980s, corpora of one million words were considered as standard size. In the 1990s, the *British National Corpus* reached a new dimension with one hundred million words, and currently the *Corpus of Contemporary American English* (COCA) and the

Corpus of Historical American English (COHA) both contain over 400 million words. At the same time and in the same shift from introspection to empirical investigations, pragmatics also developed a range of experimental methods, such as discourse completion tasks, role-plays and the like, to elicit language in controlled situations.

Historical pragmatics profits significantly from the advances in corpus technology. In recent years, considerable progress has been made in the compilation, in the search technologies and in particular in the annotation of corpora. These advances are very likely to have a major impact on research efforts within historical pragmatics. We will present the most important developments in the following two chapters.

1.3.5 Renewed interest in diachrony

The 1980s also saw a renewed interest in diachronic studies after several decades that had been dominated by synchronic linguistics, and this shift, too, is closely linked with other paradigm shifts. Language change cannot be investigated by introspection, and it cannot be investigated on the basis of internalised language. Diachronic studies rely on the externalised evidence of language from earlier periods and on empirical methods of investigating the evidence. Language change is an ongoing process, and it is reflected in the heterogeneity of language at any given point in time. Language always contains some old-fashioned elements used only by some, usually older, speakers in some situations. It also contains current elements used by most speakers in most situations, and innovative elements used by some, usually younger, speakers. Thus synchronic heterogeneity is both a reflection of and a precondition for diachronic change.

It is in this context of research interests prevalent in the early 1990s that historical pragmatics started to develop. It focused on those elements in historical sources that had very often been ignored by earlier scholars, on marginal elements and on the evidence of language use. From the very beginning it focused on the heterogeneity of the material and gave due consideration to different types of data. In hindsight this was perhaps the most significant shift for the field of historical pragmatics because it made it possible to work with a great variety of sources. Fictional language, the language of the courtroom and the language of private correspondence could be analysed within their own conditions and limitations. These sources were no longer required to be more or less perfect reflections of a homogeneous, underlying language system. Earlier scholars would not have accepted plays as possible data sources on the grounds that fictional language is artificial, constructed and does not reflect actual language use. Within the new paradigm, plays are seen as legitimate sources of data because they are interesting as one particular type of language; they are not seen as a substitute for 'the real thing'. Obviously, historical investigations rely on empirical methods of investigation, and the fact that historical corpora started to become available in the early 1990s, most notably the *Helsinki Corpus*, was a decisive factor in establishing historical pragmatics as a field of study.

1.3.6 From stable to discursive features

A more recent paradigm shift in pragmatics is the shift from stable to dynamic features or from fixed to discursive forms. Politeness, for instance, had long been taken to be a concept that can be correlated with specific linguistic forms, which are either polite because speakers who use them refrain from imposing on their addressees or because they express their appreciation of their addressees (see Chapter 7). In more recent work, however, politeness is seen as discursively constructed; it cannot be linked in a direct way to specific linguistic forms. In a similar way, gender is no longer seen to be a purely biological distinction. The more important aspect is the way in which gender is discursively negotiated, and, to give a third example, it has long been recognised that the context is always important for the interpretation of language. But context, too, is no longer seen as a fixed entity. There are far too many possible contexts for each and every utterance if both the immediate linguistic and non-linguistic as well as all sorts of larger historical, social and cultural contexts are taken into consideration. What is relevant for the interpretation by the analyst is the way in which the interlocutors discursively construct relevant contexts.

1.4 Communicative patterns of the past

The following two chapters of this book will continue the introductory survey. Chapter 2 will be devoted to data problems. Such problems have always been a major concern of historical pragmatics. Until recently, pragmatics shunned written sources as data. It was either based on intuition, for example in the philosophical investigations of speech acts, presupposition, deixis and implicatures, or it was based on recordings of spoken language. Neither of these avenues is available for historical investigations and, therefore, historical pragmaticists for a long time had to defend and justify the appropriateness of written data for their investigations. Attitudes towards the appropriateness of linguistic data for pragmatic investigations have shifted considerably in recent years, and this is the topic of Chapter 2.

In Chapter 3, we will give an overview of the range of methods available to historical pragmaticists. The various applications of these methods will reappear in the subsequent chapters, but in Chapter 3 we will present them in a systematic overview. The historical pragmaticist has access to an arsenal of tools for a range of different tasks, and it is the purpose of this chapter to present the entire arsenal or tool kit so that the tools are ready to be used later on, and the chapters can concentrate on the actual issues rather than on the introduction of the tools.

Chapters 4 to 7 are devoted to micro elements. Chapter 4 deals with discourse markers and interjections. Chapter 5 introduces terms of address. This includes not only the pronouns *thou* and *ye* and the option of choosing one or the other depending on the relationship between the speaker and the addressee in any given situation, but also nominal terms of address, such as terms of endearment, honorific titles, professional titles and expletives. Chapter 6 looks at the actions that are performed through the use of language. How do people apologise? How do they issue requests, pay compliments, or insult each other? The last chapter in this sequence, Chapter 7, is devoted to issues of politeness.

Chapter 8 is a pivot chapter that links the earlier with the later chapters. It deals with the underlying principles of language change. The first of the four remaining chapters, Chapter 9, takes a macro approach and introduces contextual issues. Communicative patterns are contextualised in larger units, i.e. genres, that is to say in texts that share characteristic features. Chapters 10 to 12, finally, present the issues of the preceding chapters in a larger context, in the context of medical discourse and news discourse, and in the context of fictional literature.

Exercises

1. The following definitions of the field of pragmatics have appeared in recent textbooks or handbooks of pragmatics. Do they define pragmatics with a theoretical (Anglo-American) or with a social (Continental-European) scope?

   Pragmatics studies the use of language in human communication as determined by the conditions of society. (Mey 2001: 6)

   [. . .] pragmatics is the study of those context-dependent aspects of meaning which are systematically abstracted away from in the construction of content or logical form. (Horn and Ward 2004: xi)

Pragmatics is concerned not just with who we are as human beings, but with how we use language to do all the various things that enable us to relate to, understand and possibly influence other people: describing the world around us, learning about how others feel about things, getting other people to do things for us, as well as many other examples. (Chapman 2011: 4)

[. . .] pragmatics may be defined as the systematic study of meaning by virtue of, or dependent on, the use of language. The central topics of inquiry include implicature, presupposition, speech acts, deixis, and reference, all of which originate in 20th-century analytic(al) philosophy. (Huang 2012: 1)

2. The *Journal of Historical Pragmatics* regularly publishes papers from both within the theoretical and the social tradition. For the following four papers, decide which tradition they belong to:

   a) One paper analyses a range of discourse contexts in which the adverbial *in fact* developed in the history of English. In Present-day English it can mean 'in practice, as far as we can tell from the available evidence', it can have an adversative meaning akin to 'certainly' and 'however', and it can be used for rhetorical purposes meaning 'what's more, indeed'. The paper traces the different uses in the history of English and identifies the pragmatic processes that are at work. (Schwenter and Traugott 2000)

   b) A second paper is devoted to the Salem witchcraft trials in 1692 and the discourse strategies adopted by the defendants. The paper uses a politeness-theoretic framework and investigates the differences between the discourse strategies that turned out to save the lives of the defendants and those that did not. It appears that cooperativeness was vital in the process, admitting the accusation but denying intentionality. (Kahlas-Tarkka and Rissanen 2007)

   c) A third paper studies expressions of sincerity, sarcasm and seriousness in the correspondence of Maria Thynne at the beginning of the seventeenth century. The paper shows how Maria Thynne used her stylistic repertoire in her interaction with various members of her family, and it speculates on the significance of such repertoires in the Early Modern period for the development of sarcasm in English. (Williams 2010)

   d) And a fourth paper traces the history of the Present-day English expletive *gee!*, which goes back to the religious name *Jesus*. The name developed gradually into the interjection *Jesus!* and from the interjection in a more abrupt change into the expletive *gee!*

The paper identifies the pragmatic processes that are at work in this change. (Gehweiler 2008)

Further reading

There are a great number of textbooks and handbooks in pragmatics. Huang (2007) and Chapman (2011) are two recent textbooks that are explicitly devoted to theoretical pragmatics (as Chapman 2011: 5 calls it) or Anglo-American pragmatics (as Huang 2007: 4 calls it). Mey (2001) and Verschueren (1999) are textbooks that adopt the broader social pragmatics or European Continental pragmatics tradition. Handbooks devoted to theoretical pragmatics are, for instance, Horn and Ward (2004), while the handbook series edited by Bublitz et al. or the handbooks by Verschueren et al. (2003) or Mey (2009) adopt the wider social pragmatics perspective.

So far there are no relevant textbooks in historical pragmatics, but a handbook has recently been published (Jucker and Taavitsainen 2010). The papers in this volume give comprehensive overviews of the state of the art in all subfields of historical pragmatics. They are useful for an up-to-date outline of research issues and current research. Good introductions to the entire field of historical pragmatics can also be found in Taavitsainen and Fitzmaurice (2007) and in several handbook articles on historical pragmatics (e.g. Brinton 2001; Jucker 2006a, 2008a, 2009a; Taavitsainen and Fitzmaurice 2007 and Taavitsainen 2012). The classic overview text in historical pragmatics, which is still regularly cited, is Jacobs and Jucker (1995). A recent somewhat more specialised book is Culpeper and Kytö (2010), which traces the vestiges of spoken language in the written data that has survived from the past.

2 The widening perspectives of the digital era: Data in historical pragmatics

2.1 Introduction

What kind of data can we rely on if we want to find out about the use of language in earlier periods and the development of usage patterns in the course of time? This question has always been a major concern for historical pragmaticists, and it is interesting to note that even in the brief history of this discipline there has been some considerable development in the way in which scholars deal with this question. At present, three different approaches to the data problem can be discerned. We shall deal with them in turn in this chapter.

The first approach, which is the one that most early historical pragmaticists adopted, assesses the different types of available sources in terms of how they are related to spontaneous speech production. This approach focuses attention on speech-related texts, such as courtroom records, witness depositions or plays, and on spontaneous, interactive texts, such as private correspondence.

The second approach relies on one of the recent paradigm changes in linguistics, that is to say, the change from homogeneity to heterogeneity. A language is no longer seen as a homogeneous entity but as a heterogeneous conglomerate of different spoken and written manifestations of language. All types of language are seen as communicative in their own right and therefore open to pragmatic analyses. In this approach a play text can be analysed not primarily because it is closely related to spoken language but because plays are interesting in themselves. They are not taken as substitutes for spoken language in general but as one specific and interesting manifestation of language in its own right.

The third and most innovative approach, finally, recognises that speech recordings themselves have now reached a sufficient time depth that allows diachronic analyses. Tape-recorded interviews and radio broadcasts are available from the early twentieth century. Some of these have already been used for diachronic linguistic analyses focusing on pronunciation and morphology but not so far – to our knowledge – for diachronic pragmatic analyses.

These three approaches are not incompatible, of course. We can analyse courtroom data in its own right and at the same time carefully assess its position on the scale from speech-like language to the formal features of written language. We can also study diachronic differences in specific radio programmes without drawing any conclusions about spoken language in general.

We shall start our survey with a discussion of the 'digital turn' in the humanities, as the developments have been rapid and a great abundance of written language materials is available to scholars online. We are at a totally different phase from the beginnings of the discipline. We have to learn what is available and how to make the best possible use of these increasing digital resources. After these recent advances, we move on to discuss problems that have puzzled researchers since the launching of the discipline. The lack of native speakers of older language forms was first seen as a significant hindrance to historical pragmatic studies as native speaker informants with their language intuitions were regarded as the only reliable data source in Chomskyan linguistics. This part is connected with the above-mentioned first approach. But attitudes have changed and the second approach represents an integrated view: once we accept our data for what it is and do not pretend it is something else, we are building on solid ground. Models of data assessment are helpful, and therefore explanations of the most widely used theoretical frames are given. We shall deal with monologic and dialogic texts, probing deeper into drama as data for pragmatic studies, with the focus on how earlier researchers saw its relation to natural spoken language. The chapter will finish with some thoughts on the most novel approach of exploring the short diachrony of speech recordings from a historical point of view. Finally, we shall point out some future directions towards which our discipline is heading as new avenues open up for historical pragmatic research.

2.2 The 'digital turn' in the humanities

Advances in technology and more liberal policies with digital imaging open up new possibilities. Purpose-built corpora are available in increasing numbers, and non-traditional sources of digital data can be used for linguistic purposes. Multimodal historical corpora are also being created, and they offer opportunities for assessing the significance of physical features of manuscripts and early printed books to complement textual analysis, thus taking the field of historical pragmatics in a new direction, (or to put it in perspective, closer to its roots in philo-logical studies). The new data pools offer us rich language materials and inspire researchers to tackle new research questions.

2.2.1 Online resources and other electronic materials

We shall begin by an overview of electronic resources that are available to researchers, though mostly subject to subscription fees. Together they cover several domains of writing and a wide array of data from various periods in the history of English. This is a fairly recent phase in scholarship and there will be more in the future, as several universities and research institutes advocate open access policies.

Newspaper archives extend from the earliest issues of news sheets or courants, to the present day, and early issues of modern newspapers are available online going back a couple of centuries. Resources like *British Newspapers 1600–1900*, the most comprehensive digital historic newspaper archive of about three million pages of historic newspapers, newsbooks and ephemera, and the seventeenth- and eighteenth-century *Burnley Collection*, offer rich data for historical studies on, for example, news discourse, but as with most digital materials, access is subject to subscription fees. *Early English Books Online* (EEBO) and *Eighteenth Century Collections Online* (ECCO) have proved immensely useful, and their text encoding versions and digital images of the originals enhance their usability for various research tasks. Chadwyck-Healey databases of literature, brought together in *Literature Online* (LION), can also be used for historical pragmatic tasks. Databases for contextualising like the *Oxford Dictionary of National Biography* provide information about authors and recipients, and *The Oxford English Dictionary* and the *Historical Thesaurus of English* (HTE) provide facts for tracing the occurrences of words and phrases in other works and dating their entries and exits, as well as placing words and concepts in their semantic fields. The *Middle English Dictionary* and the *Compendium* are indispensable tools for scholars of medieval English texts. *English Short Title Catalogue, 1475–1800* (ESTC) helps to trace the distribution of copies and assess the dissemination of ideas in written works on the same topics. Some of these resources are so recent that we have not yet seen their impact on research. For example, it can be assumed that the *Historical Thesaurus of English* will inspire a host of research articles at the interface between semantics and pragmatics, and a large project on metaphors in the history of English is underway at the University of Glasgow.

The above-mentioned digital resources and more traditional corpora can be used for various research tasks, and it is possible for an individual researcher to tailor their own material individually to uncover language use in various situations and contexts. Such corpora are often compiled to serve as material for doctoral theses. They have been called 'third-generation corpora', in contrast to the 'first-generation' multi-genre multipurpose *Helsinki Corpus*, and 'second-generation' domain- or genre-specific corpora. (See the Corpus Resource Database, CoRD.) Third-generation corpora have grown in number in recent years, and we shall refer to some of them in the chapter on methods.

With the help of new corpora like the *Corpus of Historical American English* (COHA) recent trends in pragmatics like variational pragmatics can be extended to studies on historical varieties. In sum, exciting new possibilities are offered by the availability of new electronic online resources, and these rapid developments towards open access will certainly inform future studies on historical pragmatics.

2.2.2 Digital editions: Improvements in the reliability of data

Researchers are becoming aware of multiple readings, as there is not just one way of analysing texts, and we need both narrow and wide contexts for interpretations. Manuscript texts differ from modern ones in several important ways, and it is good for all researchers of historical pragmatics, especially those with research interests in the early periods, to be familiar with the basics. Punctuation practices were different and, as is well known, the place of the comma influences sentence meanings ('eats shoots and leaves' versus 'eats, shoots and leaves', as Lynne Truss put it in her popular book). Shakespeare's folio versions differ in their punctuation; for example, *what* can be interpreted as an exclamation or interrogative depending on the punctuation (e.g. *What! Is this it?* versus *What is this? It . . .*). Texts from the early periods have fuzzy sentence boundaries, unclear scopes of modification, and discourse features like speech quotations or indirect speech are indeterminate. The discourse level exhibits other ambiguities, as texts can have multiple voices that cause major problems of interpretation. The best that researchers can do is to be aware of the pitfalls and check whether alternative readings are possible.

The authenticity of data is a focal point in all studies, and the quality and demands of genuine language use, for example in manuscripts as they reached their original readerships (as opposed to texts reconstructed by editors) have recently been discussed more extensively. Traditional philology has a great deal to offer, and we are clearly moving towards a more flexible reading of medieval texts which allows different interpretations without labelling one as 'right' and others as 'wrong'. The communicative aspects are emphasised in discussions and the value of texts as artifacts in the form they reached real audiences has been increasingly recognised. The pragmatic angle has a great deal to offer. Historical pragmatics takes into account both sides of the communication, and what was written is assessed both from the point of view of its illocutions and purposes of writing as well as its receptional side; that is to say, how it was understood by its users and how texts were appropriated in subsequent discourses. The facts are, however, mostly conjectural from the early periods as what we have in most cases is the text itself, with its physical features.

The editor's task is to render the text available and make it comprehensible to a modern reader. For this purpose, a lightly edited version with minimal intervention and with the editor's contribution clearly marked is also needed. Modern readers of medieval texts are removed by several hundred years from the original readerships, and they need help in understanding the language as well as the cultural contexts. A transcript without any intervention would not fulfil the editor's task in most cases. The electronic age offers new solutions to these problems and the field of digital editing is developing fast. The philosophy of editing texts of past periods (i.e. making them available to modern readers) is radically changing with new imaging techniques and tools for digital editing. They have been instrumental in renewing editing policies towards multilayered renderings of medieval texts. In traditional book editions, footnotes gave the alternative readings in different manuscripts, endnotes explained difficult passages, and there were glossaries at the end of the book. Electronic editions make use of these different aids to the reader, but make them accessible by links. It is easy for the reader to check the different manuscript renderings in context, a model translation may be included and, most importantly, digital images of the manuscript are present as well. The point of departure is the original text reproduced as an image displaying the hands, whether carefully executed or more quickly scribbled work-a-day notes. The layout and possible illustrations can also reveal a great deal about the purpose, target group and use of the text. All these features work together and need to be taken into account when considering how the text reached its audience. Marginal notes by later hands and other signs of use can give us further clues to reception. For example, a fifteenth-century rural doctor in Wix, Suffolk, seems to have held in esteem a verse prognostication according to the days of the moon, and consulted it for guidance. He has illustrated his manuscript (BL Harley 1735) with sketches of his baby daughter in the margin of a certain day, and depicted farm tools and brewing vessels by the side of suitable days for these activities (see Taavitsainen 1988). Further evidence of the recipient or audience side can be gleaned from comparing multiple copies of a work, and there may be references to the text in other contemporary writings.

The new editing policy is an improvement towards more reliable data sources, and we have come a long way towards authenticity from the earlier goal of editing which aimed at reconstructing a hypothetical original version that in fact never existed in reality. But having said that, we need to discuss the 'authoritative' editions like *The Riverside Chaucer* or *The Riverside Shakespeare* and their place in historical pragmatics. They are compilations, not texts that reached an audience as such, and are based on several different manuscripts. Research questions vary in respect to the need for manuscript evidence. These editions contain an extensive apparatus and there are editions in the *Variorum Chaucer* series that give minute details about each manuscript. They can be made use of if the task so requires; for example, the use of second-person pronouns should be checked against the manuscript evidence before conclusions can be drawn. Early nineteenth-century editions, especially if they were produced for historical rather than philological studies, are often unreliable in rendering linguistic variation, and scholars would be wise to check the data to avoid pitfalls. As a general trend, awareness of the extent of linguistic variation in past periods and the demand for reliable sources is growing.

2.3 Recent developments

There has been a paradigm change in linguistics and the focus has shifted to empirical studies (see the chapter on methods). Pragmatics has its roots in language philosophy based on abstract theories of language and its communicative functions, and formulated with the introspective 'armchair' method relying on native-speaker intuitions. In general, the present trends in linguistics advocate more contextualisation. Communication is seen as situated language use between people whose sociolinguistic background comes into play and whose needs have to be taken into account. As stated in the introduction, pragmatics has gained in importance in linguistics in recent years and new research paradigms, including historical pragmatics have achieved a more established and central stage in historical linguistics. It is also relevant to note here that the goals of pragmatic research have been broadened in a sociolinguistic direction especially with the Continental European way of doing pragmatics (see section 1.2 above). Conversation analysis had its roots in ethnomethodology, and in the mid 1990s the affinity was explicitly expressed in, for example, the following quotation: 'The ultimate goal of most pragmatically oriented research is the collection of ethnographic data, i.e. naturally occurring data, collected along with information about the age, sex, status, situation, culture, relationship, etc. of the interactants' (Trosborg 1995: 141). Contextual factors with sociolinguistic parameters are enhanced in this definition and that again is very much in accordance with our present concerns.

At first, with conversational analysis as the main data-driven model of pragmatic analysis in the 1960s, spoken language was considered the only legitimate data for pragmatic analysis. There are still scholars who maintain that the ultimate goal of pragmatics (and therefore also of historical pragmatics) is to find out how people use(d) language in natural and unconstrained face-to-face conversations (see 2.1). The optimal language data in pragmatics was defined as oral interaction with participants freely alternating with equal rights in communication with one another. However, this approach leaves out the majority of language production from pragmatic analysis. Strict advocators of the conversation analytical paradigm considered (and perhaps some still hold the view) that all the rest is less than 'real' language and thus of secondary value. The constraints of mediated language and, for instance, the presence of an interviewer easily alter the course of conversation and direct the choice of the language produced. Mediated language includes telephone conversations within the spoken mode, and, for example, computer-mediated communication by email counts as mediated language in the written mode. The early studies excluded forms of conversation with unequal rights, for example in institutional settings and on prescribed topics, but this has changed. In the course of time, the research paradigm has been broadened to include institutional and constrained oral language use, for example in interviews and written texts.

In recent years, the earlier dichotomy of spoken and written language has made way for more refined views. Most importantly, researchers have come to realise that there is no such thing as unconstrained language production in whatever mode. In historical pragmatics (as in historical linguistics), the focus has shifted to non-literary everyday language, as it can yield insights into interpersonal communication of past periods. Mediated language use is accepted as material, and theories have been formed how to come closest to natural spoken language and how to take the various constraints into account. The focus shift has continued, providing insights into how people used language to achieve their communicative goals and how they acted with language in past societies. We can, for example, claim that an inventory of speech act verbs of a certain period in the history of English can reveal an ethnographic view of the speech community's practices by specifying which speech acts are 'important enough to be labelled with a speech act verb which the speakers use to talk about the speech act and – in some cases – even perform the speech act in question' (Taavitsainen and Jucker 2007: 108).

2.3.1 Speech-related and spontaneous data

Historical linguists had already struggled for some time with the 'bad data problem' when historical pragmatics was launched in 1995. Much historical data has survived by chance in a haphazard way and can provide only positive evidence; negative evidence must be inferred, and therefore we cannot know for sure. For this reason historical linguistics was called the 'art of making the best use of bad data' (Labov 1994: 11). Scholars tried to access written language as close to the spoken mode as possible to gain access to the initial stages of language change, as this topic is one of the core issues in historical linguistics. According to current theories most changes (at least on the phonological level) are initiated in everyday speech by women who are mobile and have multiple ties to different networks and speaker communities. They are likely to be the leaders in the processes of linguistic change. In contrast, the most conservative speakers are non-mobile rural males who have lived in the same region all their lives and preserve the old ways of speaking in the purest form; it was precisely for this reason that such interviewees were selected as informants of early dialect projects (see below).

It is a fact that natural and unconstrained face-to-face conversations from earlier periods do not exist. Such data is not available, and thus historical pragmaticists resort to written texts of different kinds, using them in different ways according to the research questions at hand. In some studies, the goal is to come as close as possible to natural spoken language. This is the 'tape-recorder view'. Models have been developed which measure the distance between spoken and written language in various ways and these help researchers in their task of defining how closely their texts represent approximations of spoken data. In Koch and Oesterreicher's 'spoken-style view' (1985), historical data has only survived in the graphic code, but many of the surviving genres represent instances of the language of immediacy, and there is a scale from the language of immediacy to the language of distance, a scale which is of interest to historical pragmaticists. Thus, instead of a dichotomy,

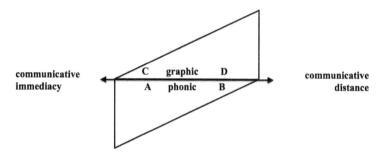

Figure 2.1 Koch and Oesterreicher's model of communicative immediacy and distance (Koch 1999: 400)

we have a continuum between the two modes, with various degrees of orality and literacy, intimacy and distance, with features realised in different ways in different texts. This model has been used fairly widely in historical pragmatic studies and it has proved to be a useful point of departure.

Figure 2.1 gives Koch and Oesterreicher's model of communicative immediacy and distance. It visualises the scale from spoken to written, placing various kinds of written data in a scale according to different distances from the spoken so that the differences are more pronounced at one end and more levelled at the other. Area A represents the language of immediacy in the phonic code, typically realised in spontaneous face-to-face conversations in everyday interaction. Area B stands for the language of distance in the phonic code, such as public lectures. Area C represents the language of immediacy in the graphic code. Present-day emails or private letters in the earlier periods fall into this area. Area D correlates the language of distance with the graphic code, illustrated by academic prose and legal language.

An analytical approach to language use takes the layers of writing into account and specifies communicative acts that take place or are embedded in texts. The model is given in Figure 2.2. S is the sender of the message and R the recipient. A letter contains several fairly conventional components, and narratives of some recent events are often included. These narratives form an embedded layer with their own actors, the people that took part in the narrated interaction. A pragmatic analysis can focus on the interaction between the people depicted in the narration or it can focus on the interaction of the letter writer with the recipient of the letter. The situation is often even more complex. The narration may contain characters who tell each other stories, which would add a further layer, and so on.

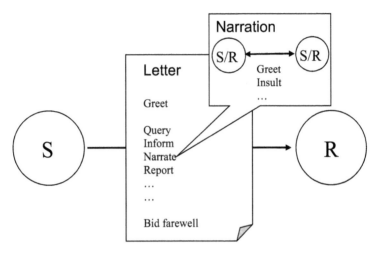

Figure 2.2 Embedding of speech acts in letters (Taavitsainen and Jucker 2007: 115)

2.3.2 Monologic and dialogic data

An alternative model to approach the same issue has been presented by Culpeper and Kytö (2010), but it is still necessary to keep the above levels in mind when analysing texts. Their questions are: 'What are written texts representing spoken face-to-face interaction like?', 'Why are written texts representing face-to-face interaction as they are?'. Having answered these questions they approach the ultimate question, 'What was the spoken face-to-face interaction of past periods like?' (Culpeper and Kytö 2010: 2–3).

Recorded language is extant in texts produced from notes taken down by an individual present during a particular speech event, such as a clerk. There are constraints in note-taking practices; for example, shorthand could be used. Reconstructed language exists in texts which purport to present dialogue which actually took place at some point in the past (invariably, the narrator was present at the speech event in question). But there is also constructed language in texts which contain imaginary dialogue. The role of the narrator, moreover, varies. There is minimal intervention in texts which present dialogue as it was supposedly spoken and where the explicit presence of the narrator is minimised (typically, his or her role is limited to speaker identification and contextual comment, such as stage directions). Narratorial intervention is more explicit, however, in texts in which dialogue is embedded in first- or third-person narration and in which the narrator's presence is

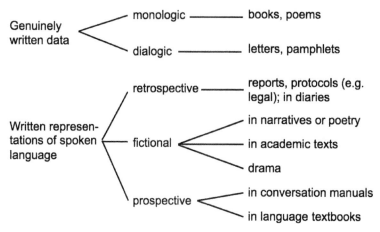

Figure 2.3 Data in historical pragmatics: The 'communicative view' (Jucker 1998: 5)

made explicit; for example, by the use of reporting clauses (see Chapter 12 on narratives). One possible way of relating different types of spoken and written language in written texts of the past is given in Figure 2.3.

It gives an outline of the data sources according to the 'communicative view' of historical pragmatics. Genuinely written data comprises texts that are intended to be read. They are of two kinds: primarily monologic texts do not expect that the average reader will respond, whereas answers are often expected to primarily dialogic texts. What is even more important is that they are themselves often written in response to earlier letters or pamphlets, and texts are in dialogue with one another, like turns in a conversation. Private letters are useful because they depict conversational exchanges, even if they are written exchanges, with formulaic language at the beginnings and ends of individual letters. The middle passages contain the more private and individual communications and they may also contain passages that are representations in one form or another of spoken language. Pamphlets were written for broad and heterogeneous audiences and they can contain quotes of direct speech or reported speech.

Representations of spoken language can be divided into three different types. Firstly, retrospective texts are written reports or protocols, as for instance depositions of witnesses, court reports or diaries of members of parliament in which parliamentary dialogues were recorded (with possibly some fictional elements). Courtroom proceedings have proved a valuable source because they give more or less faithful reproductions of actual spoken language even if the communicative situation in a courtroom is rather constrained, and scribal practices have to be taken into account as well.

Secondly, fictional accounts may occur in poems or in narrative fiction as dialogues between the fictional characters invented by the author. An opening scene of an instructional text, *The Gouernayle of Health*, from the sixteenth century, for example, negotiates authority in a conflict between a wise old man and a foolish youngster. Such a setting is typical of wisdom literature and goes back to biblical teaching and the *secreta secretum* tradition in which Aristotle teaches Alexander the Great. There is a long tradition behind such instructive texts, and it has to be taken into account in analysing the text and contextualising its language use and discourse features. The language is vivid and triggers the readers' curiosity, inviting them to read on and profit from the instruction. The *docere et delectare* function of the text is very prominent as it teaches by entertaining dialogue, songs and vivid scenes. Such non-literary treatises can contain a fictional teacher interacting with a fictional student, more or less imitating natural language (see Chapter 10).

Drama texts represent fictional data as well and consist of fictional dialogues. In many respects they provide excellent material for historical pragmatics, and drama has a special place in the data selection as it gives ample context for utterances. Action sequences give us access to the illocutions of the speaker and the perlocutions of presented speech acts, and what came before and what comes after. The characters' hierarchies are made explicit so that politeness practices become contextualised and are clearly evident, even if in a somewhat exaggerated form; for example, in Renaissance and Restoration plays. Access to inner life in psychological soliloquies in the tragedies has been pointed out as an especially helpful and even a necessary feature for a proper test of politeness theories. The special quality of drama was realised early on:

> It is, of course, a selective and inadequate representation of speech; but the more skilful the dramatist, the more skilful he will be, if presenting the normal life of his time, in authenticating the action by an acceptable version of contemporary speech. (Salmon [1965] 1987: 265)

Thirdly, there are prospective texts, that is to say dialogues, that are to be understood as models for future use. They occur in language-teaching textbooks as model dialogues which the language student is supposed to learn by heart, so that he or she can use it later on in the appropriate situation. Prospective language also occurs in politeness and conversation manuals in the eighteenth century to initiate learners or give a polished touch to polite society manners. Textbooks from the previous centuries tell us about past practices and illuminate politeness conventions. In all, the repertoire is rich and the process of analysis in matching text and context through critical reading in order to construct various levels of meaning(s), both explicit and implicit, is demanding.

2.3.3 The integrated view

The current approach to data in historical pragmatics (as explained in 2.1) is based on the argument that all language use is always contextualised and that it is not only natural spoken interaction that is worthy of pragmatic investigations, but written language should also be studied in its own right. This 'communicative view' holds that both spoken and written language are forms of communication produced by speakers/ writers for target audiences with communicative intentions, and language is always produced within situational constraints. Therefore all forms of language that have survived and provide enough information to contextualise the use, are considered potential data for historical pragmatics. However, the specific situational constraints need to be considered in pragmatic analysis, and we have to be careful not to draw unwarranted conclusions or generalise too much. According to this view, an analysis of a play tells us something about this play, but it does not tell us anything about 'language in general'. The focus is on the variability of language, and we have to be more analytical and modify our conclusions according to a particular period, the particular function of the writing, and a particular setting. Language use reveals a great deal of people's background and character: educated people speak and write differently from the semi-literate; town and country are different with regional language varieties, and so on. These distinctions are present today, but they have been present for centuries, and the underlying variables have to be taken into account.

Against this background, possible data for pragmatic analyses broaden to cover all surviving texts, as long as they are analysed for what they are and are not taken to represent something else. Thus, if we analyse courtroom data or fictional drama texts, we analyse them within their own contexts and within the constraints of their specific genres, but we do not take them to be more or less suitable substitutes for spoken, free-flowing conversations. Drama and fiction are important data sources for historical pragmatics but it is important to bear their special nature in mind. They can tell us a great deal about human interactions but in a condensed or typified form. Thus, for example, the use of interjections and discourse markers in medieval literature must have been modelled according to real language use, to give verisimilitude to the text. The occurrences of particular features are often marked with additional significance for the plot or characterisation. Thus, the moment of falling in love in Chaucer's *The Knight's Tale* is marked out by the protagonist's exclamation using the interjection 'A!' It serves its purpose in the scene in its genre frame, but does not reflect real-life behaviour in similar instances in the past or at present (see Chapter 4).

Thus language use is studied in the context of genres, with their constraints and within the more or less firmly established conventions, but scholars should take into account that we cannot generalise beyond the genre. This approach can be seen as a future step in the line of development explained earlier. Researchers are beginning to appreciate the intricate nature of written data from past periods and recognise the nature of the written code and its development from a pragmatic angle.

2.4 Pragmatics of early speech recordings

A radio programme on the BBC in which people explain what music they would choose to take with them on a desert island was launched 70 years ago and is still running. A rebroadcast of the early programmes made listeners aware of the striking difference in the way people told their stories and argued for their choices. In the same way, the following interviews with a rural male farmer, recorded in the 1970s for a dialect project, has a historical ring. The passage is given in a grammar of Cambridgeshire dialect (Vasko 2010: section 3.1.2.2) as an illustration of the use of the simple present form for vivid descriptions of past activities. This way of presentation is especially typical of narratives and jokes, and when immediacy and dramatic effect are required, but it is also used to describe more everyday tasks like farm work. The proximal tense enhances the relevance of the orderly activities in focus, and brings out their significance in the repeated cycle of farm work. Note also the use of the interpersonal second-person pronoun *you* (instead of the passive voice), which lends a slightly instructive tone to the passages by involving the listener.

> (a) Q: You ploughed, you drilled. What else?
>   CM: You **plough** the field, you **roll** it, then you **harrow** it = with harrows = and then you **drill** it, then you **harrow** it behind, **cover** the corner, use (i.e. StE used to) leave that then. That was finished. (Fulbourn)
> (b) SS: I'm had days digging fires out.
>   MH: Have you?
>   SS: Yah.
>   MH: What? Down the fen?

SS: Well you don't- you don't actually dig the fire out, 'cause you can't. What you **do** is you **start** a yard from the fire, 'cause you can't always see it, I mean 'cause i- it **goes** down. You **start** a yard away from it and **dig** the soil around it = and **go** down to the = coal. And when you **dig** it out you **have** a trench like that, so it's easy to work, een't it? Well it can't go through coal, can it? So therefore it **goes** out. Days I'm had doing that. (Willingham)

(c) Q: How did you keep your meat?

BR: Er, uset keep 'em = your meat and that what you used to have off a pig = in a pot = like that you **salt** it. See, then you can have some 'stead o' going to a shop every week = **salt** it. You can salt it and then pull the bit out and when you **come** home to tea = er i- you **want** a bit o' fried = pork, yeah, **fetch** it out, **cut** it up and = **eat** it. (Bassingbourn)

(Vasko 2010: section 3.1.2.2, emphasis original)

In the above extracts the questions were asked in the past tense, and the constructions used for past time expressions alternate: a speaker can begin with *used to* + infinitive or the simple past, and then change to the simple present, often changing the time constructions again at the end of the discourse (Vasko 2010). The above examples are quoted in a grammar of dialectal speech for their use of tenses, but the recordings are full of speech events that could also be analysed from other angles, as communication on several levels (see methods), or as narratives of storytelling, or from the point of view of discourse deictic elements and other pragmatic aspects. These recordings are solicited interviews and as a rule early tape-recorded spoken material is produced under strict constraints.

The desert island programme, *Desert Island Discs*, was mediated through the radio. Telling tales in the public sphere poses even more pressure on the 'informant' than the semi-private interview for 'antiquarian' interests, as the dialectologists described their motifs. Recordings of spontaneous speech are more recent, and this material is not usually counted as historical data, though recordings of earlier decades could also be considered in a diachronic perspective, as with the early corpora from the 1960s that are already considered historical.

2.5 Conclusions

Data problems were regarded as major obstacles for applying pragmatic approaches to historical materials, and they have been discussed from the beginning of historical pragmatics as a field of scholarly research. Written data forms the primary material, and we have come a long way from the first considerations to reach the present consensus that all material, if it is genuine, can be regarded as legitimate data for historical pragmatics. The scale extends from spoken to written, placing various kinds of written data at different distances from the spoken, and pointing out that the differences are more pronounced at one end and more levelled at the other.

Earlier periods pose their own problems, and there are several pitfalls that need special attention. It is easy to assume too much and take for granted some more recent background features and apply them to earlier periods; our modern textual practices are based on a very different culture. It takes time and effort to learn about, for example, the material circumstances of manuscript production and circulation, the transfer of manuscript practices to early printed books, development of communication networks and postal services, and even the technological advances that have revolutionised interpersonal practices within the last decades belong to the background knowledge of historical pragmatics. Once we acknowledge the restrictions of data sources and deal with them with caution, a great deal can be achieved.

Scholarship is moving fast in historical pragmatics. The basic work of making data available for other researchers' use by compiling structured corpora with contextual information or rendering manuscript texts available to modern readers in editions does not become outdated if the principles of doing it are sound and the work itself of high standard. Advances in technology have made all kinds of data in digital form easily available and restorable at a researcher's own computer. However, we have to deal with these data in an orderly way and take their special nature into account. We need to learn what kinds of texts provide the best possible material for our studies with different types of research questions, and how we should interpret our data for more reliable results. Evaluations of historical texts and genres have changed in the course of time. Traditional philologists in earlier centuries considered only literary and religious texts worthy of study, and texts belonging to other prestigious fields like surgery, and texts with curiosity value, also received some attention. Like history, moving from monarchs and aristocrats to common people, the focus of interest in historical language studies has shifted to everyday and ephemeral materials like private letters, handbooks, diaries, recipes, notes, (auto)biographies and almanacs. But fashions move in circles, and literary texts are also considered interesting and relevant material for historical pragmatics, but for very different reasons. We would not argue that speech quotations in early fiction can be taken as evidence of authentic spoken language, but they nevertheless reflect the state of language use even if in a condensed and typified form.

Exercises

1. List some of the important similarities and differences between plays and everyday communication in terms of spontaneity errors, corrections with discourse markers, and syntactic complexity.
2. The following extract of *The Trial of of Titus Oates* has been edited from a text that was taken down by a clerk at court. It contains several different communicative levels. The first turn is addressed at the same time to the previous speaker and those present at court at the time of speaking. How do we know? What are the exact phrases that reveal the addressees? The ensuing interrogation represents a third level, but between whom? What are the linguistic features that give clues for this interpretation?

> Mr. *At. Gen.* Now, my Lord, we shall go to our Evidence to prove, that all this is absolutely false: For *Ireland* went out of Town into *Staffordshire*, and did not return till after the 9th of *September*. And for this, we call *Anne Ireland.*
> *Who was sworn.*
> Mr. *Sol. Gen.* Mrs. *Ireland,* pray where did you take your leave of your Brother Mr. *Ireland,* who was executed in *Summer* 1678, and when?
> Mrs. *A. Ireland.* I took my leave of him the beginning of *August.*
> Mr. *Sol. Gen.* What day in *August,* do you remember?
> Mrs. *A. Ireland.* The 3d of *August* (HC E3 Trial Oates 1640–1710)

3. Discuss the levels of language use in the following passage taken from the Paston Letters.

> Margaret Paston to John Paston [1449?]
> [Transcribed by John F. Tinkler]
> (ii) Margaret Paston to Sir John Paston (Ibid, 363, No. 617)
> I greet you well, and send you God's blessing and mine, letting you know that last Thursday my mother and I were with my lord bishop of Norwich, ...
> and he said plainly that he had been required as often to examine her, that he might not nor would delay it any longer, and charged me, on pain of excommunication, that she should not be deferred, but that she should appear before him the next day. And I said plainly that I would neither bring her nor send her; and then he said that he would send for her

himself, and charged that she should be at liberty to come when he sent for her; and he said by his troth that he would be as sorry . . . My mother and I informed him that we could never understand by her saying nor by any language she ever had to him . . .

Further reading

Culpeper and Kytö (2000) and Jucker (2000) are early papers that focus on data problems in historical pragmatics. They carefully assess the usability of various types of historical data for pragmatic analyses. Archer (2007) provides a careful assessment of courtroom data and Kytö (2010) gives a state-of-the art overview of data issues in historical pragmatics. Kytö also lists and discusses a large range of relevant corpora and electronic tools at the disposal of historical pragmaticists. Taavitsainen and Fitzmaurice (2007) discuss the data problem of authenticity of language materials from early periods. Culpeper and Kytö (2010) discuss data problems in historical pragmatics from the perspective of the suitability of different types of sources for providing information on speech-related features.

3 Excavating usage patterns: Methods in historical pragmatics

3.1 Introduction

Pragmaticists focusing on present-day language use have several methods at their disposal that can be applied and developed to answer novel research tasks. Data-collecting methods include interviews, questionnaires, and observations with ethnomethodological approaches, to mention some of the most important ones. For historical pragmaticists these lines of investigation are not available, but we have to rely on written texts with their constraints and haphazard survival histories. In planning a historical pragmatic study the first step is to decide upon the data. The next step would be to conduct a survey of what has been done on the same or related materials, as the researcher has to chart where work has been done and where there is a gap to be filled in: the question is what is relevant and worth attention. After these considerations the researcher is ready to formulate the research questions. But an important question remains to be answered: how are research questions translated into methods?

The aim of this chapter is to provide some guidelines and illustrate how some researchers in the field of historical pragmatics have solved certain problems. The methods available offer a fairly wide repertoire of choices, and they can be combined into what is called 'triangulation'; that is, approaching the same research questions from multiple angles. In this chapter we shall survey different ways of going about pragmatic research tasks either with a synchronic or a diachronic goal, and view a range of methodologies that have been used and are being developed for studies in this field. Both qualitative and quantitative methods will be discussed, with examples to illustrate how various methods have been applied to historical data. We shall begin by discussing the prerequisites for reliable analysis and qualitative assessments. We then move on to corpus-based and corpus-driven studies and top-down and bottom-up methodologies, and to the applications of corpus linguistic methodologies. In all cases, contextualisation and qualitative assessments are needed to complement and interpret the results.

As discussed in Chapter 1, the aim of historical pragmatics is to discover and describe patterns of past language use, how the patterns developed and how meaning was made, and what factors underlie both synchronic variation in past periods and changes in a diachronic perspective. Pragmatics takes people and contexts into account, and it is the researcher's task to relate texts to people, to their authors and audiences, and provide the context, as this is what distinguishes historical pragmatic studies from historical linguistics in general. An inherent feature of all language use is its variability, and written texts display it in various ways. It is the analyst's task to uncover strategies of language use, how different features relate to one another, and define how patterns are anchored to background socio-historical developments, such as changes in the media, literacy practices, and underlying intellectual commitments. Texts fulfil different purposes in society, and genres and registers, or domains of writing, are important. Context is a multilayered notion that includes a whole range of layers from the narrow linguistic context, i.e. the immediate surroundings, to genre and register, which give the context of larger groupings of texts, to the socio-historical situation and, in the widest possible sense, the context of culture with its general outlook, attitudes, beliefs, and the whole worldview. Changes have been radical, and it is not an exaggeration to state that medieval and early modern texts were produced in a completely different culture from ours. Transition periods are of particular interest for several reasons (see Chapter 10). Contextual qualitative assessment is a complicated task in historical pragmatics, and historical knowledge of the period and culture in which the text was produced is essential, as meanings are negotiated in texts with subtle shades, implicit meanings, and even reverse meanings with irony.

3.2 How are research questions translated into methods?

When the researcher has decided upon the research questions, the next challenge is to consider which methods would be appropriate and how they should be applied. The question of how to translate research questions into methods can be answered in several ways, and we shall survey different solutions. Most studies on pragmatic research tasks dealing with historical materials employ corpora either just to retrieve the material in a readily available form, or they make use of corpus linguistic methods in various ways. Qualitative analysis used to be the rule in pragmatic studies in the earlier decades, but corpus-based studies are the main trend nowadays, and, of course, methods are combined. Quantitative methods are often used to provide a wider perspective as the backdrop of studies.

3.2.1 Tertium comparationis

Methodological innovations often spring from interfaces of different disciplines or branches of study. Parallels and models for new applications have been sought in other subfields of pragmatics. For instance, an emphasis on cultural context links historical pragmatics with contrastive pragmatics, as the cultures of past periods are very different from ours, even in the same language area. But the match is not straightforward. There are differences as well; for example, developments are not streamlined but take place at different paces in different kinds of data from one past period to the next, and generalisations easily lead to vagueness. An important methodological issue is the definition of a *tertium comparationis*, something that remains constant. It can be, for example, a speech act function, to guarantee that we are comparing like with like, and that our research question is sensible. The functions of requests, to get somebody to do something, or expressing gratitude with thanks, for instance, can be assumed to have stayed constant in the history of English, but some other speech acts are likely to be culture-bound and thus not have universal validity. Searle (1979: 29) condensed the basic functions that people do with language into the following: 'we tell people how things are, we try to get them to do things, we commit ourselves to doing things, we express our feelings and attitudes and we bring about changes through our utterances. Often, we do more than one of these at once in the same utterance'. These are fundamental aspects of human interactions, and it seems that we can assume at least the same goals for communication in past periods.

3.2.2 Philological roots: mastering language forms

Pragmatics and historical linguistics are usually given as the launching pads of historical pragmatics. Like historical linguistics, historical pragmatics uses large corpora, but there are also aspects that go back to traditional philology where the method was qualitative. For example, the requirement of a thorough knowledge of the culture and the language form (with its temporal and regional variation) of the period under scrutiny stems from the philological roots of the discipline. Reliable qualitative reading of old texts requires a mastery of the language and discourse forms of texts produced in distant periods. We need to know what the words and phrases mean, how sentences were constructed, and what genres and discourse patterns were current. These requirements become more difficult to master in the more distant periods and require special study. Luckily we have excellent dictionaries and thesauri (see Chapter 2) to help us find out the contextual meanings of lexical items and expressions. As a method, the qualitative study of texts is of value, and this is true of corpus studies as well, as all empirical studies give examples and discuss them qualitatively. In practice, translations of pre-1500 passages of texts are requested for journal articles and books, and it is impossible to explain usage patterns without a profound understanding of the language form. Another recent trend enhances the importance of manuscript studies and book history. They are gaining ground as new components of interdisciplinary studies with the historical pragmatic approach (see Chapter 2).

3.2.3 Contextual readings

Another feature inherited from philology is the requirement of contextualised readings. Meanings are negotiated, and we need to examine utterances in their context, taking various factors into account. The task of retrieving past meanings is challenging, as the mere distance of time between the locutions recorded in texts and the modern researcher's interpretations create difficulties, and misinterpretations can arise. A useful exercise in approaching the contextualisation problem is trying to reconstruct the historical conditions of text production, transmission and reception. We can begin by considering how pragmatic changes were prompted by changes in the material world. How did copying by hand influence written communication? Did the slow production of individual copies make a difference and does it or should it influence the pragmatic readings of medieval texts? Implicit meanings are difficult to catch, but clues can be found in the context. Speech acts provide the clearest examples. In addition to what the actual words in the utterance mean, we need to know a great deal more in order to interpret the utterance meaning. The checklist of things to find out resembles the script of the game 'broken telephone line' (our endeavours to retrieve past meanings often resemble it, too); or the children's game called 'diary' in which participants suggest answers to questions of who says what to whom under what circumstances, why and in what way (the answers are written down, folded and circulated after each entry and provide a funny outcome). The same utterance may have different, even reverse meanings as the same wordings can have very different shades in different contexts, especially if used with irony and sarcasm. Compliments can very easily turn into insults, and here it is not the speaker's illocutions but the per-locutions of the addressee that count. What reveals that a compliment was perceived as an insult is the addressee's or target's reaction; that is, the perlocutionary effect of the utterance. Context is the key to com-municative functions, from both the speaker's and the recipient's side. Negotiation of meaning comes out very clearly; for example, in the field of verbal aggression where insults are often negotiated (see Chapter 6).

3.2.4 Production circumstances, authors and audiences

A London food advertisement from 1781 reads:

> At the CHEAP-NOTED COVENT-GARDEN PROVISION *WARE-HOUSE*, No. 31, JAMES-STREET,
> Is this Day and To-morrow selling off Positively without Reserve, the following large Stock: Two Hundred Sides of the finest Wiltshire Bacon that ever came to Town, all Young and Warranted, well dry'd, at the uncommon low Price of Five Pence per Pound. This is without Apology known to be the best Bacon in the Kingdom, and at a Price that has never yet been offered to the Public. About Three or Four Hundred Firkins of all Sorts of Butters, which will be sold as follows: Best Dublin and Rou Cork, from Five to Sixpence per Pound. Best York and Suffolk from Sixpence Halfpenny to Sevenpence per Pound. Best Cambridge at Eightpence per Pound. Fresh Butter and Eggs. Twenty Tons of fine old rich Cheshire Cheese, Threepence Farthing by the Hundred; with the best fat Toasting Glocester after the same Price. Single Cheeses at Threepence Halfpenny, and the very best rich old Double Glocester and Northwiltshire cut at Fourpence. . . . Hams, and fine Pickled Pork in Proportion. A Trial will prove this to be the Cheapest and Best Ware-house in London.
>
> The above will surely be worth the Attention of Chandler-shops, Families, Public-houses, and Taverns, but particularly by the Country People who comes to this Market, to whom the Proprietor is greatly indebted for past Favours. All Goods of any Consequence sent hence free of Expense; but nothing till paid for, as no Day-book is kept.
>
> N.B. The above Goods will continue on Sale till all is Sold.

Background information is necessary for placing a text in its appropri-ate context. The above early advertisement for foodstuffs from 1781 is described in the following terms in the electronic database of John Johnson's *Ephemera*:

> Collection: – Advertising Document type: – Advertisements – food
> Company: – Covent-Garden Provision Ware-house, No. 31, James-Street, [London]
> Products: – bacon, butter, eggs, cheese, hams, pickled pork
> Date of publication: – 1781
> Source of date: – manuscript annotation
> Physical Form: – single sheet, [2] p., 13.4 × 21.6 cm.
> Medium: – paper
> Printing process of text: – Letterpress works
> Method of production: – Printed with display typefaces

Our modern experiences of advertisements are based on a mixture of visual and aural multimodal texts through newspapers, magazines, TV, outdoor posters and video clips. They are an outcome of a long line of development, and we have to reformulate our expectations when dealing with early examples of the genre. The first advertisements seem to have been medical or dealing with the book trade, and are often just announcements about where the goods could be purchased, but some are quite elaborate (see exercise 1). This particular one seems to have been one single sheet printed with some display types but without illustrations (for an analysis, see below). Unfortunately, no more information is available.

Anchoring language use to its context of production and reception requires background facts on the author's education, social position, gender, age and other sociolinguistic parameters; ideally the same information should be available about the target group or audience. This need has been recognised by some corpus compilers, and the trend in some philologically-oriented corpora is towards more contextualisation. For this reason, available facts are included in the text catalogues of *Middle English Medical Texts* and *Early Modern English Medical Texts* for the benefit of corpus users.

At the beginning of the modern age, transmission modes changed from manuscript to print. The change was gradual and influenced language use at various levels, from spelling conventions to larger patterns, even genres. Modes of communication developed, and it became possible, for example, to discuss controversial issues of religious reforms or medical matters in pamphlets. Polemical arguments could be developed in successive publications written pro and con; for example, the use of tobacco was debated as a health-promoting or health-destroying habit from its introduction to Europe in the sixteenth century. Pamphlets could also spread news of popular interest such as witchcraft cases. The

Gouernement of health (1595)

Author: William Bullein

Full title of text: *The Gouernment of Health: A Treatise written by William Bullein, for the especiall good and healthfull preseruation of mans bodie from all noysome diseases, proceeding by the excesse of euill diet, and other infirmities of Nature: full of excellent medicines, and wise councels, for conseruation of health, in men, women, and children. Both pleasant and profitable to the industrious Reader.*

Year of publication: 1595

Publishing information: London: Valentine Sims

Catalogue number: STC (2nd ed.) 4042

Physical description: Octavo, [8], 87, [1] ff., ill.

Source copy: WL 1151/A

File name in EMEMT: 1595_Bullein_GouernementOfHealth

Word count: 10,448

Description of the text: Medical dialogue.

Contents: The interlocutors in the dialogue are Iohn and Humfrey, a novice and an expert in medicine. They discuss the principles of medicine and curing with diet, herbs and exercise. The conversation covers the parts of medicine, complexions, elements, humours, diet, simple medicines, anatomy, diseases such as dropsy and choler, purging, baths, regiment of eating, sleeping and exercising, and the properties of herbs, flowers, fruits and different foodstuffs.

Parts included: Whole text, excluding the properties of herbs and foodstuffs.

Bibliographical notes: *Gouernement of health* was first published in 1558. The title page is written from the EEBO-image, since the copy in Wellcome Library lacks a title page.

Link to ESTC: http://estc.bl.uk/S107022

Link to EEBO: http://gateway.proquest.com/openurl?ctx_ver=Z39.88-2003&res_id=xri:eebo&rft_id=xri:eebo:citation:99842726

Biographical information: William Bullein (author)

Dates of birth and death: c. 1515–1576

About the author: William Bullein was an English physician. He was possibly educated at Cambridge and Oxford and studied medicine in Germany for some time. In 1550 he became the rector of Blaxhall, Suffolk for four years, and after his resignation, he practiced medicine in Northumberland and Durham. In 1560 Bullein was sent to prison for two years because he was charged of debts. In 1564 he was practising in London. Bullein is best known for his works on surgery, medicine, pestilence and pleurisy.

Texts by the same author in EMEMT:
William Bullein: *Bulleins bulwarke* (1562)
William Bullein: *Dialogve against feuer pestilence* (1564)

Link to Dictionary of National Biography: http://www.oxforddnb.com/view/article/3910

Figure 3.1 A catalogue description with contextual information in *Early Modern English Medical Texts*

audiences of the most popular pamphlets included semi-literate people, and almanacs belong to the same category. The numbers of such publications have been estimated in millions of copies in the early modern period. Newspapers were targeted to literate readerships and their contents were more matter-of-fact (see Chapter 11). A revolution comparable to the introduction of printing has taken place recently, as people communicate increasingly through electronic media. In language analysis, pragmatics takes people into account: both speakers/writers and hearers/readers are of importance and their illocutions and perlocutions are of interest to the analyst. The new medium lends a new kind of immediacy as the participants may be online. This rapidly developing field of research is very much connected with historical pragmatics, as besides the past, diachrony involves the present and the future.

3.3 Qualitative studies

A good point of departure for the analysis of the London food advertisement from 1781, presented above, would be the function of the text. Advertisements are aimed at enticing potential customers to buy the products. The final section points out various groups that the text directly addresses. The implication is 'this is for you'. 'Country People' are singled out by an interesting clause implicating that the vendor owes a debt of gratitude to them. Perhaps this is a means of emphasising the cheap prices and an invitation to bargain. The dates are specified at the beginning: 'this day and tomorrow'. They are deictic expressions that shift meanings according to the moment of reading the text. The implication is 'make haste', although at the end there is a face-saving note about the short timeline and sales continuing, should something remain unsold. Phrases emphasising the unique opportunity and superlatives in hyperbolic language stand out: 'at a Price that has never yet been offered to the Public – the Cheapest and Best . . . in London – the finest . . . that ever came to Town'. Prices are an important consideration and they are specified for each item. The old monetary system was complicated, and a meticulous analyst would do well to add a word about the material context as well. The end of the advertisement promises free delivery but 'nothing till paid for', which serves as a command to 'bring your money'. In sum, the advertisement is highly persuasive and we can only hope that customers found the goods as exquisite and as inexpensive as the advertisement states.

Literary works were mostly transmitted by reading aloud in earlier times, and the purely written mode and silent reading were still rare. Literacy was restricted to the upper classes of society. Even in the eighteenth and nineteenth centuries reading aloud was a popular pastime, as pictures of domestic scenes, diary entries and letters bear witness. Dialogic language use is closely related to orality. Typical interactive involvement features include first- and second-person pronouns. They provide evidence of interpersonal communication of, for example, ego-centred discourse, first-person narration, and direct instruction involving the addressee. However, it is not always as simple as that. Repertoires of linguistic features defined on the basis of modern studies on modern materials are not always applicable to older materials as such. We need to take semantic changes and developments of grammatical structures into account. In addition, there are other factors to be considered, for example cultural notions such as courtly love, politeness in conduct and rules of appropriate behaviour in general.

Below you will find a dialogic text extract with intricate negotiation of meaning. The text is *The Gouernement of Health,* published in 1595 (see Figure 3.1 for contextual information), and it will be seen that participant relations undergo a shift at the beginning. The protagonists are introduced by a contrast: an arrogant young man and a wise old man have come together.[1]

> *Iohn.* OF al pleasures and pastimes mee thinke there is none like vnto good cheere, what shoulde a man doe but passe away the time with good fellowes, and make merrie, seeing we haue but a time to liue, cast away care, wherefore is meate and bellies ordained, but the one to serue the other? The flesh that we dayly encrease is our owne. Abstinence and fasting, is a mightie enemie and nothing pleasant to mee, and bee vsed of very fewe that loue themselues, but onely of beggers, and couetous sparers, which doe spare much, and spend little. (f. 1v)

John's opening turn consists of a declaration of his lifestyle, followed by praise of his own lifestyle and contempt for that of others. He expresses his subjective stance with the impersonal phrase *mee thinke,* uses alliterative word pairs *pleasures and pastimes,* and a rhetorical question. The attitude to others is made clear with negative name-calling and contrast (*beggars, couetous sparers, much, little*).

> *Humfrey.* I know well your goodly expence of time, I wis it is no maruell, although you make your bellie your god, and boast of it. You see that all lustie reuellers, and continual banket makers, come to great estimation, as for example, Varius Hælyogabalus, which was dayly fedde with many hundred fishes and foules, and was accompanied with manie brothels, baudes, harlots and gluttons, and thus it doeth appeare by your abhorring vertue, that of right you might haue claimed a great office in Hæliogabalus court, if you had beene in those daies, but you haue an infinite number of your conuersation in these dayes, the more pitie. (f. 1–1v)

Humphrey's opening turn comments on John's previous utterance and labels it with the speech act verb (SAV) *boast* and then accuses him of extravagance. He reproaches John in moralistic terms in scholastic phrases (*I wis*), contrastive pronouns (*I-you*), exaggeration, sound play and an expression of emotion (*pitie*).

The accusation is indirect, with reference to classical learning; the Roman emperor Heliogabalus was known for his extravagance. The

---

[1] This text is discussed in more detail in Taavitsainen (2009a).

device is important for constructing Humphrey's identity and role as a learned teacher. He names the vices of gluttony and lust, and then ascribes them to John.

> *Iohn.* What? good sir, I require not your counsell, I pray you bee your owne caruer, and giue mee leaue to serue my fantasie. I will not charge you, you are verie auncient and graue, and I am but young, wee be no matches. (f. 1v)

John perceives the utterance as an insult. The perlocutionary effect shows John's hurt feelings: he reacts with a blunt *What*, an exclamatory question of surprise, not believing his ears, and the phrase *good sir* seems to have a condescending tone, perhaps in mock politeness. A request for freedom follows: the old man should leave him alone. This meaning is formulated as a negative request with a reference to a proverb. The turn is all about negotiation of face, the desire of the participant to go unimpeded. The contrast between the roles is made explicit: Humphrey is described as 'ancient and grave', John as 'young'; 'wee be no matches'. John's turn may be interpreted as a response in kind to the first insult.

> *Hum.* Good counsell is a treasure to wise men, but a verie trifle to a foole, if thou haddest seene those things which I haue seene. I knowe thou wouldest not be such a man, nor thus spend thy time. (f. 1v)

Humphrey's role as the wise man is emphasised in his response, which is delivered as a 'universal' truth, with a conversational implicature in this particular situation: he is a wise man, John a fool. The proverb works as an indirect accusation and insult, continuing the verbal duelling between the protagonists. Humphrey continues by inviting John to learn about a better life style, which is a key to the ensuing instruction.

> *Iohn.* What hast thou seene, that I haue not seene? (f. 1v)

John replies with a request for verification. It expresses doubt and continues with the contrast created at the beginning. As in real life, attitudes are not easily changed.

> *Hum.* I haue seene many notable and grieuous plagues, which haue fallen vpon greedie gluttons, as wasting their substance, disforming their bodies, shortning their pleasant daies: and in this poynt to conclude with thee, whereas gluttonie remaineth, from thence is moderate diet banished: and those bellies that follow the lust of the eyes (in meates) in youth, shall lacke the health of all their bodies, in age if they liue so long. (f. 1v–2)

A narrative of experience follows with a cumulative list of vices with negative consequences in the vein of 'universal' truths.

> *Iob.* Mee thinke thou canst giue good counsell, thou seemest to be seene in phisicke. I pray thee, is it so great hurt to delight in plentie of banquets? (f. 2)

The turning point of the plot occurs in the above turn which shows a change in John's attitude. The difference is striking. John pays Humphrey a compliment, expresses appreciation, and continues with a polite request. He is ready to learn more.

> *Hum.* Sir, if it will please you to [/4./] bee somewhat attentiue, I will tell you. It is the verie graine whereof commeth stinking vomits, sausy faces, dropsies, vertigo, palsies, obstructions, blindnes, flixes, apoplexis, caters, and rheumes, &c. (f. 2)

Humphrey's tone of voice changes, too. He begins with a polite address, *Sir*, the polite pronoun, *you*, and a promise that he will comply. A hyperbolic list of illnesses and misfortunes serves as a guarantee of his positive impact on John's life from now on. Dreadful hardships can be avoided by paying heed to Humphrey's teachings.

   The above analysis serves as an example of qualitative analysis and shows how co-occurring linguistic features in a text work in the same direction and contribute to the didactic goals of the dialogue. The function of first- and second-person pronouns is to exhibit interpersonal relations that change in the course of the dialogue. The text begins with contrasts between wise and foolish, old and young. The speech act verbs of boasting and the long lists of negative items, whether labels for people or names of diseases, build up a sense of conflict that is then reconciled. There is then a turning point, and the dialogue continues in harmony and mutual respect in a pleasant learning environment, leading to a positive outcome.

3.4 Corpus linguistics and historical pragmatics

At present corpus linguistic methods are applied in the great majority of studies in all branches of English linguistics. The advent of electronic corpora and corpus linguistics has changed the whole research paradigm of linguistics. Handwritten slips of paper belong to history, whereas data collection with computerised methods is fast and efficient. Corpus linguistic methods for historical pragmatics are becoming more fine-tuned and new applications can bring new precision to studies in this field. For assessments overlapping with historical linguistics (like grammaticalisation) and for historical stylistics, corpus methods are well established, but some other areas may present problems, as pragmatic units do not easily lend themselves to corpus studies. Recent advances have had a significant impact on historical pragmatics, and historical corpus pragmatics has grown to be an innovative and dynamic field of study.

3.4.1 Advantages and pitfalls

The advantages brought about by corpus linguistic methods are undeniable, including more transparent practices. The availability of a fairly large number of electronic historical corpora and the increasing sophistication of corpus linguistic tools have opened up a whole range of new research opportunities that allow us to tackle research questions that could not have been asked before. One of the benefits of corpus linguistic methodology is that it has brought language studies to a more objective level by making the criteria of exact sciences applicable to the humanities. Replicability as a scientific criterion was launched with the dawn of the new science in the latter half of the seventeenth century, and experiments were described in detail so that they could be repeated. In principle, different investigators should achieve the same results by applying the same method to the same data. Replicability applies to studies that overlap with historical linguistics to a large extent, but it is not self-evident in other subfields of historical pragmatics, as the contexts are seldom identical or self-explanatory, and there is always a subjective element in the interpretations. As a rule, grammaticalisation studies employ corpus linguistic methods, and they are at the core of both historical pragmatics and historical linguistics. Material for tracing the development of discourse markers, for example, can be efficiently retrieved with lexical searches. In such cases and in other studies that take a lexical item as the point of departure, the process is similar to that found in mainstream historical linguistics. In the other branches of historical pragmatics replicability is not as straightforward. Past cultures had different societal norms of politeness and contexts may be deficient. There are, however, some means to reduce the haphazard element in interpretations. For example, two people can code the same examples and their results can be compared; their inter-coder reliability indicates how replicable the results are. This method has been used in some speech act studies (Jucker et al. 2008, Jucker and Taavitsainen forthcoming).

But there are downsides as well, for electronic corpora encourage a shift away from contextual assessments when a great deal of material is available in an easily accessible form. The corpus user may not be familiar with the background facts of texts, and without this knowledge qualitative analysis of examples cannot be performed without risking the integrity of the study. The problem of decontextualisation has been noticed as a drawback and a shift seems to be taking place in linguistics towards pragmatic approaches (as noted before), with context playing a more prominent role than before. Corpus compilers are trying to remedy this by including detailed descriptions of pertinent background features to help future scholars.

3.4.2 Top-down and bottom-up methodologies

In corpus linguistics, there are two main approaches to research planning. The first is called 'top-down', as the point of departure is a linguistic feature or grammatical category such as modal verbs. The second, the 'bottom-up' method, sees what the material yields as a means of expressing the researched feature, such as modality or expressions of stance. The former relies on the deductive method and takes a list of features to be studied as its point of departure, while the latter is inductive and explores the material without preconceived ideas about what it might yield. Top-down assessments of modality, for instance, begin by searches of modal auxiliaries or semi-modal verbs and rely on lists of items from earlier studies. The bottom-up method takes the text itself as its point of departure, and a good way of doing it is to assess the word lists of the data to see which items in the repertoire could be used in modal expressions. Often it is the researcher's own familiarity with the data that helps them pay attention to recurrent patterns that have been ignored or passed by in earlier studies. This is the case with 'hidden manifestations' of speech acts, for instance. Another dividing line has been drawn between corpus-aided or corpus-based studies and corpus-driven studies. The former refer to top-down methodologies, while corpus-driven studies are based on bottom-up investigations. In historical pragmatics, it is common to begin with the top-down method, but this is complemented by checking whether the material contains additional items which might be overlooked. For example, when studying discourse markers and interjections, the lists in modern grammar books is not enough and the material itself has to be consulted as well.

3.5 Different types of corpora, research questions, and suitable methods

Chapter 2 introduced electronic databases, but it is pertinent to go into more detail here and relate the different types of corpora to different research questions and methods. Distinctions between general-purpose corpora and one-genre, one-domain corpora suggest different uses. Some years ago the types of historical corpora were characterised as 'long and thin' (with few text samples in a long diachrony) versus 'short and fat' (broad coverage of texts within a short timeline), but this is not applicable any longer as the newest historical corpora belong to the generation of mega corpora with billions of words.

The first electronic corpora on Present-day English were compiled in the 1960s, and the first historical corpus, the *Helsinki Corpus* (HC hereafter), was released in 1991. It is a multigenre-multipurpose diachronic corpus of 1.5 million words, covering the time from the first emergence of vernacular English texts c. 750 to 1710. Today, more than twenty years later, it still serves its purpose, but researchers have learned to use it in a different way. In the early days the research questions were fairly modest and could focus on a few individual texts, while nowadays studies draw on large databases and combine an increasing number of different corpora. The composition of recent studies often follows an ambitious line: HC is taken as a point of departure to provide an overall view and show which genres and registers are likely to provide interesting material for further exploration. Results of such preliminary surveys can indicate how the question under scrutiny can best be researched, whether it is optimal as such, to be modified or developed in some other direction. The next step is then to search other larger or more specific corpora in order to find more material and to detect and verify larger patterns of variation. In all cases, qualitative methods are needed to complement the studies for reliable results.

There are several 'second-generation' genre- or domain-specific corpora that were compiled after HC to provide materials for more specific research questions posed by the compiler teams. The *Corpus of English Dialogues* (CED) was created especially for historical pragmatic studies, and has proved fruitful for a number of research questions particularly on dialogic language use (see Culpeper and Kytö 2010). The *Corpus of Early English Correspondence* (CEEC) was compiled to shed light on issues of language change to answer sociolinguistic research questions about how and by whom the changes were initiated, how they spread and diffused in time and how the new forms began to be used by various groups of people, and when the changes were completed. These studies were conducted in the frame of correlational sociolinguistics, but letters have proved a fruitful data source for (socio-)pragmatic studies as well, as formulaic language renders itself easily to corpus linguistic studies, and the passages in the body text may give access to more individual and informal language use (see below). The *Corpus of Early English Medical Writing* (CEEM) was created to trace the development of scientific thought styles and study the dynamics of genres within the register of scientific and medical writing (see Chapter 10). The *Lampeter Corpus* (1640–1740) contains shorter tracts and pamphlets and has been used for various pragmatic research purposes. There is a comprehensive Late Modern English multigenre corpus (the *Corpus of Late Modern English Texts*), and a number of other specialised historical corpora on genres or varieties of English. The large literary databases can also be used as historical corpora mainly to retrieve material for qualitative studies. The trend of mega corpora has come to historical materials as well with the *Corpus of Historical American English* (COHA) with some 400 million words of historical American English (1810–2009), and American English Google Books is even larger with 155 billion words. They can be used to explore frequencies of expressions or concepts, to provide a larger cultural context, and to establish a time frame that would be worth studying further. A very recent trend is to begin a study by showing the overall timeline of the feature in focus with these mega tools.

An example of the application of a large variety of both literary and non-literary corpora can be found in Laurel Brinton's recent book *The Comment Clause in English: Syntactic Origins and Pragmatic Development* (2008). She traces the diachronic development of comment clauses like *I think* and *I mean*, with the first person pronoun and a common verb of perception and cognition. They function as causal pragmatic markers expressing stance, and they can be found in texts throughout the history of English. Brinton's corpus-based study relies on a representative array of digital corpora over a millennium (2008: 20). For Old English, she used the *Helsinki Corpus* and the *Dictionary of Old English Corpus*. For Middle English, she used the *Helsinki Corpus*, the *Middle English Dictionary* and Chaucer's works. For the Early Modern period, she used the *Helsinki Corpus* and the *Lampeter Corpus*, complemented by the literary corpora of *Early English Prose Fiction*, *The University of Virginia Electronic Text Center, Modern English Collection* (1500–present), Shakespeare's works and the *English Drama* corpus. On the basis of corpus evidence, Brinton was able to show how these expressions undergo grammaticalisation, acquire subjective and intersubjective meanings, and become used for pragmatic and politeness purposes in communication. The earlier view of their development was that they originated in syntactically indeterminate matrix clauses and become reanalysed as parenthetical clauses. This explanation proved inadequate, and on the basis of her thorough study on comprehensive historical corpora, Brinton was able to propose a more varied and complex development.

3.6 Applications of corpus-linguistic methods

In recent years there has been rapid progress and increasing sophistication as new corpus linguistic software tools make it possible to scru-
tinise more subtle aspects of meaning-making processes and provide
new means of studying the linguistic diversity of the past. For several
applications, however, normalised versions of the text and the reference corpus are needed. Good results have been achieved with the
automatic standardisation of spelling variants, which was developed for
this purpose.[2] The development has been rapid and it is now possible
to gain deeper insights into textual patterns than before, as they are not
discernable with the naked eye and qualitative reading alone. The tools
are easy to apply, as the user can rely on the expertise of the program-
mers and the refined statistical methods that underlie these programs.
Some research questions in historical pragmatics lend themselves easily
to traditional corpus linguistic searches, while some others call for more
innovative approaches and applications. The field of historical discourse
analysis is closely connected and overlaps with historical pragmatics
and is often considered its subfield. Discourse studies have traditionally
relied on qualitative readings, and corpus-linguistic applications are
newcomers in the field. In the following sections, we shall present some
case studies to illustrate how corpus linguistic methodologies have been
applied to historical pragmatics. There are several tools that provide
useful corpus linguistic applications. The programs are easy to apply by
following the instructions. AntConc, a freeware concordance program
by Laurence Anthony, can be downloaded onto a personal computer.
Wordsmith contains the same functions but needs a licence. Both
perform the KWIC (keyword in context) concordance searches and
word lists efficiently. They are very useful for getting better acquainted
with the data, and researchers often play with these tools to explore the
data and form their research questions in an optimal way.

3.6.1 KWIC concordances

KWIC (keyword in context) concordance lines are perhaps the easiest
corpus-linguistic means to approach a research question; keyword in
this application simply means the search term the researcher is interested in. These lines show the context of an expression: the narrow
context is readily seen on the screen, and a larger context can easily be
accessed by clicking.

---

[2] See http://www.comp.lancs.ac.uk/~barona/vard2/

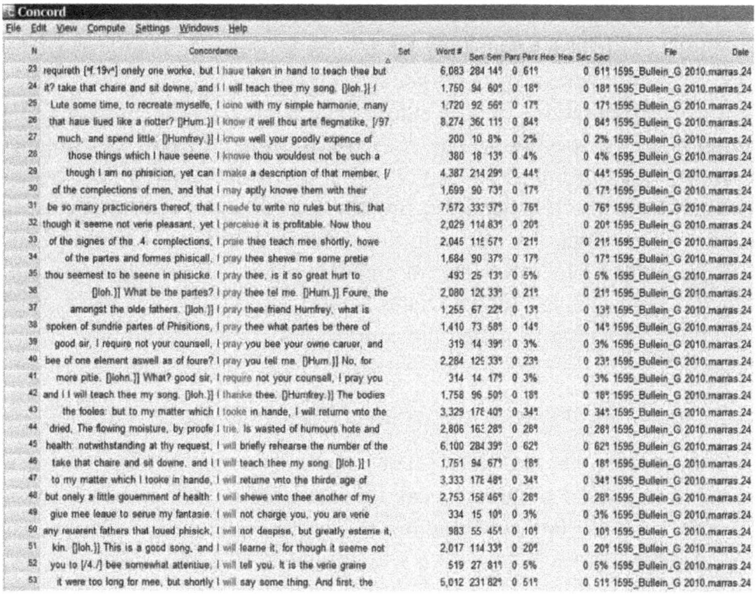

Figure 3.2 KWIC concordance of the first-person singular pronoun *I* in the *Gouernement of Health* (1595)

The screenshot exhibits lines 23–62 of the concordance. Several polite speech acts (*I pray thee*, *I thank thee*) can be detected, but there are lines that also reveal conflict talk (*I require not your counsel*). See the qualitative analysis above.

The method has been successfully applied to various kinds of research tasks even in discourse studies. One of the early applications aimed to find out how refugees and asylum seekers were presented in two different kinds of corpora: British newspaper articles and in publications by the United Nations High Commissioner for Refugees office. An assessment of concordance lines revealed clear differences. In the newspapers, the prominent semantic concepts associated with refugees included 'quantification' often in terms of water metaphors such as 'flood' for refugees, presenting them as an out-of-control mass, whereas the United Nations documents were more concerned with refugees returning home (Baker and McEnery 2005). This study has inspired others as it showed how corpus techniques can fruitfully be combined with discourse analysis, and they can be applied to historical data for studying the representations of, or attitudes towards, groups of people. The same techniques combined with the theoretical framework of critical discourse analysis was used in an article on the mid-seventeeth-century Glencairn Uprising, a military rebellion by Scottish Highlanders, against the English government (Prentice and Hardie 2009). This study probes into the presentations of both sides of the conflict in the contemporary London newspaper data. The material was analysed by concordance lines extracted using a wide set of search terms like 'enemy', 'the Scots/ the Scottish', 'the Highlanders', and 'the English'. The texts made use of greatly contrasting discourses in their representations of Glencairn and others, resulting in 'discourses of empowerment and disempowerment', where Glencairn and his associates were discredited, while the English and their associates provided the contrast with credit attribution.

3.6.2 Keyword analysis, collocations and clustering (WordSmith)

Another study by McEnery (2006) shows how novel research questions of historical pragmatics can be answered by advanced statistical methods. In the late seventeenth and early eighteenth centuries bad language was associated with a wide range of sins and sinful acts, and societies were founded to abolish bad language and legally charge its users. These societies developed a particular style that made use of 'spirals of signification' by associating bad language with other, not necessarily related, sources of moral offence. A special corpus called the Society for the Reformation of Manners Corpus was compiled for this study, and the *Lampeter Corpus* of contemporary shorter tracts and pamphlets of various fields was used as the reference corpus. The keyword method provided a means to demonstrate the discursive construction of 'moral panic' about language use by revealing the obsessive nature of moralistic discourse. The WordSmith tool was used to define positive and negative keywords; that is, words that were significantly more or less frequent in the assessed corpus than in a reference corpus. Keywords serve to distinguish these texts from general English, or even texts written in a similar register/genre but not conveying moral panic. Keywords themselves are ranked by the WordSmith program and given a keyness score to denote the strongest to weakest negative and positive keywords. In general, they are of three kinds: names, topic words and grammatical items. Most keywords fell into the topic area, but the first non-register positive keyword *and* proved to be of particular significance because of its function in creating spirals of signification by chains of collocation. *And* was used to bring together objects of offence in coordinated noun phrases. Moral panic was shown to occur in clusters, and the collocational networks contributed to a signification spiral within the Society for the Reformation of Manners Corpus. For example, *swear* was collocated with *blaspheme, curse, damn, game, hector* and *rant*. *Swearing* was systematically coordinated with disapproved verbal acts, lawlessness, frivolous pursuits and sexual activity. Its negatively loaded collocates included *backbiting, blaspheming, blasphemy, chambering, contention, cursing, damning, dancing, drinking, drunkenness, fiddling, gaming, injustice, intemperance, lewdness, lying, perjury, profanation, rioting, sabbath-breaking, slandering, thieving, wantonness* and *whoring*. Swearing on its own may be objectionable, but in convergence with other sins, a signification spiral is created in the text and moral panic becomes amplified with a strong negative semantic prosody.

Other new corpus linguistic tools also provide methodological innovations. For example, recurrent patterns in language use in terms of lexical bundles were relied on to answer the research questions of what gentlemen of Early and Late Modern England could say about themselves in the first person and whether differences in typical self-reference patterns could be detected in the *Corpus of Early English Correspondence* (Palander-Collin 2009). The cluster facility of WordSmith tells what company words keep most frequently in the text under scrutiny. The method was used to reveal the words that co-occur with the self-referential first-person pronoun *I*. The study combined quantitative and qualitative methods in the analysis of recurrent word clusters. The salient functional categories included the opening or closing formulae, humiliative and polite phrases, requests, attitudes and contextual expressions typical of personal correspondence. The analysis was extended to situate writers as the persons responsible for what is uttered. It also investigated what participants attribute to themselves, and how that varies in letters by the same person to different addressees in the family and outside it, in contexts where the participants' rights and obligations are different. A significant increase was found in the frequency of *I* from the sixteenth to the eighteenth century. In particular, self-referential stance expressions conveying the writer's personal feelings and assessments with mental verbs (for example, *think, know, wish* and *hope*) became more prominent. The results confirmed similar observations in stance marking by other researchers, and the explanation for this was discussed in terms of general cultural changes and the increasing freedom to express subjective opinions and feelings more openly.

3.7 A possible research agenda

To come back to the agenda proposed in 3.1 we would like to suggest the following research steps which combine corpus methodology with qualitative analysis:

1. Begin with the data that interest you most. You should also have a general idea of your research interests at this stage. Familiarise yourself with the texts by qualitative reading and explorations by corpus searches (KWIC concordances, wordlists, etc.)
2. Survey previous research: what has already been done and where can you find untrodden paths to explore?
3. Formulate your research question(s).
4. Decide upon your methodology. Can quantification illuminate some background aspects or frequencies of expressions? Can ready-made corpora be used? Are there suitable checklists of features in grammars or previous research that you could use? Are there previous studies that can be used as a model for your own study? Can you combine qualitative and quantitative methods?
5. Perform the empirical analysis.
6. Interpret the results. Show illustrative examples and explain them with qualitative analysis. Diagrams, tables and figures can also be very useful.
7. Contextualise your findings by considering larger issues, and by relating your findings to the multilayered context from the microlevel to the macrolevel of culture.

3.8 Future prospects

We are at a dynamic phase in historical corpus pragmatics. One of the new trends is annotation; that is, marking the words of the corpus for word class or parsing the corpus for grammatical functions. It is being developed for pragmatic research tasks by marking, for example, speech acts in the corpus. At present, pragmatic annotation has been applied to only a subsection of the *Corpus of English Dialogues 1560–1760* with comedy plays, drama and trials, but the *Sociopragmatic Corpus* (1640–1760) has already given encouraging results that indicate that this is the way to go in the future (Archer and Culpeper 2009). Another new trend moves at the interface between semantics and pragmatics. The *Historical Thesaurus of English* was made available only recently, and researchers are already developing new methods, making use of the rich data offered by this new tool. Some time ago, macro and micro approaches were seen as opposites, but now they are increasingly combined and like qualitative/quantitative, macro/micro approaches are seen as complementary. The above examples of concordance lines and keyword analysis show that it is possible to gain insights by applying quantitative assessments, complemented with qualitative analysis. Often the analysis proceeds from the microlevel of the narrow linguistic context of the utterance to discourse and genre and all the way to the large context of culture to account for the variability of language. What is certain is that experiments of cross-fertilisation with other branches and methods of pragmatics and neighbouring fields will continue in the future, and methods will develop and become more transparent.

Exercises

An advertisement for a beauty lotion from the year 1734 reads:

> So exceedingly valued by Ladies of Quality, and all who have used it, for its transcendent Excellency in Beautifying the Face, Neck, and Hands to the most exquisite Perfection possible, is to be had only at Mr. Radford's Toyshop, at the Rose and Crown against St. Clement's Church-yard in the Strand.
>
> It gives an inexpressible fine Air to the Features of the Face on the Spot, and a surprising Handsomeness to the Neck and Hands, which it immediately makes exceeding smooth, fine and delicately white.
>
> Nothing in the World can sooner or more certainly take away all disagreeable Redness, Spots, Pimples, Hear, Roughness, Morphew, Worms in the Face, Marks of the Small Pox, Sun-burn, or any other Discoulouring, nor remove all Wrinkles so perfectly; for it quickly makes the Skin become so incomparably fine, clear, plump, soft, and beautifully fair, as to cause Admiration in the Beholders.
>
> It really gives a most engaging resplendent Brightness to the whole Countenance, and causes sparkling Life, Spirit, a juvenile Bloom to reign in every Feature, and yet is nothing of Paint, but exceeds it, by its bringing the Skin, whether of the Face, Neck, or Hands, and tho' brown, red, or rough, to a natural youthful Fairness, Smoothness, and charming Delicacy, which Paint only faintly imitates; neither is this ROYAL BEAUTIFYER prepared from the least Particle of Mercury, or any Thing Metalline, but is perfectly harmless, and may be given inwardly even to Children. It has also a pleasant Scent, will not soil the finest Lawn, and is very agreeable to use.
>
> But these its admirable Properties, by which it vastly exceeds any Thing whatever for the like Purpose, have occasioned many to imitate it under various other Names, beware therefore of such Impositions, the true ROYAL BEAUTIFYING FLUID, that has given such universal Satisfaction to so many Ladies of Distinction, being only to be had at Mr Radford's Toyshop abovementioned, at 3 s. 6 d. a Bottle, with Directions, and no where else in England. (John Johnson's *Ephmera*)

1. Analyse the text, paying special attention to the adjectives and nouns. The following questions are posed by Leech and Short (2007: 61) in a checklist devised to help researchers in their work. Not all are applicable to the present task, but they indicate the way in which linguistic stylistic research is conducted:

> Are the adjectives frequent? To what kinds of attribute do adjectives refer? Physical? Psychological? Visual? Auditory? Colour? Referential? Emotive? Evaluative? etc. Are adjectives restrictive or non-restrictive? Gradable or non-gradable? Attributive or predicative?
>
> Are the nouns abstract or concrete? What kinds of abstract nouns occur (e.g. nouns referring to events, perceptions, processes, moral qualities, social qualities)? What use is made of proper names? Collective nouns?

2. How does this text compare with modern advertisements of cosmetics? What similarities can you find? Can you find culture-specific or period-specific details?

3. Discuss the details of the catalogue description of the above text given below. Which of them would you include in a research paper? Are there points that should be further elaborated?

> Collection: – Advertising Document type: – Advertisements – advertisement
> Title: – The Royal Beautifying Liquid Advertiser: – Radford, Mr, Mr. Radford's Toyshop at the Rose and Crown against St. Clement's Churchyard in the Strand, [London]
> Products: – beautifying liquid Brand Names: – Royal Beautifying Liquid Date of publication: – [1734] Source of date: – manuscript annotation
> Physical Form: – single sheet, [1] p., 12.5 × 7.9 cm. Medium: – paper
> Printing process of text: – Letterpress works Country: – England
> Subject (LCSH): – Cosmetics Early works to 1800 Patent medicines; Early works to 1800 Beauty, Personal ; Early works to 1800 Notes: – Advertisement cut from unidentified newspaper. Additional information: has prices

Further reading

The handbook *Historical Pragmatics* (Jucker and Taavitsainen 2010) contains 22 comprehensive chapters giving an overview of the different branches of the field and the methodologies used in research. Methods in historical pragmatics have also been discussed by Taavitsainen and Fitzmaurice (2007) and in the articles of the volume, edited by Fitzmaurice and Taavitsainen (2007).

For corpus linguistics, see Baker (2006) and McEnery and Wilson (2001) and for applications of both qualitative and quantitative methods to various research tasks in historical pragmatics, see the *Journal of Historical Pragmatics* (for example, the above discussed examples in 3.6.1 and 3.6.2 were published in the journal).

Useful textbooks for the interface between language and literature are listed in Further readings for Chapter 12.

4 'Lo, which a greet thyng is affeccioun!': Discourse markers and interjections

4.1 Introduction

In the middle of the eighteenth century, Horace Walpole, 4th Earl of Oxford, writes in a letter to Sir Horace Mann:

> **Oh!** how shall I do about writing to her? **Well**, if I can, I will be bold, and write to her to-night. (CLMET 1 314, Letter 101. To Sir Horace Mann. Arlington Street, 25 March 1743.)

Walpole contemplates on whether to write to Madame Grifoni, whom he calls 'my Princess' in one of the preceding sentences, and then makes up his mind to do it. In these two sentences, he uses the elements *Oh!* and *Well* which give the passage an informal and indeed a spoken character. Walpole writes at this point as if he were talking to his friend. Such elements as *oh* and *well* are variously described as discourse markers or interjections. They are typical of spoken language but they also occur in a wide variety of written texts.

In a different register of writing some two hundred years earlier, a section of a professional medical text with a teaching function begins with *now*:

> *The .ii. Chapter. Of the Elementes.* NOw after that I haue declared and opened the sectes and opynions of the mooste noble and moost auncient Physitions, I thynke it verye mete to shewe the nature of the Elementes, whyche be iiii. in numbre: the fyre, ayer, water, and earth. (EMEMT, Langton, *Introduction into phisycke*, 1550, f. 11r)

Originally, *now* is a temporal adverb but in the above passage it has a summing-up function, and, as we will show below, it can also be described as a discourse marker, which here has a register-specific function. In such uses it is often accompanied by metatextual comments as in the above example. The other more common function in historical texts is forward-looking, foregrounding the unfolding discourse, which is also the prevailing function in modern spoken English.

In the history of English, both the repertoire of linguistic elements, which function as discourse markers or interjections, and their specific functions in specific genres and registers are subject to change and variation. In this chapter we want to give an overview of how discourse markers and interjections developed in different genres and provide two case studies. But first we shall deal with some difficult issues of delimitation. How are these elements defined and how do they relate to other similar elements?

4.2 Definitions: Discourse markers and interjections

Discourse markers and interjections both belong to the class of words called inserts by Biber et al. (1999: 1082–6). Inserts are invariable stand-alone words, syntactically independent from the rest of the utterance, and they have textual and interpersonal functions. Besides discourse markers and interjections, the class of inserts comprises greetings and farewells (such as *hi*, *hello* or *good morning*), attention signals (such as *hey* or *hey you*), response elicitors (such as *right?*, *eh?* or *okay?*), response forms (such as *yeah*, *yes*, or *yep*) and a few others. Discourse markers, which include elements such as *well*, *now*, *right*, *I mean*, *you know* or *you see*, have the textual function of structuring elements in a discourse. They indicate transitions, beginnings of new elements, the closing off of current elements and so on. They also have an interpersonal function, signalling various aspects of the relationship between the speaker, the addressee and the message. Discourse markers regularly have homonyms in other word classes, and this sometimes leads to ambiguity. *Now* can also be a temporal adverb, *you know* can also be the subject and the verb of a normal sentence rather than a discourse marker, and so on. Interjections, on the other hand, have primarily an exclamatory or expressive function, and they include elements such as *oh*, *ah*, *wow*, *oops*, *Heavens* or *Good Lord*. Sometimes a distinction is made between primary and secondary interjections. Primary interjections, such as *oh*, *ah*, *wow* and *oops*, do not have homonyms in other word classes, whereas secondary interjections, such as *Heavens* or *Good Lord*, do. But definitions used by different scholars vary. Discourse markers and interjections are often seen as overlapping groups of elements with fuzzy boundaries, and they have been categorised under many different names. Besides 'discourse particles' or 'pragmatic markers', discourse markers have been called 'mystery particles' and 'implicit anchoring' devices, offering 'windows (with different degrees of opacity)' to what is being communicated below the surface level (Östman 1995: 99–100), and interjections have been described as 'those seemingly irrational devices that constitute the essence of communication' (Ameka 1992: 101).

Discourse markers and interjections can also be related to the concept of pragmatic noise, a term introduced by Culpeper and Kytö (2010: 199). Pragmatic noise includes items such as *ah, ha, hah, o, oh, ho, um, hum*, as well as reduplicative forms like *ha, ha* or *ha, ha, ha*. What they have in common is that they do not have homonyms, they are not part of a sentence construction, they are morphologically simple, they have no propositional or referential meaning, and they are often sound symbolic to a degree. Figure 4.1 provides some key features of inserts and pragmatic noise in overview.

In Figure 4.1, inserts and pragmatic noise are represented along a continuum. Some inserts, such as discourse markers and polite speech act formulae, are made up of regular words that have adopted specialised meanings but they still carry – to some extent at least – a residue of their original meaning. At the other end of the scale, we can find vocalisations, such as laughter, which do not have word status and which do

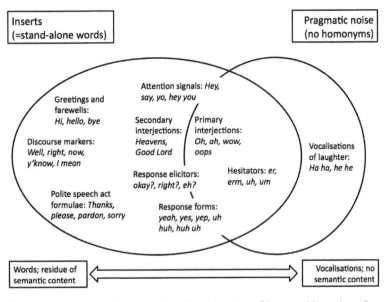

Figure 4.1 Inserts and pragmatic noise (based on Biber et al.'s notion of 'inserts' (1999: 1082ff) and Culpeper and Kytö's notion of 'pragmatic noise' (2010: 199))

not have any semantic content. Many elements are somewhere between these extremes. Attention signals, for instance, include elements that are more word-like (*say*, *you*) and elements that are more like vocalisations (*hey*). In the case of interjections, the boundary between primary and secondary interjections actually coincides with inclusion and exclusion as pragmatic noise.

In historical pragmatics, the emphasis is on the functions of communication and negotiation of meaning, and thus the distinction between primary and secondary interjections, especially if etymology is considered, seems somewhat artificial. It seems better to adopt a prototype approach (see also Chapter 9) as it fits well both discourse markers and interjections in a historical perspective: items are more or less core or peripheral, and the two categories overlap. The same lexical item can serve as a discourse marker (with primarily textual and interpersonal functions) or as an interjection (with primarily emotive functions). The overlap is evident, and a prototypical approach takes this into account. Core members of the categories of discourse markers and interjections display all main features of their class. Prototypical discourse markers are in accord with the features defined as typical of discourse marker use in the literature: *well* is one of them, though it too has been called an interjection by some scholars. Less prototypical ones have fewer of those features or exhibit them to a more limited extent only: *y'know* and *like* are marginal to the extent that they have a residue of semantic meaning (Jucker 2002: 213). The less prototypical members overlap with other categories. Brinton's (1996: 32) list of discourse markers – or pragmatic markers as she calls them – contains some peripheral items, like *and*, *then*, and *therefore*, as their most common uses are different from those of more typical discourse markers. Several of her items, like *ah*, *oh*, and *uh huh*, are counted as interjections or pragmatic noise in other studies. A good example of the fuzziness of the borderline is *oh!*, which can be treated either as a discourse marker or as an interjection. When it has a text-structuring function, *oh* can be treated as a discourse marker, but when it expresses emotion, such as admiration or surprise, it is an interjection. Some others are prototypical discourse markers and core members of the category with multiple discourse marker functions, *well* being a case in point here.

Interjections in turn reflect the speaker's mental state, and their functions have been taken as a point of departure for a classification that groups them into three main types (Ameka 1992: 113–14). They have been noticed to apply to historical materials as well. The first function consists of expressive uses with emotive and cognitive subfunctions and can be further subdivided into emotive interjections like *Yuk!* 'I feel disgust' or *ouch!* 'I feel pain', and cognitive interjections, which pertain to the state of knowledge reception of new knowledge, in utterances like *aha!* 'now I know'. Manipulation of social relations, or one's own behaviour, can be attested in uses of *Oh!* and *Well!* as in Walpole's letter cited at the beginning of this chapter. The expressive function is particularly important in historical data, but other functions occur as well. The second function is conative. Such expressions are directed to an addressee (or addressees) with an action-demanding purpose, or directed at someone to attract their attention or to elicit a response; for example, *shh!* to demand silence or *eh?* in anticipation of an answer, and *Hey!, Ho!, Look!* to attract attention. Similar expressions are used in historical texts and their repertoire is even wider with the biblical *Lo!,* for example. Conative uses of interjections can be found in a broad range of texts. The third function is phatic; that is, expressions to keep the conversation going. Hesitators signal planning difficulty, but indicate that the speaker wishes to continue with their turn. Backchannels, such as *mhm!* or *uh-huh!* encourage the speaker to continue. All these elements are common in Early Modern English plays.

4.3 Genre-specific developments

Discourse markers and interjections, as pointed out above, are typical of spoken language, but their conventionalisation in written genres in the history of English is intriguing, especially because these additional functions have not been established in present-day spoken language and they open up a new perspective. The repertoires of discourse markers and interjections vary in different periods of the history of English and there is room for more studies in this area, as only some interjections and some lines of development have received attention so far. In this section we will cast some spotlights on relevant issues and developments.

In written texts the functions of discourse markers and interjections can deviate from present-day spoken uses. For example, they were particularly important marking turn-taking in dialogues at a time when literacy was rare and reading aloud the rule. They served as signposts for speaker changes, making it easier for the audience to follow turn-taking in dialogic passages. This function is evident in medieval romances that served as entertainment in public readings at court and noble households. Imagine the following passage read aloud in front of an audience. In the medieval period, punctuation had not developed the conventions it has today, and discourse markers and interjections served much the same purpose as modern punctuation in the written language:

'A,' seyde Balyne, 'I know that knyghtes name . . .'
'Well,' seyde hys oste, 'I shall telle you how . . .'
'Than I promyse you,' seyde Balyn, 'parte of his bloode to hele your sonne withal.'
'Than we woll be forewarde to-morne,' seyde he.
So on the morne they rode . . . (Malory, *The Knight with the Two Swords*, pp. 82–3)

Items of pragmatic noise often cluster together, and it is not unusual for passages to contain items of different sorts in a sequence. It is their joint effect that makes the audience react.

In comedies such passages often release laughter. An example can be found in William Congreve's comedy *The Double-Dealer* (1694). It contains several interjections and mild swearing, and the pragmatic noise items are particularly frequent. In the following passage, the first turn begins with vocatives, containing repetition and a sequence of direct questions, finishing with *ha* used like a tag question, demanding an answer. After a witty exchange of turns with an accusation and its return in kind, Brisk's turn begins with *Pooh* followed by laughter given as *ha, ha, ha*. The phrase *By the Gods!* is an exclamation and mild swearing. Another accusation, this time elaborated and emphasised, follows. *Pox* belongs to the same category as the previous mild swearings. Brisk's triumphant twisting of words into another insult finishes with an ascription of the next turn to Mellefont. In the phrase *O' my word*, the *O* is an abbreviation for 'on', but the following turn begins with *my dear* prefaced by the interjection *Oh!* to denote a change in the mental state of the speaker. The effect is enhanced by 'let me perish'. What comes after reveals that the utterance is ironical, with a modification of a common pattern employed even today by stating the opposite of what is really meant.

> *Brisk.*   Boys, Boys, Lads, where are you? What do you give ground? Mortgage for a Bottle, ha? *Careless*, this is your trick; you're always spoiling Company by leaving it.
> *Care.*   And thou art always spoiling Company by coming into 't.
> *Brisk.*   Pooh, ha, ha, ha, I know you envy me. Spite, proud spite, by the Gods! and burning envy. – I'le be judged by *Mellefont* here, who gives and takes Raillery better, you or I. Pox, Man, when I say you spoil Company by leaving it, I mean you leave no body for the Company to Laugh at. I think there I was with you, ha? *Mellefont.*
> *Mel.*   O' my word, *Brisk*, that was a home thrust; you have silenc'd him.
> *Brisk.*   Oh, my dear *Mellefont*, let me perish, if thou art not the Soul of Conversation, the very Essence of Wit, and Spirit of Wine, (CED, Congreve, *The Double-Dealer* (1694), p. 2

Some Old English discourse markers, episode boundary markers, and interjections have been discussed in the literature. *Hwat!* as an interjection assumes the initial position and co-occurs with a first- or second-person pronoun. Interjections are used for interpersonal functions, to sequence discourse and mark turn-taking in dialogues, and for general emphasis. *Eala* is the most frequent of them in Old English literature. It occurs in a fairly broad range of genres, especially in verse and in religious texts, but it is also found in fiction. It is often combined with features of interactivity, like the second-person pronoun and term of address, and these features work together to create involvement. An example can be found in Aelfric's homilies in which *eala* is used to involve the addressee and the real audience. Note also the vocative use of *O*, according to the Latin model, with the address term which also works in the same direction.

> Drihten andwyrde. þam chananeiscum wife. and cwaeð; Eala, ðu wif micel is ðin geleafa. (AECHom 70) 'The Lord replied to the woman from Canaan and said, O you woman, great is your faith.' (translated by Hiltunen 2006: 98, 114)

In the case of *eala,* Latin texts provide the model, but in the case of *la,* which is also frequently present in the Bible and in homilies, no interjection is found in the Latin original. Biblical language and religious texts are an obvious source for studying these features in Old English, and fiction is interesting as well. Markers of text deixis and *witodlice* or *soplice* 'truly' have received some attention. We can assume that, for example, *nu* occurs in the discourse-marker function modelled after the Latin *nunc,* for example in biblical prose, but studies have not been conducted yet on a larger scale and discourse markers are still a fairly understudied area.

One of the most researched discourse markers in the early periods is the time adverbial in the discourse marker use *than* 'then'. It has received a great deal of attention as a narrative marker both in Old and Middle English from the 1970s onwards. In addition to the foregrounding function established in the early studies, many other functions have been assigned to it: it can mark the peak of the narrative, and act as a dramatiser, or as a topic shifter. In Middle English it serves to sequence a narrative. A recurrent pattern in early romances like Malory's is *so (whan) ... than ... and ... anone ... (and) ...* where *than* acts as a result marker (Fludernik 2000). Some saints' legends show similar features to medieval romances and contain an abundance of interjections and discourse markers. *Than,* for instance, is extremely frequent in the legend of *St. Katherine of Alexandria* in MS Southwell Minster 7 (ed. Nevanlinna and Taavitsainen 1993), reaching 1.2 per cent frequency in one section where almost all episodes begin with it. In addition, the text contains frequent exclamations with *a, alas, lo,* and *loo.* Often they are used in the narrator's metacomments where he explains to the readership what was happening and they serve to heighten the emotions of the storyteller, as in the following passage:

> A lord, what ioye was felt in this holy virgyne at this tyme! Ther was neu*er* ioye like befor, out-take the ioy þat our lady had, when scho bar Ihe*s*u, the kyng of blis (lines 540–3)
> 'Oh Lord, what joy this virgin felt at this time! Never was joy like this felt before except the joy that Our Lady felt when she was pregnant with Jesus, the King of Bliss.'

Late medieval narrative genres contain several other discourse markers and some of them have very clear genre-specific functions. For example, *whilom* 'once upon a time' serves to create 'horizons of expectation' (Jauss 1979), and depending on the continuation, whether set in noble surroundings in the past or contemporary homely environment, the audience knew right away what was to follow, whether a romance or a fabliau (see Chapter 9). Authors can use these devices, especially interjections, to appeal to fictional addressees within the text, but also to manipulate readers in the real world. Often several functions occur simultaneously, and the communication takes place at two levels: in the fictional discourse world between its characters, and between the author and his audience, who become addressees in several cases. The functions of discourse markers and interjections focus on meaning-making practices in interaction on the frame level between the author/ narrator and the reader, as in the above example, or in the embedded level between the characters of the story. In Geoffrey Chaucer's *The Miller's Tale,* the narrator intervenes with ironic remarks like '*Lo,* which a greet thyng is affeccioun!' (MilT 3611)[1] beginning with an interjection that had biblical connotations. In this genre context, it is used ironically to underline 'fabliau justice' in accordance with the burlesque and carnivalistic nature of the genre. In such examples, the interjection alerts the reader to pay attention to what follows. Thus interjections can act as markers of ironic connotations or additional meanings. In Chaucer's texts, interjections and other exclamations have developed genre-specific vocabulary: in sermons, saints' lives and romances *alas, lo* and *o* are common, while fabliaux have a wider repertoire with *fy, harrow, out, tehee* and *weylaway* (Taavitsainen 1995). Passages with several interjections and mild swearing mark turning points in the plot or give a summary as the culmination of the story:

And gan to crie 'Harrow!' and 'Weylaway!
Oure hors is lorn, Alayn, for Goddes banes,
Step on thy feet! Com of, man, al atanes!
Allas, our wardeyn has his palfrey lorn.' (*The Reeve's Tale* I 4072–5)
'And he cried "Harrow!" and "Weylaway!
Our horse is lost, Alain, for God's bones,
Get on your feet! Come along, man, at once!
Alas, our warden's horse is lost!"'

On Chaucer's genre map, romances provide the counterpoint of fabliaux. They are set in the distant past with idealised characters, gardens and pastimes, and with courtly love as the overarching theme. Falling in love at first sight in *The Knight's Tale* is marked by the interjection *A!* which represents a spontaneous outburst of emotion and typifies the intensity of the feeling:

He cast his eye upon Emelya,
And therwithal he bleynte and cride, 'A!'
As though he stongen were unto the herte. (*The Knight's Tale* I 1077–9)
'He cast his eyes upon Emily,
And thereupon he grew pale and cried "Ah!"
As if his heart had been stung.'

The late medieval period provides an abundance of material for studying discourse markers and interjections, whereas early Elizabethan prose is almost devoid of them.

Well is one of the prototypical discourse markers and has received perhaps more attention than any other discourse marker in Modern English, and its attestations have also been well researched in the various periods of the history of English. In Present-day English, *well* can be used as a frame device to introduce a new topic or preface direct reported speech. In both cases, it functions mainly on the textual level as a text-structuring device, but it entails a deictic reorientation. *Well* can also qualify as a reply and signal that only a partial answer to a question can be given for some reason. It occurs as a face-threat mitigator when it prefaces a disagreement indicating some problems on the interpersonal level. This function has been much discussed in the literature: *well* implies that the answer is not optimal for some reason (see above). It can also be used as a pause filler to bridge a silence and keep up the interaction. Of these four present-day uses only two were found in historical texts in data drawn from the *Helsinki Corpus* (Jucker 1997). However, an interesting line of development emerged, as the discourse marker *well* developed from predominantly textual to predominantly interpersonal uses. Framing was the oldest function, attested regularly from the Late Middle English period onwards. The function as face-threat mitigator is found in Early Modern English, for example, in Shakespeare's plays, and the interpersonal functions become prominent. The following exchange contains several discourse markers. It begins with *Why ay*, which in the early modern period had a discourse marker function, but *you see* is here juxtaposed to *and we all see* and is thus not as clearly a discourse marker as in Present-day English. The following turn begins with *Well*, qualifying the answer, and demanding more explanation. *Why then* is again a discourse marker, in response to *well*, expressing the idea that the speaker finds it somewhat unnecessary to explain his previous utterances:

> *J. U.* Why ay this is true; but you see, and we all see, that here is nothing come of it. Therefore I intend to undertake
> the Business my self, my dear *State Rogue* : And first, I'll know
> of our wise Senate how many Millions *per An.* they will give
> me to do it; and how many Years they are willing to allow
> me to humble this great and mighty Monarch of *France* .
> *S. R.* Well, and what then?
> *J. U.* Why then, for Six Millions *per An.* and Seven Years
> to effect it, I'll undertake the Business. (CED, Anon. *State Rogue* (1695), p. 2)

After a meagre beginning in the sixteenth century, the use of interjections and discourse markers again increases, and an interesting continuum of usage patterns has been suggested to the present day (see the case studies below). In the Late Modern English period, the use of interjections to create a romantic emotional mood was so common that William Cowper (1731–1800) parodies the device and gives tongue-in-cheek guidance for achieving the desired effect: 'In order to write pathetical … get together a large quantity of Oh's and Ah's! and introduce them as – thus – Ah Me! Oh Thou!' (ed. King and Ryskamp 1986: 35–7; see also Taavitsainen 1998). In Jane Austen's early prose, interjections are used in various ways for various purposes: they have a peak-marking function, a foregrounding function and, to a lesser extent, a turn-taking function, and serve as a mechanism for increasing the reader's emotional involvement. Characterisation of fictional people using interjections is a fairly late phenomenon, and is found in some of Jane Austen's novels. Interjections are particularly prominent in *Northanger Abbey*, her parody of the gothic novel (see Taavitsainen 1998). The protagonist, Catharine, talks with Henry Tilney, the romantic hero of the story, about the imaginary horrors of the Abbey. Her reaction to Henry's hair-raising accounts employs an interjection and a discourse marker in a humorous sequence:

> '. . . but scarcely have you been able to decipher "Oh! Thou – whomsoever thou mayst be, into whose hands these memoirs of the wretched Matilda may fall" – when your lamp suddenly expires in the socket, and leaves you in total darkness.'
> 'Oh! No, no – do not say so. Well, go on.' (*Northanger Abbey*, p. 126)

In another example from the same novel, interjections mark the peak of suspense in narrative passages like the following, describing the heroine's nightly explorations, where *Alas!* provides the culmination point:

> The dimness of the light her candle emitted made her turn with alarm; but there was no danger of extinction, it had yet some hours to burn; and that she might not have any greater difficulty in distinguishing writing than what its ancient date might occasion, she hastily snuffed it. Alas! It was snuffed and extinguished in one. A lamp could not have expired with more awful effect. Catherine, for a few moments, was motionless with horror. (*Northanger Abbey*, p. 135)

4.4 Two case studies: *Oh!* and *Alas!*

4.4.1 *Oh!*

In the theory part of this chapter we pointed out that *Oh!* falls into the two overlapping areas of inserts and pragmatic noise. It is a primary interjection because it does not have a homonym in another word class. The N-gram viewer of Google Books can give us a first approximation of the frequency of this element across the centuries (see Figure 4.2), but this new tool has to be used with caution, as the optical character recognition software used for the compilation of this corpus may give false results. The early centuries seem particularly untrustworthy because of their unstandardised spellings and letter forms.

Discourse markers have long been one of the foci of conversation analysis, but the application of the method to historical data is only recent. Pragmatic variables include transient states of mind expressed with discourse markers and interjections and the study below shows how dependent interpersonal negotiations of meaning are on situations and how momentary shifts in mental processes can be expressed in discourse. They are important in modern Conversation Analysis (CA) that pays attention to how readers co-produce meaning in interaction in unfolding discourse without preconceived notions of how turns should

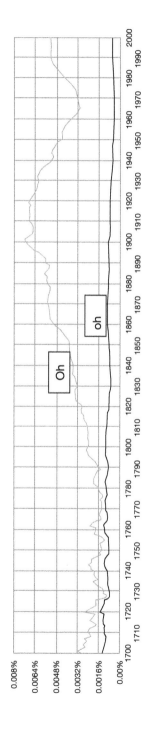

Figure 4.2 *Oh, oh* 1700–2000 with N-gram viewer (http://books.google.com/ngrams/)

be or how they usually are expressed. Person (2009) analysed the works of Shakespeare from this angle, and pointed out that all the various uses of *Oh!* observed in conversation analytic studies of contemporary English talk-in-interaction could also be found in historical material. In the following we shall survey some examples where the underlying assumption was that at least some of the conversational Elizabethan uses of *Oh!* must have been present in order for the earliest audiences of the plays to understand these verbal exchanges. The study claims to have demonstrated a degree of continuity of the use of *Oh!* in conversation over the last 400 years (Person 2009: 103). All functions established in CA for the discourse marker *Oh!* were identified in these plays. Nonresponsive uses are most common and they occur most frequently in the opening position of a turn, or in the middle of a character's speech or within an interactive conversation between characters, and topic change or a change of addressee is often signalled. In these cases it suggests a change of state in the speaker's thoughts. The following example comes from *A Midsummer Night's Dream*. Lysander produces an *oh* to mark a shift in topic from asking a question of Helena about Demetrius' whereabouts to self-reflection on his loathing of Demetrius.

> Lys.   And run through fire I will for thy sweet sake.
> Transparent Helena, nature her shewes art,
> That through thy bosome makes me see thy heart.
> Where is Demetrius? Oh how fit a word
> Is that vile name, to perish on my sword! (MND 758–62, as quoted in Person 2009: 88)

In an example from *Hamlet*, *Oh!* marks the beginning of a soliloquy. King Claudius thanks Polonius, who exits. Claudius then begins his soliloquy marking the change of addressee from Polonius to the audience with *Oh!*:

> Pol.   . . . Fare you well my Liege,
> Ile call vpon you ere you go to bed,
> And tell you what I know.
> King   Thankes deere my Lord. [exit Pol.]
> Oh my offence is ranke, it smels to heauen,
> It hath the primal eldest curse vpon't,
> A Brothers murther. (Ham. 3. 3. 33–8, as quoted in Person 2009: 89)

Another type of use of *Oh!* occurs in contexts in which it acknowledges a response to information or knowledge in interaction with the other speaker, in informings and repairs. It is common for the recipient to express a change of state resulting from the information, interpreting it as good or bad news. In such utterances, *Oh!* is invariably in the initial position. The generic use of *Oh!* as a change-of-state token in response to new information acknowledges the receipt, giving epistemic authority to the other speaker. *Oh!* indicates a marked shift of attention or orientation, but it also suggests that the speaker's own original perspective was superior. In this way, the statement prefaced with *Oh!* is not so much an acknowledgment of new information but a negotiation of authority. In an example from *Othello*, Desdemona asks Iago the question 'What would'st write of me, if thou should'st praise me?' after having heard Iago strongly criticise Emilia and then declaring him a 'slanderer' because of this criticism. In this way Desdemona's question has a biting challenge.

> Desde. What would'st write of me, if thou should'st praise me?
>
> Iago.   Oh, gentle Lady, do not put me too 't,
>   For I am nothing, if not Criticall. (Oth. 2. 1. 119–21, as quoted in
>   Person 2009: 93)

Iago's response clearly questions the wisdom of Desdemona's asking him such a question, but does so in a way that throws some criticism upon himself. His response implies that she should know better and should not have asked the question at all. Therefore, even though it appears that he is being respectful by not giving his honest opinion of her, he does so in such a way that really asserts his superiority. Sarcastic and ironical uses are always intriguing, and the following analysis has to do with such a case. In *Antony and Cleopatra*, Charmian is being ironic or sarcastic in her response to the Soothsayer's prediction with the mocking response 'Oh excellent'.

> Sooth. You shall be more belouing, then beloued.
>
> Char.   I had rather heate my Liuer with drinking.
>
> Alex.   Nay, heare him.
>
> Char.   Good now some excellent Fortune: Let mee
>   be married to three Kings in a forenoone, and Widdow
>   them all: Let me haue a Childe at fifty, to whom Herode
>   of Iewry may do Homage. Finde me to marrie me with
>   Octauius Caesar, and companion me with my Mistris.
>
> Sooth. You shall out-liue the Lady whom you serue.
>
> Charm. Oh excellent, I loue long life better then Figs. (Ant. 1. 2. 24–34,
>   as quoted in Person 2009: 102)

4.4.2 Alas!

The interjection *Alas!* provides an interesting case study in many respects. Although etymologically derived from two words (Old French *ha las*, 'ah' + 'wretched'), it acquired the interjection status early (the first example in OED from c. 1260) and its meaning has remained constant throughout the centuries, expressing 'unhappiness, grief, sorrow, pity, or concern' (OED). It is always an interjection with a conventionalised meaning. Google Books' N-gram Viewer allows us to trace the relative frequency of *alas* (and separately for the capitalised version *Alas*), the following graphs showing a steady decline in use especially from the twentieth century onwards (see Figure 4.3).

It must have become a stereotypical expression of sorrow and grief early on, as Middle English lyrics (to be performed with music) contain examples like:

> 'Alas, alas, Alas!' is my chief song!
> ffor peyne and woo none other can y syng. (Robbins (ed.) 1952: 150)

The most recent examples in the Chadwyck-Healey poetry corpus of LION quotes twenty-first-century poets (born in the 1960s). The meaning of *alas* has remained constant, as the following example testifies:

> As any newsagent will explain, it is only, alas,
> when their businesses collapse en masse that they
> themselves are the news. The public-spirited tear
> open the serrated pages in search of names
> long wreathed in puzzling, clinging mists, now ablaze
> with fame. The print smudges the fingers. Streams
> of disjointed syllables cleave the air, and threaten
> the passer-by . . .
>
> (Ford, Mark, 1962– : A poem called 'I Wish'
>   from the collection *Soft Sift*)

And it is still used today both in spoken and in written English. The *Corpus of Contemporary American English* records about one instance per one million words in the spoken material, and frequencies between four and eight in the written genres of the corpus. The following is a relevant example from the spoken section.

> Oh, OK, I had Pittsburgh by seven. That's OK. Let's get to Oakland and New England. Now this should be the last game of the year for both teams. But, alas, one of them will win, and I'm going to guess it's the

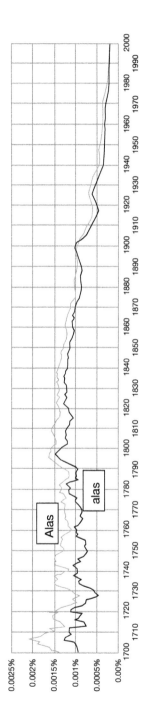

Figure 4.3 *Alas, alas* 1700–2000 with N-gram Viewer (http://books.google.com/ngrams/)

Raiders by a field goal, but by the grace of Jerry Rice. (COCA: NPR-Saturday, Analysis: Predictions about the National Football League playoffs, 2002)

4.5 Conclusions

Modern language use can give us insights, and we can learn a great deal from present-day features of discourse markers and interjections, but here, as in other historical interpretations, we have to avoid simplistic explanations and one-to-one fits. A classification based on structural form and etymology was discussed, but we do not consider it very significant for historical pragmatics and opted for the prototype view instead. Both discourse markers and interjections have an important role in managing and sequencing information. Discourse markers display the speaker's understanding of the situation, how it is negotiated and how created by sequences of utterances and how it develops. In addition or simultaneously, discourse markers serve a structural function by dividing discourse into sequences, and they also provide a way to maintain conversational continuity. Our interpretations cannot rely on prosodic features of speech, which are often used as an aid in interpreting the functions of present-day interjections, and metacomments specifying the way the utterance was spoken are rare. What we do have is the context in all its aspects, and it must be relied on for ascribing meanings to these fairly elusive components of communication. Situations provide the keys, but we need guidelines for interpretation. In historical pragmatics, we are dealing with written materials from the past and the expressions may have developed their modern meanings later (see Chapter 8). There can also be other functions typical of the written mode that cannot be found in present-day spoken discourse. The importance of context is vital to the interpretation, as irony can reverse meanings and the use of a discourse marker can serve as a guideline for the audience to understand the utterance in the right way. Through context the properties of pragmatic variables become clear.

Note

1. Extracts from Chaucer are quoted from *The Riverside Chaucer*, Benson (1987). Translations are our own unless otherwise specified.

Exercises

1. Below you will find two text extracts. The first is from the fifteenth century, the second from the seventeenth century. What function(s) can you find for the use of *alas* in the following extracts? Can you provide a context for the first extract?

    a) 'Alas,' seyde the knight, 'I am slayne by thys traytoure knyght that rydith invisible.'
    'Alas,' seyde Balyne, 'thy ys nat the first despite that he hath done me.' (Malory I: 81)
    'Alas', said the knight, 'I am slain by this traitor knight who rides invisibly.'
    'Alas', said Balyne, 'this is not the first hostility that he has done to me.'

    b) When *Rush* was banished out of the house of Religion,
    and was turned into the same likenesse that he was,
    then he wandred abroad in the worlde with an heauie heart,
    & these words he said: Alas, alas, what shall I doe, I wote not
    now whether to goe, for all my seuen yeres labour is left. (CED, Anon.
    The Historie Of Frier Rvsh (1620)

2. Identify the discourse markers, interjections and pragmatic noise in the following passage. How would you analyse their functions? Do they have multiple functions in some cases? Is the classification into discourse markers/ interjections/ other categories clear in all examples, or can you find borderline cases?

    Enter *Servant*, who whispers: Primrose.
    Prim. Very well; bid 'em go up one after another, the Scotch Woman first.
    Enter Beaumont
    Beau. Hist! Primrose, is the Coast clear?
    Prim. Yes, yes, old Argus is employ'd above.
    Beau. Well, and how are we? how came you off with your Scene of Quackery?
    Prim. As Quacks of all sorts do, Sir; with flying Colours. I soon routed the Doctor, and run away with his Business.
    Beau. Bravely said! But where's our Squire? what's doing with him?
    Prim. Oh! we are doing very handsomly by him above Stairs.
    Beau. Is the Farce we contriv'd, in Action now, then?
    Prim. Yes; Ha, ha, ha! He'll have enough of Wives, I'll warrant him.
    Beau. Well, but what have you for me to do now?
    Prim. Let it be your Business to contrive the Winding-up of the Play, while I play my Scenes with him.– You understand.

Beau. Ay, ay.

Prim. And as soon as I have planted him as I would –

Whispers Beaumont

Beau. Very well; that will do the best of any thing in the World.

Prim. But here he comes. – Get you gone quick, for we mustn't be seen together.

(CED, Miller, *The Mother-in-Law* (1734), pp. 70–1)

Further reading

Brinton's book-length study *Pragmatic Markers in English* (1996) is a classic in the field. It deals with, among other items, *gan, anon, I gesse* and episode boundary markers, and it describes them in terms of grammaticalisation processes. Interjections have also received the attention of several scholars. The range is wider in Middle English than it is in Old English, e.g. *ah, alas, hey, weylaway, pardee* and *what.* They serve a variety of textual functions, such as turn-taking, foregrounding and narrative segmentation (see in particular Taavitsainen 1995, 1997, 1998). Taavitsainen (1998), for instance, looks at the function of interjections – primarily *ah, oh/o* and *alas* – in the Romantic novel of the late eighteenth / early nineteenth century. Jucker (1997) provides a long-term diachronic perspective on selected discourse markers. Brinton (2010) and Gehweiler (2010) provide useful handbook accounts of historical analyses of discourse markers, interjections and expletives. For discourse markers and interjections in Old English, see in particular Hiltunen (2006) and Sauer (2009). Culpeper and Kytö (2010) analyse interjections, which they subsume to some extent under the more general heading of pragmatic noise, as they call them, in the *Corpus of English Dialogues, 1560–1760.*

5 'For I thou thee, thou Traitor': Terms of address

5.1 Introduction

Addressing someone is an efficient means of attracting attention and one of the most prominent interactive features of language use. With terms of address speakers appeal directly to their hearer(s), and two principal kinds can be distinguished: pronominal and nominal address. Both provide powerful means of expressing social and attitudinal meanings embedded into the terms, and often both forms are used together; for example, *thou Traitor*, *Your Excellency*, *you rascal*. In the history of English, pronominal address is particularly intriguing as the choice of the second-person pronoun could express subtle shades of meaning, depending on the context. This system has undergone radical changes in the course of time, with *you* as the normal standard pronoun and *thou* in some archaic uses in religious contexts in Present-day English. The more familiar and intimate pronoun could become contemptuous and abusive, or the pronoun could be used in a more distant and respectful way, or it could be used in mock respectful address. According to textual evidence, *thou* had virtually disappeared by 1700 (Walker 2007: 63). The use of nominal terms of address has also changed considerably both in terms of their frequency and in terms of the semantic types. Some words like *Madam* are most commonly used in the address function, *Sir* is both a title and address term, but most nominal terms of address are also used as referring expressions to talk about people. The scale extends from more familiar and intimate terms of endearment to – on the one hand – more distant and polite terms used with deference and – on the other hand – to terms of abuse and derogative name-calling.

Both pronominal and nominal terms of address have attracted a great deal of research. Much of this research focuses on Early Modern English, especially on Shakespearean terms of address and address lines in private letters. But there is also a fair amount of research on older phases of English and on present-day practices.

5.2 An overview of pronominal and nominal address terms

The choice of the pronoun of address in the second person used to be similar to that in Modern French or Modern German, in which interlocutors use *vous* or *Sie* if they address somebody in a more formal manner, while they use *tu* or *du* if they address somebody in a less formal or more familiar manner. Similar distinctions exist in many languages, even if the precise rules of when to use the more formal and when to use the more familiar pronoun differ from one language to the next. Present-day English does not have this distinction. Only the pronoun *you* can be used to address an interlocutor, except for some very specialised usages in religious contexts or in a few rural dialects, where *thou* is still used. However, from the thirteenth to about the seventeenth century, speakers of English had a choice of two different pronouns. It appears that the motivations for choosing one or the other were complex and liable to change within these three or four centuries, and they also differ from the present-day systems in languages such as French or German. It is, therefore, important for the modern reader of Chaucer or Shakespeare, for instance, to understand the pragmatics of pronoun choices in particular historical and fictional contexts.

Brown and Gilman (1960) provided the groundbreaking research on pronominal terms of address in a broad range of European languages, such as German, French, Spanish and Italian. Unlike English, these languages still distinguish between a more familiar pronoun and a more polite and distant pronoun. On the basis of the French pronouns *tu* and *vous* they abbreviated the more familiar pronoun with the letter T and the more polite and distant pronoun with the letter V. They argue that the distinction goes back to the Latin spoken in the fourth century when there were two Roman emperors, one who resided in Rome, the other in Constantinople. Words addressed to one were understood to be addressed to both. In the course of time the Latin plural pronoun *vos* was also used for other power figures and ultimately led to a system in which a socially superior person was addressed by V and a socially inferior person by T. This system of nonreciprocal power semantics, according to Brown and Gilman, applied throughout much of medieval Europe. Equals of the upper classes exchanged mutual V, while equals of the lower classes exchanged mutual T, but Brown and Gilman (1960: 255) conceded that 'there was much inexplicable fluctuation between T and V'. This system had its foundation in the strictly hierarchical societies of medieval Europe up to the time when more egalitarian societies began to take the place of the earlier hierarchical systems. In these societies the asymmetrical power semantics in which the superior person received V and used T in return was replaced by a more symmetrical system in which a high degree of solidarity or familiarity leads to the reciprocal use of T, while social distance, unfamiliarity and politeness leads to reciprocal V.

Address terms serve as subtle indicators of interpersonal relations, but they also reflect attitudes and concepts of prestige and politeness. In the late fourteenth century address terms were included as status symbols: 'It is ful fair to been ycleped "madame",/ And goon to vigilies al before,/ And have a mantel roialliche ybore' ('It is very nice to be called madam, and go to church before everyone, and carry your cloak like a queen'; The CT, *General Prologue* 376–7). Five hundred years later, in Dickens's *Little Dorrit*, Mrs General teaches refined manners to Little Dorrit in a somewhat ironic scene:

> 'Papa is a preferable mode of address,' observed Mrs General. 'Father is rather vulgar, my dear. The word Papa, besides, gives a pretty form to the lips. Papa, potatoes, poultry, prunes, and prism are all very good words for the lips . . .' (Book the second, Chapter 5)

To illustrate the use of nominal address further, we surveyed the *Helsinki Corpus* for some of the most common terms. *Madam* occurs 101 times in 14 texts, mostly in address function but also as a title. Robert Mannyng's *Handlyng Synne* classifies the desire to enhance one's social esteem by using fine address as a sin: 'Or ȝe wymmen also, comunly, wulde be kallede "madame" or "lady;" Al þys comþ of grete pryde' (lines 413–15). *Sir* occurs 844 times in 58 texts, but mostly as a title when referring to people. The earliest text is the anonymous *Brut* from c. 1333. The following extract contains *Sir* both as a title and an address term. Both T and V pronouns of address occur in the passage,

> Þo ansuerede Sir Andrew of Herkela, and saide: '**Sir Thomas**! þat wolde y nouȝt do, ne consent þerto, for no maner þing . . . for þan shulde y be holde a traitoure for euer-more.' And when þe noble Erl Thomas of Lancastre saw þat he nolde consent to him for no maner þing, '**Sir Andrew**,' he saide, 'wil ȝe nouȝt consent to destroye þe venyme of þe reaume, as we bene consented? At on worde, **Sir Andrew**, y telle þe, þat or þis ȝer be gon, þat ȝe shal be take and holde for a traitoure . . . ' (lines 441–50)

> 'Then answered Sir Andrew of Herkela and said: "Sir Thomas! I would not do that, neither would I consent to that, for anything at all, because then I should be considered a traitor for ever." And when the noble Earl Thomas of Lancaster saw that he would not consent to his plan in any way, he said: "Will you not consent to destroy the poison of the realm,

as we agreed? At one word, Sir Andrew, I tell you that before this year is gone you shall be taken for a traitor."'

The anonymous Early Modern English *Penny Merriments* (1684) includes 'A Merry Dialogue between Tom the Taylor, and his Maid Joan' with several terms of address in a short passage. Nominal forms include *Huswife, Madam, Master, Sir* and the proper name *Joan*; the pronoun use is primarily *you*, which is in accordance with the late date of the text:

> *Tom.* Why how now **Huswife**, do **you** snap at me? do **you** grudge me my Victuals? Pray **Madam Joan**, what is it to **you** how much I eat and drink, do I not provide it? be it known to **you Joan**, that your Mistris when she was living, would not have said so much to me poor Soul.
>
> *Joan.* No truly Master, no more would not I if I was **your** Wife, but as I am **your** Maid, I am not bound to **you**, and therefore I take the greater priviledge, but if **you**'d Marry me, I know what I know.
>
> *Tom.* Why, what do **you** know **Joan**? suppose I should Marry **thee**:
>
> *Ione*[1]. Indeed **Sir**, I'de be the lovingest Wife that ever was made of flesh and blood, i'le be so kind.
>
> *Tom.* How kind wouldst **thou** be?
>
> *Ione.* Ah master, so kind as my mistris us'd to be to **you**, if not kinder, **you** may remember **Sir** that in her days I us'e to lye in the Truckle bed; O then master. (lines 337–53)

In the following, we shall survey some of the most important factors and methods used in assessing address terms, whether pronominal or nominal, or a combination of both. We shall begin chronologically with a short passage on Old English, proceed to Middle English which is the period when the T/V distinction entered the language, and proceed to Early Modern English, which has perhaps received more scholarly attention than any other period. We shall finish with some observations on Present-day English. In the examples we shall pay attention to both pronominal and nominal forms, as it is the joint effect that really counts when interpreting the forms.

5.3 Old English

Anglo-Saxon society was strictly hierarchical, but the pronominal T/V system had not entered the language yet, as no instances of the

---

[1] The spelling of the name changes in the text.

V-form address to a single person can be found in Old English (Burnley 1983:28). In Old English, address terms are mainly found in sermons and poetry, and kinship terms and religious designations are particularly common in extant data. The following scene from the anonymous *Apollonius of Tyre*, for example, contains an address to the King, with respectful nominal terms accompanied by the T-form:

> ... and eode into þam cynge and cwæð: **Hlaford cyngc**, glada nu and blissa, forðam þe Apollonius him ondræt **þines** rices mægna swa þæt he ne dear ... (lines 179–81)

> '... and went to the king and said: Lord King, be glad and happy now because Appolonius is so much afraid of your kingdom's greatness that he dare not ...'

Address terms have been found to be sensitive indicators of appropriate behaviour and politeness between various social classes, but in Old English address was not used in the same way as in the periods that follow. Kohnen (2008c) studied the distribution of some central nominal address terms, like *leof, hlaford*, and *ealdorman*, using the *Dictionary of Old English Corpus*. He wanted to find out whether polite and courteous behaviour was expressed in these terms and what the typical communicative settings were. The general picture was not quite homogeneous. On the one hand, friendship and affection invoking family bonds prevails in the data. The term *hlaford*, on the other hand, is authoritative and in secular contexts it indicates a fixed rank in a hierarchical society. Kohnen did not find the same kind of face work that occurs in the later periods in Old English, and negative politeness seemed to be absent. Instead, the use of address terms reflects mutual obligation and kinship loyalty as well as the Christian values of *humilitas* and *caritas* in Anglo-Saxon communication.

5.4 Middle English

In Middle English, the choice between *ye* and *thou* is particularly intriguing. Compared to the T/V systems in other languages, 'the English seem always to have moved more freely from one form to another than did the continental Europeans' (Brown and Gilman 1960: 265), but in contrast to these other languages, English has given up the contrast and today only uses what used to be the V (Y) form. Burnley (1983) also draws attention to the variability in the English system:

> Although general hints on the factors governing the choice of *ye* or *thou* can be given, it is important to realise that no unbreakable rules exist. The

choice between *ye* and *thou* when addressing a single individual is not a grammatical one, but a stylistic one governed not only by institutional-ised forms of social structure, but also by transient emotions and attitudes arising from a relationship. (Burnley 1983: 19)

Burnley (1983) presents the underlying system of the choice between *ye* and *thou* in the form of a flow chart, which first distinguishes between a courtly style and a non-courtly style. In the non-courtly style, speak-ers always choose *thou*. In the courtly style further distinctions are made. For unfamiliar addressees, *ye* is chosen and for friends *thou*. For familiar non-intimates, a further distinction is made between younger addressees for whom *thou* is appropriate, while for older address-ees the distinction is made between those of a lower social class, for whom *thou* is appropriate and those of a higher social class for whom *ye* is used. This means that *thou* is the default option except in cases of an unfamiliar addressee or a familiar addressee who is older and of a higher social status. However, Burnley's flowchart leaves the option of switching between the two forms for reasons of affection, rhetoric and style. This scheme is illustrative of the main principles, but we would like to argue that the issues are more complicated and the choices need to be studied in their microcontext on a turn-to-turn basis.

Middle English fictional writings, for example, Chaucer's texts, employ a wide range of address terms, but non-literary writing also provides ample examples. Private letters emerge as a new genre in the fifteenth century, and they have proved a particularly fruitful source for the study of address terms in their social context. Chaucer's characters do not make the choice between *ye* and *thou* on a default basis for each possible interactant, but instead they take on-the-spot decisions, deci-sions that are crucially based on the question of deference and respect. On the one hand, the choice of *ye* as a pronoun of address for a single addressee expresses the speaker's deference, but the use of *thou* in the same situation indicates that deference in this situation is not neces-sary. Affection and intimacy, on the other hand, do not play the role that is often assigned to them. On the basis of modern T/V systems in languages such as German, French or Italian, we may find it odd that married couples address each other with *ye* because in the modern systems intimacy always calls for the T-form rather than the V-form, but Chaucer's characters use a different system. Deference and intimacy are not contradictions. Husband and wife, if they are of a higher social class, address each other with respect and politeness, that is to say with deference and therefore they use the pronoun *ye*.

We can gain access to the imaginary world of late fourteenth-century England with Geoffrey Chaucer's *The Canterbury Tales* with its rich array of characters and address terms. The work contains a wide range of very diverse tales held together by a frame narrative. In this frame a group of pilgrims travel together to Canterbury and on their way each pilgrim tells a story. They set out on their journey from an inn in Southwark, in south London. The innkeeper joins the group and organises the story telling as a contest. The narrator who tells the best story will on their return get a free meal at his inn. The group of pilgrims consists of a cross section of fourteenth-century society which was still split up into the three medieval estates. The first estate, the clergy, is represented, for instance, by a Pardoner, a Friar, a Monk, a Prioress, and a Parson. The second estate, the aristocracy, is represented by only two pilgrims; a Knight and his son, a Squire. The third estate, the commons, is represented, among others, by a Miller, a Reeve (a manager of a manor), a Cook, a Merchant, a Man of Law, a Yeoman (a servant in a noble household), and a Manciple (a person in charge of food supplies at a monastery or a college). In the frame narrative these characters interact with each other. They discuss the various tales and whose turn it is to be the next narrator. The Host acts as master of ceremonies and appears regularly, interacting with virtually every single pilgrim, while the pilgrims may appear only once in the introduction to their own tale or several times.

This constellation of characters provides an interesting context for the analysis of the use of address terms. Obviously, these pilgrims are fictional characters. Even when they argue or when they hurl insults at each other, they speak in perfect, rhymed pentameters, and thus they should not be mistaken for real fourteenth-century speakers of English. But they provide a fascinating picture of Middle English (fictional) dialogues within and across social classes. Each of the three estates in medieval Britain was hierarchically organised. There was a considerable difference, for instance, between the Archbishop at the top of the clergy and a simple priest of a rural parish at the bottom. Chaucer's Canterbury pilgrims include only members at the lower ends of the hierarchies of each of the three estates, but they are nevertheless stratified.

The character who is highest in the social hierarchy is the Knight. Only the Host addresses him and he always uses a Y pronoun for the Knight "'Sire Knyght" quod he, "my mayster and my lord"' (GP, I 837). There are three women pilgrims; the Prioress, the Wife of Bath and the Second Nun. The Second Nun is never directly addressed by any of the pilgrims, but the other two always receive a respectful Y.

Among the commons there are several pilgrims who are always

addressed with T both by the Host and by the other pilgrims who interact with them. These include the Miller, the Reeve, and the Shipman.
They are of a low social status and therefore T seems appropriate for
them. The clergy pilgrims are also, within their own estate, rather
low down in the social hierarchy, but their estate already demands
some respect and, therefore, the address form Y. However, while
the Summoner receives only T, all the other clergy are sometimes
addressed with Y and sometimes with T, and often it is one and the
same character, usually the Host, who sometimes uses Y and sometimes
T to them. Thus it cannot be their social status alone which decides on
pronoun usage. We therefore need to work out in more detail when the
Canterbury pilgrims use T, when they use Y and when they switch from
one pronoun to the other even if they still talk to the same interlocutor.
Contextual microanalysis of the unfolding discourse is needed to catch
the shades of meaning of such switches.

In the prologue to *The Monk's Tale* the Host addresses the Monk and
appoints him as the next speaker, but first he politely asks him for his
name. 'But by my trouthe, I knowe nat youre name. Wher shal I calle
yow my lord daun John, Or daun Thomas, or elles daun Albon?' (MkP
VII 1928–30). *Daun* is a title of respect that was often used for priests. At
this point the Host shows respect and deference, or perhaps just mock
politeness, and uses the Y pronouns to address the Monk. However, his
speech to the Monk soon shifts into jocular banter. He asks him for his
profession within the clergy and expresses astonishment that the Monk
is in religious orders when he could have been a prolific procreator.

> I pray to God, yeve hym confusioun
> That first thee broghte unto religioun!
> Thou woldest han been a tredefowel aright.
> Haddestow as greet a leeve as thou hast myght
> To parfourne al thy lust in engendrure,
> Thou haddest bigeten ful many a creature. (MkP VII 1943–8)

> 'I pray to God to confound those
> Who first put you into monastic life!
> You would have been a chicken-copulator, all right!
> Had you as good a chance as you have power
> To perform your desire in procreation;
> You would have begotten many a creature.'

In this kind of banter, the Host obviously feels no need to show respect
or deference. He uses T pronouns throughout, and at the very end he
ironically apologises for his banter:

But be nat wrooth, my lord, though that I pleye.
Ful ofte in game a sooth I have herd seye! (MkP VII 1963–4)

'But be not angry, my lord, as I am joking;
Very often I have heard a truth said in jest.'

The Parson provides another good example. In the General Prologue of the *Canterbury Tales* he is described as a very serious character who cares for his flock and avoids all the mistakes that many other parish priests are guilty of. In the prologue to his own tale he is addressed by the Host in a rather jocular fashion when he asks him for his status using T forms of the verb 'to be' ('artow a vicary? Or arte a person?' (ParsP X 22) 'are you a vicar or are you a parish priest?') and he prompts him with a light-hearted oath to 'Telle us a fable anon, for cokkes bones!' (ParsP X 29) 'Tell us a fable, by cock's bones' (a euphemism for God's bones). But the Parson refuses to tell a fable or any other rhymed narrative. Instead, as a parish priest he will deliver a tale of morality in prose, in fact, he will preach a sermon. The pilgrims agree to this, and the Host now invites the Parson in a much more respectful and sober manner, beginning with the polite nominal address with *Sir* and the occupational name:

'Sire preest,' quod he, 'now faire yow bifalle!
Telleth,' quod he, 'youre meditacioun.
But hasteth yow; the sonne wole adoun;
Beth fructuous, and that in litel space,
And to do wel God sende yow his grace!
Sey what yow list, and we wol gladly here.' (ParsP X 68–73)

'"Sire priest," he said, "good fortune may now come to you!
Tell us your meditation," he said.
But make haste; the sun is about to go down;
Be fruitful, and that in a little space of time,
And may God send you his grace for you to do well!
Say what you like, and we will gladly hear it.'

The tales told by the different pilgrims range from burlesque fabliaux to a serious sermon and from fairy-tale romance to beast fable. The diversity of genres represented is reflected in the diversity of characters that occur in these tales. While the fictional characters in the frame story create the impression of life-like characters that might have lived in Chaucer's England, there are characters, such as talking farmyard animals in *The Nun's Priest's Tale*, that are clearly fictional. But these characters, too, consistently distinguish between the address terms *ye*

and *thou.* For instance, Chauntecleer, a farmyard cock, and his favourite wife, Pertelote, are depicted as aristocratic characters engaged in
a philosophical dispute. They, predictably, address each other with Y
pronouns. Later in the story, Chauntecleer encounters a fox who sets
out to trick him. At first they use the polite pronouns Y. The fox initially
succeeds and carries Chauntecleer away, who addresses him humbly
and respectfully using the polite address term *Sire* with *ye.* "Sire, if that I
were as ye" 'Sir (…) if I were you' (NPT VII 3407) and tricks the fox to
taunting his pursuers. The unwary fox replies "In feith, it shal be don"
'I'll do just that' (NPT VII 3414). Chauntecleer grabs the opportunity
and flies into a tree top. He has outwitted the fox and thus clearly gained
the upper hand, and with the new power situation the opponents also
change their pronouns of address. The fox now addresses Chauntecleer
very humbly with *sire* and *ye.* The nominal address in the passage
is given in the vocative with the interjection *o* before the name, and
another interjection, *allas,* to express misery and mock repentance:

> And whan the fox saugh that the cok was gon,
> 'Allas!' quod he, 'O Chauntecleer, allas!
> I have to yow,' quod he, 'ydoon trespas, …
> But, sire, I dide it in no wikke entente.
> Com doun, and I shal telle yow what I mente
> I shal seye sooth to yow, God help me so!'
>   'Nay thanne,' quod he, …
> If thou bigyle me ofter than ones.
> Thou shalt namoore thurgh thy flaterye
> Do me to synge and wynke with myn ye;
> (NPT VII 3418–32)
> 'When the fox saw that the cock was gone,
> He cried, "Ah, Chanticleer! Alas!
> I fear I behaved very badly to you …
> But, sire, I meant no harm;
> Come down, and I'll tell you what I intended –
> And so help me God, I'll speak the truth!"
> "Oh no," returned the cock …
> If you trick me more than once!
> You're not going to flatter me
> Into singing with my eyes shut again!'

In only seven lines of direct speech he uses five Y pronouns to underline his respect and submission. Chauntecleer, however, is not taken in.
With his newly-gained dominance over the outwitted fox he can now
safely use T pronouns.

5.5 Early Modern English

The pronominal system was in a flux in the early modern period. The T/Y distinction still existed, but it was not the same as in the previous period and scholars have tried to detect regularities of a different kind especially in Shakespeare's works. Another complication is presented by the forms *ye* and *you* as the distinction between the subject and the object forms became blurred and the two forms were used interchangeably. A study on the progress of the change in the *Corpus of Early English Correspondence* (CEEC) showed that about 60 per cent of letter writers vacillated in their choice at the most rapid phase of the change (Nevalainen and Raumolin-Brunberg 2003: 97). Letters and other texts of the early modern period display a wide range of nominal address terms including kinship terms, titles, rank and occupational terms in addition to a wide range of terms of endearment and terms of abuse. The most fruitful sources for studying address terms are drama, fiction, trial records and correspondence, but address terms also occur in religious texts and teaching dialogues.

Two hundred years after Chaucer the functions of address pronouns had changed noticeably. In fact, in many contexts the Y pronouns had become the standard choice and the use of a T pronoun could be seen as insulting. In a trial that took place in 1603, the English aristocrat, explorer and courtier, Sir Walter Raleigh, was tried for high treason. The attorney addresses him with a T pronoun combined with a nominal term of abuse ('For I thou thee, thou Traitor', see p. 1). This was highly inappropriate and insulting, given the social class of the addressee and the formality of the situation. It is in this period that we find explicit comments about the use of *thou* as a derogatory term. In Shakespeare's *Twelfth Night*, Sir Toby Belch advises Sir Andrew Aguecheek to use the insulting *thou* in the challenge that he is writing:

> Sir To. Go, write it in a martial hand, be curst and brief. It is no matter how witty, so it be eloquent and full of invention. Taunt him with the license of ink. If thou thou'st him some thrice, it shall not be amiss; and as many lies as will lie in thy sheet of paper, although the sheet were big enough for the bed of Ware in England, set 'em down. Go about it. Let there be gall enough in thy ink, though thou write with a goose-pen, no matter. About it. (Shakespeare, *Twelfth Night*, 3. 2. 42–50)[2]

From these examples it becomes clear that *thou* can be used as a term of abuse to insult the addressee, and even in milder cases in trial records

[2] Quoted from *The Riverside Shakespeare* (Evans 1974).

it has been noticed to stress the social divide (Walker 2007: 318), for example, the judge instructs a witness 'Speak as loud as thou would'st do if thou wer't at home' (CED; *The Tryal of John Giles* 1680: 36). Against this background it does not seem surprising that the use of *thou* disappeared almost entirely over the next 100 years or so.

5.5.1 Shakespeare's characters

Shakespeare seems to use a slightly archaic system, which already shows signs of erosion. This is very clear on the level of case marking. Shakespeare no longer consistently distinguishes between the subject and the non-subject forms of the pronouns of address (see U. Busse 1998). Such a mixture can be found, for example, in the following passage, where *you* is used in subject position in 'if you should deal', and in non-subject position in 'Pray you', 'I told you' and 'bid me inquire you'. And *ye* is used both as a direct object and as a subject in 'let me tell ye, if ye should deal double'. Here Juliet's nurse is addressing Romeo:

> Pray **you**, sir, a word: and as I told **you**, my young lady bid me inquire **you** out; what she bid me say, I will keep to myself. But first let me tell **ye**, if **ye** should lead her in a fool's paradise, as they say, it were a very gross kind of behavior, as they say; for the gentlewoman is young; and therefore, if **you** should deal double with her, truly it were an ill thing to be off'red to any gentlewoman, and very weak dealing. (Shakespeare, *Romeo and Juliet*, 2. 4. 162–70)

Shakespeare's address terms have received a great deal of attention, and different approaches have been applied. Any attempt to ascertain the consistency of Shakespeare's system presupposes, of course, that we know the details of the underlying system from which he might have deviated. One approach is based on the markedness of the pronominal terms of address in Shakespeare's *As You Like It* and *King Lear* (Stein 2003). Stein combines general usage patterns with micro-pragmatic analyses, and deviations from these patterns receive special attention. He identifies socially defined dyads of fathers and daughters, servants and aristocrats, or lovers, and establishes the unmarked use of pronouns for each of them. Deviations from norms often occur in dramatic contexts and show emotional involvement. The sociolinguistically informed approach examines the relative frequencies of pronouns taking the relations between dyads of characters into account. The occurrences are accounted for on a sociolinguistic basis, focusing on their relative frequencies over longer stretches and often over entire plays.

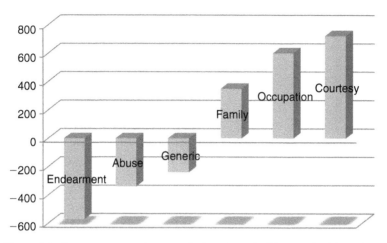

Figure 5.1 Co-occurrence of pronominal and nominal forms of address in Shakespeare's plays (source: U. Busse 2003: 214)

Terms of address in *King Lear*, *Othello* and *Hamlet* have been studied by Mazzon (2003), and she also establishes usage patterns for specific types of relationships between characters, such as husband and wife, father and daughter or the relationship between equals. She includes nominal terms of address in her study, and pays special attention to contexts in which the characters deviate from the expected patterns.

The correlation of pronominal and nominal terms of address has been developed even further by U. Busse (2003), who established a fairly complicated measurement system. He distinguishes six categories of terms of address, presented in Figure 5.1. The terms of address that co-occur more often with the pronoun *thou* are indicated on the left. Terms of endearment (e.g. *bully*, *chuck*, *heart*, *joy*, *love* or *wag*) show the highest predominance of *thou* over *you*, terms of abuse (e.g. *devil*, *dog*, *fool*, *knave*, *rascal*, *rogue*) come next, and generic terms of address (*boy*, *friend*, *gentleman*, *gentlewoman* etc.) also co-occur more often with *thou*. The three categories on the right co-occur more often with *you* than with *thou*. Terms indicating family relationships (*brother*, *cousin*, *coz*, *daughter*, *father* or *husband*) and occupational terms of address (such as *captain*, *doctor*, *esquire*, *justice*, *knight* or *nurse*) fall into this category, and titles of courtesy such as *Your Grace*, *Your (royal) Highness*, *Your Honour*, *Your Ladyship*, *Goodman*, *goodwife*, *lady*, *lord* or *sir*, represent the extreme end of the *you*-fullness scale.

The order reflects Brown and Levinson's (1987) politeness scale with titles of honour and courtesy standing at the extreme end of negative politeness or deference, and terms of endearment at the extreme end

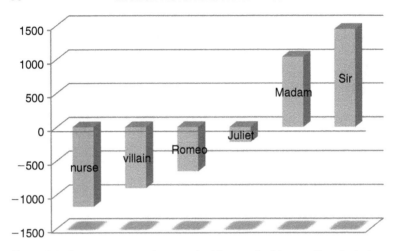

Figure 5.2 Co-occurrence of pronominal forms of address with selected nominal forms of address in *Romeo and Juliet* (Jucker 2012a: 88)

of positive politeness. The fact that terms of family relationship also occur more often with Y pronouns than with T pronouns indicates that solidarity in the sense used by Brown and Gilman (1960, 1989) does not automatically call for T pronouns.

Patterns of co-occurrence of nominal and pronominal address terms in *Romeo and Juliet* illustrates the scale of '*thou*- and *you*-fullness' (U. Busse 2003) in this play in a slightly simplified form. The six most frequent terms of address include the occupational term *nurse*, the proper names of the protagonists, and the term *villain*; they co-occur more often with T than with Y. In contrast, the terms *Madam* and *Sir*, co-occur more often with Y.

The fact that the extreme values in Figure 5.2 are considerably higher (or lower) than in Figure 5.1 is probably due to the much smaller basis on which these figures have been calculated. Only the data of single characters (the Nurse, Romeo, Juliet) and only one single term used to address a range of different characters (*villain, Madam, Sir*) have been included.

5.5.2 Address terms in letters

Another perspective on address terms can be achieved by studies of address terms in letters; this is the genre that has received most attention in this respect in non-literary writings. Address is a compulsory component of both public and private letters and occurs from the very beginning of letter-writing in English. The model of chancery letters was adopted in private correspondence with patterns such as 'Right trusty and wellbeloved', which could also occur without a nominal headword (Nevalainen and Raumolin-Brunberg 1995: 545). In general, the repertoire of nominal address forms is fairly limited, with kinship terms, names, and words denoting social and occupational standing forming the stock.

Nominal address terms in private letters have been placed on Brown and Levinson's politeness scale from negative to positive, and the results are very similar to the scales presented above of Shakespeare's '*thou*- and *you*-fullness'. The extreme end of negative politeness is occupied by honorific titles, then come other titles, family kinship terms, and the positive end is occupied by nicknames and terms of endearment (Raumolin-Brunberg 1996: 171, Nevala 2004). Diachronic changes of address forms have also been explored. Nevala (2004) found that positive politeness increases in the course of time from the fifteenth to the seventeenth century as the use of terms of endearment and nicknames becomes more common. Among social groups, the gentry lead this change, and royalty lags behind; this was also the case in a follow-up study on the late modern period.

5.6 Present-day English

Present-day English has a more reduced selection of kinship terms and – in some special contexts – occupational terms (*driver, waiter*). *Sir* is commonly used as an address term for men and in particular for men in authority (especially in American English) as in the following example:

> 'You doubt my ability to best a barbarian, soldier?' // The smaller man backed up a pace, hastily sheathing his weapon. 'No, sir. Of course not. My apologies, sir.' (COCA, 2008, Fiction, Bk:DeepMagic)

Cultural differences in the varieties of English can be detected in terms of politeness, address terms being a sensitive indicator of the degree of formality in interaction. As a result of intercultural contact and development of interactional patterns, Indian English is often described as fairly formal because of its administrative history and use in legal, educational, military and media contexts (see McArthur 2002: 313–26). It has acquired a more complex system of address terms than most other varieties. Nominal address terms are frequent and include titles alone (*Sir, Madam, Doctor, Professor*, etc.), titles and honorific suffixes, and honorific tags, in addition to kinship terms and pet names (Dodiya

2006: 210–11). Address terms can be used in different ways and in fiction they can achieve some special effects; for example, the expression 'Your Honour' is a vocative typical of the legal register, but when used in everyday communication it sounds bookish (ibid.).

5.7 Conclusions

English started to use a plural pronoun of address for a single addressee in the thirteenth century under the influence of French, but about four hundred years later this usage was no longer found. In fact, the erstwhile plural pronoun came to be used both in situations in which a single person was addressed and in situations in which two or more people were addressed, and there was no longer a choice between a more formal and a less formal pronoun of address for a single addressee. It is still not entirely clear why this distinction disappeared while in many other European languages; for example, German, French, Spanish or Italian, it has survived until today. The 400-year history of the distinction is in itself fascinating for the historical pragmaticists. The usage patterns deviate considerably from the modern systems that we are familiar with today, and many of these patterns are still unexplored. So far, research has mainly focused on works by Chaucer and Shakespeare. In Chaucer's work, the singular T form seems to be the default. The plural Y form was used whenever the situation required deference, and this in turn depended on the complex interaction of the social status of speaker and addressee, their relationship in general and the current situation. Nominal forms of address have changed in the course of time as well, and the system has become simpler. At the same time, however, special developments in some varieties of English provide opportunities to, for example, authors of fiction to exploit the system and add shades of formality to character description.

Exercises and research projects

1. The following extract is taken from Chaucer's *The Canterbury Tales*. It occurs in the prologue to *The Monk's Tale*. The Host, Harry Bailly, addresses one of the pilgrims, the Monk, and asks him to take his turn and tell a tale. Read this extract carefully and note not only the pronominal terms of address but also the nominal ones. How does Harry Bailly address the Monk? Is he polite or impolite? Note that he finishes off by protesting that he is only jesting. How does this relate to his use of *thou* and *ye* to the Monk, and why do you think he switches his form of address?

'My lord, the Monk,' quod he, 'be
  myrie of cheere,
For ye shul telle a tale trewely.
Loo, Rouchestre stant heer faste by!
Ryde forth, myn owene lord, brek nat
  oure game.
But, by my trouthe, I knowe nat youre
  name.
Wher shal I calle yow my lord daun
  John,
Or daun Thomas, or elles daun Albon?
Of what hous be ye, by youre fader kyn?

I vowe to God, thou hast a ful fair skyn;

It is a gentil pasture ther thow goost.

Thou art nat lyk a penant or a goost:
Upon my feith, thou art som officer,
Som worthy sexteyn, or som celerer,
For by my fader soule, as to my doom,

Thou art a maister whan thou art at
  hoom;
No povre cloysterer, ne no novys,
But a governour, wily and wys,
And therwithal of brawnes and of bones

A wel farynge persone for the nones.
I pray to God, yeve hym confusioun
That first thee broghte unto religioun!

Thou woldest han been a tredefowel
  aright.
Haddestow as greet a leeve as thou
  hast myght
To parfourne al thy lust in engendrure,
Thou haddest bigeten ful many a
  creature.
Allas, why werestow so wyd a
  cope?
God yeve me sorwe, but, and I were
  a pope,
Nat oonly thou, but every myghty man,
Though he were shorn ful hye upon
  his pan,
Sholde have a wyf; for al the world is
  lorn!
Religioun hath take up al the corn

'My lord, the Monk,' said he, 'cheer up,

For you must tell a tale truly.
Lo, Rochester stands here near by!
Ride forth, my own lord, do not interrupt
  our game.
But, by my pledged word, I know not
  your name.
Which shall I call you – my lord Don
  John,
Or Don Thomas, or else Don Albon?
Of what monastic order are you, by your
  father's kin?
I vow to God, thou hast a very handsome
  complexion;
It is a noble pasture where thou goest to
  eat.
Thou art not like a penitent or a ghost:
Upon my faith, thou art some officer,
Some worthy sexton, or some provisioner,
For by my father's soul, according to my
  judgment,
Thou art a master when thou art at home;

No poor cloistered monk, nor no novice,
But a governor, wily and wise,
And, in addition to that, of muscles and of
  bones
A very handsome person indeed.
I pray to God, give him ruination
Who first brought thee unto the monastic
  life!
Thou wouldest have been a chicken-
  copulator indeed,
If thou haddest as much permission as
  thou hast power
To perform all thy desire in procreation,
Thou would have begotten very many a
  creature.
Alas, why wearest thou so wide a
  cope?
God give me sorrow, unless, if I were a
  pope,
Not only thou, but every mighty man,
Though he had a tonsure very
  prominently upon his head,
Should have a wife; for all the world is
  lost!
Religion has taken up all the best

Of tredyng, and we borel men been shrympes.	At copulating, and we laymen are shrimps.
Of fieble trees ther comen wrecched ympes.	Of feeble trees there come weak offshoots.
This maketh that oure heires been so sklendre	This makes our heirs to be so scrawny
And feble that they may nat wel engendre.	And feeble that they can not well beget children.
This maketh that oure wyves wole assaye	This makes it that our wives want to try out
Religious folk, for ye mowe bettre paye	Folk in holy orders, for you can better pay
Of Venus paiementz than mowe we;	Venus' payments than we can;
God woot, no lussheburghes payen ye!	God knows, you pay with no inferior coins!
But be nat wrooth, my lord, though that I pleye.	But be not angry, my lord, though I am joking.
Ful ofte in game a sooth I have herd seye!'	Very often I have heard a truth said in jest!'
(MkP VII 1924–64)	

Translation from http://courses.fas.harvard.edu/~chaucer/teachslf/mkt-par.htm

2. The following passage comes from Izaak Walton's *The Compleat Angler* (Chapter II). Analyse the instances of address from the point of view of interpersonal relations and unfolding teaching dialogue:

Viat. My friend *Piscator*, you have kept time with my thoughts, for the Sun is just rising, and I my self just now come to this place, and the dogs have just now put down an *Otter*; ... ; look, you see all busie, men and dogs, dogs and men, all busie.

Pisc. Sir, I am right glad to meet you, and glad to have so fair an entrance into this dayes sport, and glad to see so many dogs, and more men all in pursuit of the *Otter*, lets complement no longer, but joyn unto them; come honest *Viator*, lets be gone, lets make haste; I long to be doing: no reasonable hedge or ditch shall hold me.

Ven. Gentleman Huntsman, where found you this *Otter*?

Hunt. Marry (Sir) we found her a mile from this place a fishing; ... I am to have the skin if we kill her.

Ven. Why, Sir, what's the skin worth?

Hunt. 'Tis worth ten shillings to make gloves; the gloves of

an *Otter* are the best fortification for your hands against wet
weather that can be thought of.

Pisc. I pray, honest Huntsman, let me ask you a pleasant
question, do you hunt a Beast or a fish?

Hunt. Sir, It is not in my power to resolve you ... (EEBO, 1653)

3. Use a corpus of Present-day English, for example, the *British
   National Corpus* (BNC) or the *Corpus of Contemporary American English*
   (COCA) and search for instances of the pronoun *thou* (including the
   case forms *thee, thine* and *thy*) and/or the nominal address term *Sir*.
   Carefully analyse twenty examples in their context and try to find
   what these contexts have in common. Can you detect a number of
   different contexts, for example, quotations from older texts, religious
   writings, jocular use of an archaism, and so on?

Further reading

Finkenstaedt (1963) provides an early comprehensive and book-length
study (in German) of the dual terms of pronominal address from the
emergence in the thirteenth century to its final decline in the sixteenth
and seventeenth centuries. It also deals with the Quaker use of *thou* and
reactions towards this usage in the seventeenth and eighteenth centuries.
More detailed studies tend to focus on the fictional writings of Chaucer
and Shakespeare. Recent studies on Chaucer include Mazzon (2000),
Honegger (2003), Jucker (2006b) and Knappe and Schümann (2006).
Shakespeare has received even more scholarly attention. Brown and
Gilman's (1989) seminal paper on four major tragedies has influenced
much of the later work on address terms. U. Busse (2002) provided the
most comprehensive study of the variability of second-person pronouns
in Shakespeare's plays. Other relevant studies are, for instance, Stein
(2003) and Mazzon (2003). B. Busse (2006) also provides a book-length
study, but she focuses on vocatives and, therefore, adopts a slightly different perspective. There are also studies that do not focus on fictional
language or not exclusively on fictional language. Hope (1994), for
instance, analysed the Early Modern English use of pronouns in depositions in the Durham ecclesiastical court records. Walker's (2007) study
on Early Modern English pronoun usage is based on data from trials,
depositions and drama. Nevala (2004) focused on forms of address in
Early English correspondence. U. Busse and B. Busse (2010) provide a
handbook overview of historical pragmatic analyses of Shakespeare's
plays and Mazzon (2010) of address terms in general.

6 'No one can flatter so prettily as you do': Speech acts

6.1 Speech act theory: From philosophical reflections to corpus searches

Speech act theory begins with the work of two philosophers: J. L. Austin and John Searle. As philosophers they were concerned with the recognition of different types of speech acts and their logical status. They did not work empirically but dissected speech acts with philosophical rigour. Austin drew attention to the three facets of an utterance. First of all, an utterance is an act of uttering certain words, and as such it is a locutionary act, as he called it. Second, an utterance is also an act of doing something; that is, the act of asking a question, of greeting someone, of making a promise or of ordering the addressee to do something. This aspect he called the illocutionary act. And third, an utterance may have an intended or unintended effect on the addressee. The addressee may feel insulted, persuaded, convinced, enlightened and so on. This is called the perlocutionary act. The speaker may intend his or her utterance to have a specific effect on the hearer but the realisation of a specific perlocutionary act depends on whether the addressee is actually persuaded, convinced or enlightened.

In the huge amount of work on theoretical aspects of speech acts and more practical work on specific speech acts, it was always illocutionary acts that received the bulk of scholarly attention. John Searle proposed a particularly influential way of thinking about the illocutionary force of utterances. He worked out what kind of conditions must be met for a certain utterance to count as a promise, a greeting or a question. He called these the felicity conditions of a speech act, and he proposed a taxonomy of illocutionary acts (Searle 1979: Chapter 1). According to this taxonomy, directives are speech acts in which the speaker tries to get the hearer to do something, and commissives are speech acts in which the speaker undertakes to do something himself or herself. In both cases the speaker's words describe a state of affairs that is to come about in the future through the actions of either the hearer (directives) or the speaker (commissives). The direction of fit – according to Searle – is from word to world. For assertives, on the other hand, the direction of fit is from world to word. The speaker describes a state of affairs. In expressives he or she expresses her feelings, and in declarations, finally, are speech acts which, if performed successfully, bring about the state of affairs that they describe. Searle gives the examples of appointing a chairman or nominating somebody as a candidate.

It did not take long for linguists to see the potential and power of this new way of thinking about utterances, and in addition to the theoretical approaches to speech acts based on the researchers' intuition, they started to develop more empirical methods. In order to find out how realisation patterns of speech acts differed across languages, researchers developed methods to elicit specific speech acts from informants. They gave them questionnaires with short conversations that led up to a specific speech act, such as a request or an apology and asked them to fill in the missing speech act. The responses to these questionnaires could be compared across languages in order to find out about language-specific ways of issuing requests or apologies (Blum-Kulka et al. 1989). Another method to obtain empirical results was the use of role-plays. The researcher describes a particular scene to two participants who then have to role-play this situation in which typically one of the participants has to apologise or complain to the other participants about some everyday misdemeanour committed by the speaker or the addressee (see, for example, Trosborg 1995). On the basis of the transcripts of these staged interactions the researcher can then investigate different ways of apologising or complaining, depending, for instance, on the gravity of the misdemeanour or the role relationship between the speaker and the addressee.

It has turned out to be more difficult to use corpus evidence for specific speech acts because there is no straightforward way of searching for a speech act, such as an apology or a complaint, in a corpus, irrespective of whether it is a corpus of written language or a corpus of transcribed spoken language. Apologies, complaints, and almost every other type of speech act, may come in countless different guises. They cannot be recognised on the basis of their syntactic or lexical form alone. Within the last ten years or so, however, some researchers have developed methods to locate specific speech acts in large computerised corpora.

Deutschmann (2003), for instance, in a pioneering study located apologies in the *British National Corpus*. He argues that apologies in English are to a large extent conventionalised. They typically come in a small range of formats and generally include one of a small set of lexical

items, including words such as *sorry, pardon* or *excuse*. A search for these
items, therefore, will recover most of the apologies that are included in
the corpus. He then proceeds to categorise the apologies in the found
set on the basis of the nature and the gravity of the offence for which
speakers apologised, the demographics of the speakers and the recipients of the apology and their mutual relationship, to mention just a few
relevant factors to be taken into account.

6.2 Typical patterns, IFIDs and metacommunicative expressions

In historical pragmatics, the available research tools are more restricted.
Experimental approaches, such as discourse completion tasks or role-
plays, are not available, and researchers have to rely on the available
corpus data. For investigations with a limited data set, it is possible
to read the available texts and to search them for instances of specific
speech acts. With this method, the researcher can bring his or her
philological understanding of the original texts to bear on the analysis
in order to locate both the more obvious and more indirect or marginal
realisations of a particular speech act. But this method is time con-
suming, and it sets limitations on the amount of material that can be
considered.

For larger scale investigations, electronic retrieval tools have to
be used. However, speech acts, as we have pointed out above, are
functional entities which cannot be searched for directly. There are,
however, search techniques that will retrieve at least some of the relevant instances from a historical corpus. These search techniques can be
visualised in three overlapping circles (see Figure 6.1).

The first circle contains searches for patterns that are known to be
typical of specific speech acts. Compliments, for instance, often contain
positively connotated adjectives. A search for such adjectives is therefore likely to retrieve some compliments, even if it is very unlikely to
retrieve all compliments in the corpus. In the words of corpus linguists,
the recall is limited. At the same time the search will find a lot of positively connotated adjectives that are not used in the context of a compliment. In the words of the corpus linguists, the precision is also severely
limited. The method may, however, be good enough to retrieve some
relevant examples from the corpus. In other cases, it might be possible
to get higher levels of precision and/or recall. Kohnen in several of his
publications (for example, 2008b) has tried to establish an inventory
of typical patterns for directives in Old and Middle English in order
to provide a (partial) history of directives in English (see section 6.6
below).

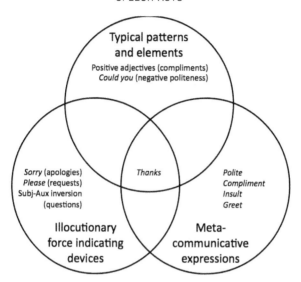

Figure 6.1 Three circles of corpus-based speech act retrieval

The second circle contains those linguistic expressions and syntactic features which are not only typical of a specific speech act but which reliably indicate the illocutionary force of the speech act. These are called illocutionary force indicating devices (often abbreviated as IFIDs). In Present-day English, for instance, *please* is an IFID for a request, *sorry* is one for an apology and the inversion of subject and auxiliary is an IFID for a question. This circle is more focused than the first circle. Positive adjectives, for instance, may be fairly typical for compliments but they are not sufficiently indicative of compliments to count as proper illocutionary force indicating devices. This circle also contains speech act verbs that are used performatively. Expressions such as 'Let me compliment you on . . .' or 'I wish to thank you for . . .' do not only report but actually perform a speech act of complimenting and thanking, respectively. Such formulations may be clear illocutionary force indicating devices but they may also be fairly untypical ways of performing the speech acts that they name.

The third circle takes a slightly different approach. The search strings in this circle do not search for speech acts directly but for meta-communicative expressions, that is to say expressions that are used to talk about communication. Communicators do not only pay each other compliments, give directives to each other, apologise to each other or insult each other, but they also, from time to time, talk about these activities. They may do this for all sorts of reasons: to evaluate, or just to report, or indeed to negotiate the intended force of an utterance ('Was this a compliment?', 'Do you wish to insult me?'). Such instances of communication about communication, i.e. metacommunication, may be very helpful for the researcher because it gives him or her a direct insight into the speaker's perception of specific speech acts.

Some search strings may, in fact, appear in the section where all three circles overlap. The following examples taken from the *Helsinki Corpus* illustrate this with the expression *thank*, which is at the same time a speech act verb and an illocutionary force indicating device.

1. and he meniþ ful hertly **þankyng** to God, for þe worþines and þe 3ift of his beyng, (HC M3 1350–1420, *The Cloud of Unknowing*, lines 702–3)
   and he remembers to thank God with a full heart for the worthiness and the gift of his being
2. Deare S^r – I **thanke** you for your letter which you sent me from Tuddington (HC, E2 1570–1640, *Letters of the Lady Brilliana Harley*, lines 22–3)
3. **Thanks**, Harry, saies he; (HC E2 1570–1640, Armin, Robert: *A Nest of Ninnies*, line 385)

In (1) the expression is used to report an instance of thanking God. Here *þankyng* is a metacommunicative expression. In (2), the expression is used performatively. Lady Brilliana Harley uses it and thereby performs the act of thanking her husband for a letter that she had received. And in (3) the speaker ('he') uses the abbreviated form 'thanks' in order to thank Harry. In (2) and (3), therefore, the expression 'thank' is both a typical expression for the speech act of thanking and a device that clearly indicates the illocutionary force of the utterance in which it is contained (see exercise 1 for further examples).

In the following we will present four case studies of specific speech acts or speech act classes in the history of English. However, our focus will be more on the research methodologies that have been employed rather than on a comprehensive history of any of these speech acts. At present such comprehensive histories do not yet seem possible, but these case studies may give an idea to what extent the methodologies might be powerful enough to bring us closer to a comprehensive history of speech acts.

6.3 From 'God be with you' to 'goodbye'

The first case study concerns a specific linguistic form of a speech act and its etymology, namely *goodbye* as a routinised leave-taking formula at the end of an interaction. In Present-day English, it is not only a typical pattern but also an illocutionary force indicating device for this particular speech act. It may perhaps express good wishes or it may be a mere formula devoid of any propositional content, as suggested by Searle for greetings in general. Only a few people are probably still aware that the origin of *goodbye* was a pious blessing, the phrase 'God be with you' uttered at the beginning, at the end or even during an interaction. In the course of time *good* was substituted for *God* presumably on the analogy of greetings such as 'good morning' or 'good evening'. As a result, it is not possible to use the phrase *goodbye* to express a pious wish in Present-day English. If people indeed want to use a blessing, they have to go back to the expanded form and say 'God be with you'.

Arnovick (1999: Chapter 6) has provided a detailed study of this farewell expression as a case study of pragmatic reanalysis. She shows in detail in what contexts and how this expression lost its religious meaning and became a strictly secular farewell expression. Her study is corpus based. She uses the Chadwyck-Healey database of 2,700 plays by 580 authors, first performed between 1290 and 1949 (Arnovick 1999: 97).

It has to be noted, however, that her approach is more specific than the model introduced above. Her research question does not concern the speech function of a parting salutation in general. In this particular chapter she does not look at expressions such as *farewell* and other ways of taking one's leave or finishing a conversation. Instead she is interested in the changing function of one specific linguistic form, and thus her approach is not a case of function-to-form mapping but rather a case of form-to-function mapping. This is so in spite of the fact that the linguistic expression itself did not remain stable. In the course of time it underwent a process of contraction, but all the spelling variants across time can still be seen as instantiations or rather developments of the same original form.

According to Arnovick (1999: 98), the first attestation of the phrase 'God be with you' can be found in the late fifteenth century. In the late sixteenth century, the phrase was contracted and merged into one word, and it was in the seventeenth century that *good* was substituted for *God*. At the beginning of its development the phrase 'God be with you' functioned both as a blessing and as a parting salutation at the end of a conversation. A blessing was a ritualised speech act that could be performed not only by ordained clergy but by anybody who believed in the power evoked by the blessing. In Arnovick's corpus such blessings are regularly used in closing sections of conversations. The anonymous play *A Warning for Fair Women*, first published in 1599, contains several extended closing sequences with a combination of 'God be with you' with other parting salutations, as for instance in (4).

4. *Bro.* Now afore God, this bloud was ill espied?
             But my excuse I hope wil serve the turne.
             Gentlemen, I must to London this forenoone,
             About some earnest busines doth concerne me,
             Thankes for my ale, and your good companies.
    Both. Adieu good maister Browne.
    Bro.   Farewell unto you both.   *Exit.*
M. James. An honest proper Gentleman as lives:
             God be with you sir, Ile up into the Presence.
    Yeo.   Y'are welcome *M. James*, God be with ye sir.   *Exeunt.*
             (Anon. *A Warning for Fair Women*, ed. by Ch. D. Cannon, Mouton de
             Gruyter, 1975, p. 141)

Captain Browne, Master James and the Yeoman of the Buttery are here engaged in a lengthy parting sequence with the blessing 'God be with you/ye', with thanks and with other parting salutations, *adieu* and *farewell.* The conversation comes to an end and the characters depart, as indicated by the stage directions *exit* and *exeunt.*

In the early attestations, the phrase 'God be with you' regularly served as a 'parting blessing-greeting that helps to close that conversation' (Arnovick 1999: 103). However, in the course of time, the blessing function receded and through its regular association with closing sequences, the function of the phrase shifted to a mere parting salutation, and at the same time – Arnovick times this to the end of the seventeenth and beginning of the eighteenth century – the spelling *Good-bye* superseded the spelling 'Good be with you', and it is exactly the seemingly random variation of the spelling of *Good* and *God*, sometimes even by the same writer, that provides evidence for the loss of the religious meaning. It is interesting that after the phrase had lost its function as a blessing and had adopted the modern spelling, the original blessing, 'God be with you' re-emerged towards the end of the nineteenth century but this time not as a parting greeting but as an independent blessing. Arnovick (1999: 110) gives the following example to illustrate that *Goodbye* can no longer be used as a blessing:

5. Closing Section:
    Explicit Blessing followed by Closing Sequence:
    A: Go with God.
    B: Thank you.

A: Bye
B: Bye
Arnovick (1999: 110)

The two illocutionary forces of blessing and leave taking cannot be merged into one utterance and therefore two independent speech acts are necessary to carry out both functions.

Arnovick describes this change as a case of an illocutionary split. The blessing function and the leave-taking function became separated and adopted independent spellings. The development of *goodbye* in itself, furthermore, is seen as a case of 'discursisation'. This term is proposed by Arnovick (1999: 117) on the analogy of pragmaticalisation. Where the process of pragmaticalisation enlists lexical material and adopts pragmatic meanings, the process of discursisation recruits illocutionary material, such as the leave-taking function of 'God be with you', and adopts this for a specific discourse function.

6.4 Promises

With a promise a speaker undertakes to do something in the future. According to Searle, a promise is a speech act of the commissive type. The direction of fit is from word to world. The speaker uses words to describe the world that will come about as a result of making the promise come true. Several conditions need to obtain for an utterance to qualify as a prototypical promise.

6. I promise to give you the greatest album of this decade, just for you. (COCA, *Rolling Stone*, 2011)

7. I promise to practice my French before my next visit. (COCA, *American Scholar*, 2010)

In a prototypical promise, the speaker must believe that the hearer actually wants the promise to be carried out. The speakers in (6) and (7) must take it for granted that the addressees want them to bring out a great album and to practise French. This is called the preparatory condition. And in order for these utterances to be sincere promises, the speakers must have the intention of actually doing what they promise. This is called the sincerity condition. The formulation, moreover, must be recognisable as an undertaking of bringing out an album and of practising French. This is called the essential condition (Searle 1969: 60, see also Pakkala-Weckström 2005: 184).

However, it has to be noted that the verb 'promise' is often used to carry out speech acts that are not prototypical cases of promising.

8. It wasn't a dream, Dad. I promise it wasn't. (COCA, *Christmas at Hostage Canyon*, 2011)
9. Don't take another step. Put your hands up, or I promise I'll blow you away! (COCA, *Ray of Hope*, 2011)

In extract (8) the verb 'promise' is used in the sense of 'I assure you'. What is being promised is not an action of the speaker in the future but something that happened in the past and that the speaker claims to have been real rather than a dream. In (9) 'promise' is used to threaten the addressee. There can be no question that the future action described in the 'promise' might be in the addressee's interest. (8) and (9), therefore, are not promises in the intended sense in spite of the fact that the verb 'promise' is used performatively in these utterances.

An investigation of a particular speech act, therefore, must distinguish carefully between the different shades of meaning that a speech act verb such as 'promise' can have and the functional profile of an illocutionary act. In a historical investigation the problem may be exacerbated by the fact that functional profiles of specific illocutionary acts may change. In the section above, we have seen that in earlier times a farewell greeting often included a pious blessing. In this section, we shall take a look at how prototypical promises changed their functional profile from Middle English to Present-day English. Two types of Middle English promises have been particularly well researched: the promise of restored health at the end of a medical recipe, and the literary promise in the world of courtly love. Both of them differ significantly from the prototypical promise in Present-day English exemplified in (6) and (7) above.

Middle English medical recipes often finished with an efficacy statement which promised the success of the prescribed measures (Alonso-Almeida and Cabrera-Abreu 2002). They often had the general form of 'he shal be hol' ('he will be healthy'). Extract (10), for instance, is the end of a medical recipe for headaches. It describes how a plaster can be made consisting of breast milk, ale and various spices, such as camomile and cumin, and it finishes as follows:

10. let yt þer as þe hed ys sorest & vse þis medycyne iij dayes & euery tyme newe & he schal be hool bi godes grace.
    'put it where the head is sore. Use this medicine three days, a new one each time, and he will be healthy by the grace of God.' (Alonso-Almeida and Cabrera-Abreu 2002: 147)

Such promises obviously differ from Searle's prototype of a promise. Here it is not the writer of this promise who undertakes to do something in the future, but he assures the reader that, if the instructions of the recipe are faithfully carried out, the desired effect will be obtained, that is to say the patient will recover from the ailment. Alonso-Almeida and Cabrera-Abreu (2002: 148) also discuss the significance of the final phrase 'bi godes grace' ('by the grace of God'), and whether this actually diminishes the strength of the promise. Thus, more than just a faithful observance of the recipe is necessary; God's help is also required. Moreover, should it turn out that the patient does not recover in spite of the medicine, the lack of success can still be blamed on the lack of God's grace.

In *The Franklin's Tale*, one of Chaucer's *Canterbury Tales*, promises play a particularly significant role. This tale is about Arveragus and Dorigen, who are happily married, and Aurelius, who courts Dorigen against her will. In order to get rid of the unwanted suitor, she promises her love if he can remove all the rocks on the coast of Brittany, rocks which threaten the safe return of her husband. To her this means that she will never love him because the task is impossible. However, Aurelius manages to secure the help of a magician by promising him the princely sum of £1,000. The magician removes the rocks and, thus, puts Dorigen in the dilemma of keeping her promise to Aurelius and at the same time her loyalty that she promised her husband Arveragus. Promises, as Pakkala-Weckström (2005: 186) has pointed out, were considered binding even if they were only made orally and even if they were made in jest: 'Among the consequences of breaking a promise were public and private shame.' Confronted with the dilemma Dorigen and Arveragus agonise over a solution, but Arveragus decides that Dorigen must be true to her promise and therefore commit adultery. In the end, Aurelius is so impressed by the true love between Arveragus and Dorigen that he releases Dorigen from her promise to love him, and the magician is so much moved by Aurelius' story that he releases him from his promise to pay the enormous sum. Dorigen's 'promise', on closer analysis, turns out not to be a promise at all. By combining it with what she considers to be an impossible condition, she makes clear that she has no intention of doing what she promises. The promise does not fulfil the felicity conditions. But it is so strong and binding that even her husband forces her to be true to it. Pakkala-Weckström (2005: 194) concludes:

> The tale's roots lie in the tradition of folktales, romance and courtly love, and the generic rules that govern these also affect the behaviour of the characters. Furthermore, the nature of promises has undergone fundamental changes over the centuries that have passed between the compilation of the *Franklin's Tale* and its sources, and the appearance of speech act theory. It is not enough that Dorigen herself has no intention of loving

Aurelius, and that she can easily set conditions if she believes they will never be met. In the fictional society where the tale is set, Dorigen's truest intentions become irrelevant when measured against her husband's honour and the value of *trouthe*.

Thus, Searle's profile of a prototypical promise helps us both to identify promises in historical contexts and it allows us to pinpoint the fundamental changes in the nature of promises over the centuries. In the two studies of promises in medical recipes and in Chaucer's tale, the researchers identified the promises by reading the source texts and by their philological understanding of texts of the period in question and their sociocultural or literary context. With this method it is difficult to trace long diachronies, and, therefore, methods have been developed that allow the researcher to find specific speech acts with more or less automatic corpus searches. Such approaches will be introduced in the following section with the example of directives.

6.5 Directives

Directives are used to get the addressee to do something in the future. They comprise a large group of speech acts that range from unmitigated commands and polite requests to simple suggestions, vague hints and instructions in cookery recipes. There are countless different ways in which directives can be formulated. Depending on the specific type of directive, on the relationship between the speaker and the addressee, and on the general situation, some of these forms may be very direct and unmitigated while others may be elusive and vague. As yet it is not possible to provide a comprehensive repertoire of all possible directives at any given time and even less to tell the precise history of how this repertoire changes over the centuries in the history of the English language.

However, some considerable advances have recently been made in this direction; for example, by Thomas Kohnen. In a methodological paper he has set out the necessary steps for an investigation of directives in the history of English (Kohnen 2008b). He points out that the crucial first step must consist in establishing the inventory of directives in a narrowly defined text genre. As an example he uses sermons, because of their primary function of religious instruction, which he presumes to consist at least to some extent of directives and which persists throughout the entire history of the English language. Thus sermons provide a stable context for a diachronic analysis. The researcher can investigate how people were told how they should act morally at different stages in the history of English. Within this genre, Kohnen then proceeds to establish the inventory of all directives. This has to be done manually by subjecting the texts to a careful philological analysis and by highlighting relevant instances. Such an analysis must necessarily be based on a limited amount of data because of its labour-intensive nature. But once an inventory has been established for a particular period, the analysis can proceed with corpus-based technologies, at least for the recurring patterns. This means that the method will provide the most reliable results for those patterns that are most frequent and most conventionalised, and it is far less reliable for rare and creative patterns. The method also depends on the availability of a sufficient amount of relevant data throughout the period under investigation.

With this method, Kohnen (2008b: 298) established that there are basically four manifestations to be accounted for. The first type are performative directives, which typically contain a directive speech-act verb in the first-person singular or plural indicative active as in extract (11), which contains the performatives *pray* and *beseech*. By using these verbs in this context, the author performs the act of praying and beseeching.

11. Wherefore **we pray and besech thy maiesty**, that at no tyme thou suffer vs to be vnthankefull vnto these exceding great benefites, not yet vnworthy of thy greate merytes, . . . (Cuthbert Tunstall, *Certaine godly and deuout prayers*, Kohnen 2008b: 298, Kohnen's emphasis)

The second type of directives are the imperatives, which comprise various types of first, second- and third-person imperatives, including forms such as *let us* or *let's* and Old English *uton we* with a similar meaning:

12. . . . **let vs never gruge** therat but take in good worth and hartely thanke hym as well for aduersytie as for prosperytie. (Thomas More, Letter to his Wife, Kohnen 2008b: 299, Kohnen's emphasis)
13. And **utan** ðurh æghwæt Godes willan wyrcan swa we geornost magan. (Helsinki Corpus, Wulfstan, *Homilies*, 184)
    'And let us in every way perform God's commands as carefully as we may be.' (Kohnen 2008a: 36)

Extracts (12) and (13) illustrate the so-called first-person imperatives with the form *let us*, and *uton*. Kohnen (2008b: 37) points out that the *uton* construction was regularly used for exhortations to love and adore God, to pray, keep the peace and so on. Standard second-person imperatives also belong to this group.

The third group of directives, the modal directives, are formed by modal expressions denoting obligation, permission or possibility.

They can again occur in the format of expressing an obligation for the addressee or as first-person directives as in extract (14):

14. **We must** take heed how we scoff at Religion. (Tillotson, *Sermons*, Kohnen 2008b: 299, Kohnen's emphasis)

The last group, the indirect directives are the most diverse group and contain, for instance, hearer-based interrogatives ('could you ...'), hearer-based conditionals ('if you would like to ...'), speaker-based declaratives expressing volition ('I'd like ...'), and so on. Kohnen (2008b: 300) ventures that 'the four basic classes seem to cover most, if not all, the manifestations of directives in the history of English'. He also hypothesises that these four forms probably cover most of the directives in other genres, too. If he is right that his search strings cover most manifestations of directives, it should be possible to locate a high percentage of all directives in his data. He then proceeds to provide statistics on the frequency of directives at the various periods covered in his data (see Figure 6.2).

Figure 6.2 indicates that performatives and second-person imperatives have increased considerably, while first-person imperatives and to some extent modals have decreased over the centuries. Kohnen (2008b:

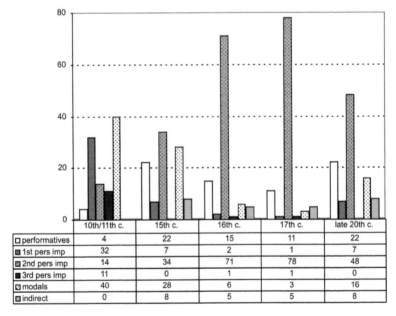

	10th/11th c.	15th c.	16th c.	17th c.	late 20th c.
□ performatives	4	22	15	11	22
▨ 1st pers imp	32	7	2	1	7
▩ 2nd pers imp	14	34	71	78	48
■ 3rd pers imp	11	0	1	1	0
□ modals	40	28	6	3	16
▨ indirect	0	8	5	5	8

Figure 6.2 Distribution of manifestations of directives in the data (in percentages) (Kohnen 2008b: 301)

309) concedes that the class of indirect directives is most problematic because it is least predictable. It is difficult to draw the line between speech acts that can still be taken to be directives and other speech acts. In addition, there may be examples of directives in his corpus that were not retrieved by his search strings. This means that we cannot establish with certainty the entire inventory of directives and their precise number at a given time, and as a result we have to be very cautious about the changing importance of specific directives because we cannot compare the frequency of these types with the overall frequency of all directives.

6.6 Insults and compliments

What insults and compliments have in common is that they are speech acts that express – in a very general sense – the speaker's evaluation of the addressee. In the case of an insult it is a negative evaluation, and in the case of a compliment it is a positive evaluation. In Searle's classification, they are expressives. They also have in common that their status as a positive or negative evaluation is not always clear or that they can be misunderstood. On occasion, one may even be mistaken for the other. An ironic compliment may be intended as an insult, and a compliment that comes across as inappropriate may be perceived as an insult even if it is not intended as one. To some extent at least, insults and compliments depend on how they are understood by the addressee. If somebody does not feel insulted it may well be argued that the utterance was not really an insult, and if the recipient is not pleased about a compliment, the utterance is not really a proper compliment. Finally, what the two speech acts also have in common is that the conventionalisation of their realisation is very limited. While greetings, apologies and thanks have a range of conventionalised linguistic forms that are regularly used for their realisations, this does not seem to be the case for insults or compliments.[1]

At different periods, insults and other forms of verbal aggression can be found in different types of texts. In order to account for the diversity of forms of verbal aggression, the framework of the pragmatic space of insults with a multi-dimensional grid can be used (see Jucker and Taavitsainen 2000). This grid distinguishes, for instance, between ritual- or rule-governed forms of insults and creative forms. In the Old English heroic tradition, for instance, Anglo-Saxon warriors followed strict rules in what is called 'flyting'. It consisted of sequences of Claim, Defence, and Counterclaim. The Claim and the Counterclaim often consisted of boasts and insults. The contestants boasted of their own deeds and belittled those of their opponents (Clover 1980: 452). These contests either ended in violence or in silence, but they were ritual in terms of their structure and content. In this they resemble the twentieth-century practice of 'sounding', the ritual insults of urban African-American adolescents also known as 'playing the dozens', 'screaming', 'joining' or 'signifying' (see Arnovick 1995: 604).

This grid also distinguishes between ludic and serious forms of insults, and according to this dimension, the sounding of African-American adolescents can be described as mostly ludic. The purpose is to better one's opponent with caustic and humorous insults but it is part of the game that they have to be patently unrealistic and untrue. However, many forms of verbal aggression are not ludic but very serious indeed. In seventeenth-century courtrooms, for instance, insults seem to have been used as a systematic means of intimidation in the interrogation of defendants and witnesses, as in the following extract taken from the proceedings of the trial of Lady Alice Lisle in 1685. Dunne, a baker and a messenger for Alice Lisle was interrogated by the Lord Chief Justice, who grows increasingly impatient at what he sees as Dunne's evasive, confusing and contradictory answers:

> 15. *L.C.J.* Why, thou vile Wretch didst not thou tell me just now that thou pluck'd up the Latch? Dost thou take the God of Heaven not to be a God of Truth, and that he is not a Witness of all thou say'st? Dost thou think because thou prevaricatest with the Court here, thou can'st do so with God above, who knows thy Thoughts, and it is infinite Mercy, that for those Falshoods of thine, he does not immediately strike thee into Hell? Jesus God! there is no sort of Conversation nor human Society to be kept with such People as these are, who have no other Religion but only Pretence, and no way to uphold themselves but by countenancing Lying and Villany: Did not you tell me that you opened the Latch your self, and that you saw no body else but a Girl? How durst you offer to tell such horrid Lyes in the presence of God and of a Court of Justice? Answer me one Question more: Did he pull down the Hay or you?
> *Dunne.* I did not pull down any Hay at all. (p. 114) (HC E3 XX TRI LISLE; Jucker and Taavitsainen 2000: 87–8)

Dunne has no way of defending himself against this onslaught of insults hurled at him in the official context of a courtroom and gives a very brief answer. He is certainly not in a position to insult the Lord Chief Justice in return. A return of insults, however, is regularly appropriate both in the case of Old English flyting and the sounding of African-American adolescents.

Such a grid allows the analyst to focus on similarities and differences of related speech acts across different centuries and different cultures. Speech acts are seen as dynamic. They may change their communicative profiles as well as their linguistic realisations, but they can be described with the help of appropriate dimensions in a multi-dimensional pragmatic space. So far it is only possible to trace very partial histories of specific speech acts, such as insults, but ultimately larger scale studies of forms of insults may lead to a better understanding of the inventory of speech acts in the pragmatic space of verbal aggression and its development over time.

Taavitsainen and Jucker (2008: 207) report on an attempt to locate compliments in historical corpora by searching for adjectives that regularly express positive evaluations, such as *beautiful, nice, great, lovely*, and lexical strings, such as *really nice, really great, well done, like/love your, what a, you look/'re looking* and so on. While these searches did indeed provide relevant hits, they also returned a lot of passages that did not contain any compliments (very low precision).

In the absence of typical words and expressions and in the absence of relevant illocutionary force indicating devices, the analysis has to turn to a metacommunicative expression analysis (Figure 6.1 above), that is to say to the search for terms that describe insults and compliments. A search for the term 'compliment' (including spelling variants and related forms such as *complimentary*) retrieves passages in which the term is used performatively as well as passages in which it is used discursively:

16. 'Will you do me the honor of exchanging cards with me?' he said to Elizabeth. 'You have shown yourself so competent here this afternoon, and your work has been so skilfully done that I want to **compliment** you upon it, and to say that I am sure you have before you a promising future.' (COHA, 1911, Florence Finch Kelly, *Emerson's Wife and Other Western Stories*)

17. Tis believed the Pope will order him to **compliment** the Duke of Mantoua upon his late Marriage with the Princess of Guastala. (ZEN, 1671, 1671lgz00518)

18. *De R.* Lady Clanarlington, permit me to congratulate you on your excellent looks this morning. But I must not forget to ask after your fair daughters – though daughters, indeed, appear impossible, when such a mother blooms before us.
    Lady C. Really, Monsieur, you are too **complimentary**; no one can flatter so prettily as you do. (Stuart-Wortley, Emmeline, Lady, *Moonshine* (1843), pp. 35–6; Taavitsainen and Jucker 2008: 215)

In extract (16), the speaker uses the verb *compliment* performatively to pay Elizabeth a compliment. In extracts (17) and (18) the term compliment is not used performatively but is used either descriptively or discursively. Extract (17) is taken from a seventeenth-century newspaper which reports the audience of an abbot with the Pope. The abbot received several favours and was ordered to pay compliments to the Duke of Mantua on his recent marriage. The reader of this newspaper is not told with which words the abbot complimented the Duke of Mantua. But the report reveals the circumstances of the compliment, who is to make it and who will receive it. The compliment, in this case, differs from those we are familiar with in Present-day English. It is a ceremonious act of diplomacy. Such compliments were common in the seventeenth and eighteenth centuries, and newspapers regularly reported them. Dignitaries received compliments not only on their marriages but also on the births of their children, on their accession to power and even on occasions of bereavement. In Emmeline Stuart-Wortley's comedy *Moonshine*, Monsieur de R. pays a rather elaborate compliment to Lady Clanarlington. He compliments her on her looks and after an enquiry about her daughters hints that Lady Clanarlington looks so young and beautiful that it seems impossible for her to have daughters. The receiver of the compliment responds gracefully with an ambiguous countercompliment. She praises the complimenter but also calls it flattery. In this case it is the term *complimentary* which retrieves the extract in a corpus search. The term is used discursively in that the speaker uses it to assign a discourse value to the preceding utterance, and it reveals that the speech acts of complimenting and flattering could be seen as being very close together.

A metacommunicative expression analysis reveals passages which may tell the researcher a great deal about the nature of a specific speech act at a given time. Who used this particular speech act, to whom and on what occasions? How was it evaluated by the speakers and the recipients? In addition the search will often reveal the wordings of the speech act itself in close vicinity to the search term as in extract (18) above.

6.7 Conclusions

In this chapter, we have looked at a range of speech acts and how they have changed over the centuries. The case studies reviewed above have also revealed rather different approaches in the attempt to trace speech acts in historical contexts. Illocutionary acts are defined in functional terms. A greeting, a promise or a directive are instances of their category, not because of their linguistic form, but because of their functional profile, because of their purpose in an interaction. Such functional profiles can be found in historical contexts by a careful and philologically trained reader, but this method has its limitations if we want to gain an understanding of the larger picture of developments across centuries and across a broad range of different genres. In the case of the farewell greeting *goodbye*, the starting point of the investigation was the linguistic form. In spite of the changes in the spelling, the early form 'God be with you' and its spelling variants can easily be identified as the precursor of *goodbye*, and the analysis focuses on the functional change which turned a pious wish that often occurred at the end of an interaction into an entirely secular marker that finishes a conversation. The promises that occur as efficacy statements at the end of medical recipes and the literary promises in *The Franklin's Tale*, on the other hand, had to be located manually on the basis of their functional profile (but see Valkonen 2008 for an attempt to use corpus searches to identify promises in historical contexts). In the case of directives we have focused on work that tried to locate a large number of relevant speech acts via an inventory of relevant linguistic manifestations. For insults and compliments, finally, we reviewed approaches that used speech act verbs in order to locate discursive passages in these speech acts.

Note

1. Manes and Wolfson (1981: 120) have argued that American English compliments are very formulaic. They claim that three syntactic patterns account for 85 per cent of all the compliments in their data ('NP {is/looks} (really) ADJ', 'I (really) {like/love} NP' and 'PRO is (really) (a) ADJ NP', where '(really)' is an optional intensifier and ADJ a positive adjective). However, it seems very likely that their data collection method (diary reports collected by their students) is at least partly responsible for the stereotypical nature of their compliments.

Exercises

1. Look at the following examples from the *Helsinki Corpus*. In which cases is the expression 'thank' used as a performative speech act verb? Do the thanks offered to God pose any problem in the analysis? In which cases is 'thank' a metacommunicative expression?

    1. And Iesus lift vp his eyes, and said, Father, I thanke thee, that thou hast heard me. (HC E2 1611, *The New Testament* (Authorised Version), lines 1821–3)
    2. But oh! she disarms me with that modesty and weeping, so tender and so moving, that I retire, and thank my stars she overcame me. (HC E3 1640–1710, Behn, Aphra: *Oroonoko*, lines 368–70)

3. I do heartily thanke God for it, and will endevor myselfe to put it in practise continually. (HC E2 1570–1640, Brinsley, John: *Ludus Literarius*, lines 414–16)

4. In charitee, ythanked be oure Lord! (HC M3 1350–1420, Chaucer, Geoffrey: *The Summoner's Tale*, line 83)

5. and thereupon I drinke to you, and I thanke you for my good cheere with all my heart. (HC E2 1570–1640, Deloney, Thomas: *Jack of Newbury*, lines 147–9)

6. My Lord of Cant: gave me greate thanks for the advertisement I sent his Grace in October (HC E3, 1640–1710, *Diary of John Evelyn* lines 469–70)

2. The following passages contain several strategies commonly used in performing apologies. Extract (1) is one of Blum-Kulka et al.'s (1989: 290) illustrative examples. Extract (2) has been retrieved from the *British National Corpus*.

   1. I'm sorry, I missed the bus, and there was a terrible traffic jam. Let's make another appointment. I'll make sure that I'm here on time.

   2. I shall have to apologize to the council, cos I mean I did do the, the survey of the erm residents and of course I had flu last month, I do apologize, I didn't actually manage to get that done. But if you still want me to do it I will do it. (BNC H49 910–11)

   Which words belong to the IFID, which provide the explanation, express responsibility, and promise forbearance and repair?

3. The following extract is taken from the autobiography of John B. Gough (1817–86), an American temperance orator. In this extract he gives a humorous account of an overly polite landlord he met on one of his visits to London. Provide a speech act analysis of the utterances attributed to the landlord.

   The proprietor of the lodging-house where we were entertained on our first visit to London, was so excessively polite, that it was embarrassing at times. He would insinuate himself into the room at breakfast time, and, bowing very gracefully, would say: "I beg your pardon—excuse me—I'm much obliged to you—thank you—but, hem!—what would you like for dinner?" These expressions he used on all occasions. The committee had presented him with tickets to the lecture at Drury Lane Theater, and on my return he met me at the door and said: "I beg your pardon, sir," etc., "but, hem! —I've been to your lecture, and—I beg your pardon—thank you—but, hem!—I've been very much disappointed, sir."

   "Ah! Mr. ———, I'm sorry for that."

   "Oh, my!—thank you—I beg your pardon—but, hem!—to look at you, nobody would think you could speak on a stage—hem!—I beg your pardon—thank you, sir—but, hem!—when Lord Shaftesbury introduced you—you know, sir—hem!—that he is a very noble-looking gentleman, so tall, you know, and so—hem—I beg your pardon, but really—thank you, sir—when you stood up, you looked so-hem!—so very—I beg your pardon, but really I pitied you—I did indeed, now—to look at you nobody would think you could speak on the stage—hem!—I beg your pardon." (John Bartholomew Gough: *Autobiography and Personal Recollections* by John B. Gough, San Francisco: Francis Dewing, 1870, p. 238–9, Google Books)

Further study

1. Use the *Corpus of Historical American English* (COHA) to search for the term 'compliment'. Look at the first ten or fifteen hits for the decades headed 1810, 1900 and 2000.
   a. Try to categorise the hits according to whether the term *compliment* is used performatively (to carry out a compliment), descriptively (to describe a compliment), or discursively (to negotiate the status of a preceding utterance).
   b. Are the compliments positive evaluations of the addressee or can you find any ceremonious compliments (compliments of diplomacy)?
   c. Can you find out what the addressee is complimented on (appearance, performance, possession, personality)?
   d. Can you find a development from 1810 to the most recent compliments?

Further reading

The classic text in speech act theory is still Austin's (1962) posthumously published book of his lecture series in which he develops some of the foundations of speech act theory. Searle's (1969) work is the second foundation stone of speech act theory. Soon after the work of these language philosophers, linguistic work on speech acts began to proliferate. In the text above some pioneering research efforts were highlighted that introduced empirical methods into the study of speech acts: Blum-Kulka et al. (1989), Trosborg (1995) and Deutschmann (2003). None of these titles, however, considers speech acts from a historical perspective. In fact, historical speech act analyses are still somewhat scarce, but Arnovick (1999) is an early example. She studied the illocutionary histories of a range of speech acts in English, not only the history of *goodbye* referred to above but also the illocutionary histories of the agonistic insult, promises, curses and the sneeze blessing. In 2008 a volume of articles was published on speech acts in the history of the English language (Jucker and Taavitsainen 2008).

The most relevant references for the speech acts of the case studies above have already been mentioned in the text. For promises, we have relied mainly on Alonso-Almeida and Cabrera-Abreu (2002) and Pakkala-Weckström (2005: Chapter 7). Kohnen has studied directives from a diachronic perspective in many of his publications. The best overview of the problems of locating directives in historical corpora is provided by Kohnen (2008b). Compliments have been investigated from a historical perspective by Taavitsainen and Jucker (2008), Jucker and Taavitsainen (forthcoming), and insults by Jucker and Taavitsainen (2000) and Taavitsainen and Jucker (2007).

7 'For your curteisie': Forms of politeness and impoliteness

7.1 Introduction

In Present-day English the following utterances are typical ways of asking somebody to do something.

1. Er, could you tell me where you were born? (BNC FXV 2)
2. Would you mind shutting up for a minute? (BNC HV1 389)
3. I wonder if you could provide me with the following information? (BNC AP1 697)

The speakers of these utterances use the format of a direct or indirect question to inquire about the addressee's ability or willingness to perform a certain action, but in the context these utterances are not understood as genuine inquiries. It is clear that these are requests for the addressee to comply and to answer a particular question in (1), to be quiet in (2) and to provide some relevant information in (3). It appears to be more polite to give the addressee an option, even if the option is only pretence. The speaker projects the illusion of not imposing on the addressee. As a result, such forms may also appear to be insincere or even hypocritical, but they are certainly widely used in Present-day English. However, they are a fairly recent phenomenon. Earlier stages of the English language relied much less or not at all on such formulations for making requests.

Does that mean that during these earlier stages speakers of English were less polite? The answer to such a question can only be, no, they were not less polite but they had different ways of interacting with each other in a socially acceptable manner. For the historical pragmaticists it is interesting to trace the changing manifestations of politeness. How did people interact courteously? How did they make polite requests and how did they compliment each other? It is equally interesting – or perhaps even more fascinating – to see how people used language to be impolite at different points in the history of English. How did they insult and offend each other? How did they criticise and hurt other people using linguistic means?

In all these questions, it is clear that politeness and impoliteness describe a secondary language function. They are superimposed on primary functions, such as conveying information, asking a question, getting another person to do something, and so on. As such, elements of politeness and impoliteness are more elusive and, therefore, more difficult to pin down. In the following sections, we want to give a brief overview of the research that has so far been carried out in the development of politeness and impoliteness in the history of the English language. This picture is still patchy with many gaps, especially in the case of impoliteness, but in recent years some notable insights have emerged. However, in order to tackle these questions, it is necessary to first establish more clearly what the term 'politeness' and its opposite 'impoliteness' refer to.

7.2 Approaches to the study of politeness and impoliteness

The words 'politeness' and 'impoliteness' are both part of our everyday language but like many words they have no clear-cut delimitation as to what exactly they refer to. What appears to be polite for one speaker may appear as insincere and therefore not particularly polite or even downright rude to another. At the same time, these words are also used as technical terms, and this often leads to confusion. The technical terms are sometimes taken to be as fuzzy as the everyday notions. For this reason, it has become customary to refer to the everyday notion of politeness as first-order politeness or politeness$_1$ and to the technical term as second-order politeness or politeness$_2$.

Politeness$_1$ and impoliteness$_1$ are susceptible to change in the course of time. What people believed to be polite or impolite a few centuries ago may be evaluated differently today as we will see later in this chapter. Nevertheless, politeness$_1$ offers unique opportunities for diachronic research. It is extremely revealing to investigate not just the words 'politeness' and 'polite' and their antonyms 'impoliteness' and 'impolite' but a whole range of terms in the semantic field of courteous and discourteous interaction. This will tell us a great deal about how people at a particular time evaluated particular forms of social interaction.

Politeness$_2$ and impoliteness$_2$, on the other hand, are analytical tools. They are as precise and stable as we manage to make them by formulating precise definitions. Once we have established one or several

definitions of politeness₂ or impoliteness₂, it is an empirical question
to find out whether the forms of behaviour described in the definitions
exist in a particular society at a given time or not.

The best-known classification of different types of politeness (politeness₂) was introduced more than 30 years ago by Brown and Levinson
(first edition 1978, second edition 1987). They distinguished between
positive politeness and negative politeness, which were directly related
to their notion of positive and negative face. Face as a technical term
was based on the everyday notion of face in such phrases as 'save someone's face', 'lose face' or 'maintain face'. Positive face consists of a person's wish to be appreciated by others. We generally prefer to get praise
for what we do and for who we are, rather than criticism. Negative face
consists of a person's wish to be unimpeded in their actions. We generally prefer not to be bossed around – we would rather do things our
own way.

Positive politeness and negative politeness are forms of (linguistic)
behaviour that pay respect to the addressee's positive or negative face
wants, in particular in situations where one or the other of these are
in some way threatened. If parents ask their child to eat up his or her
dinner or if teachers ask students to move chairs and tables, the negative face of the addressee is threatened because the request interferes
with the addressee's wish to be free from imposition. In (4) the speaker
chooses a token of positive politeness, the term of endearment *honey*, to
mitigate the face threat and in (5) the speaker uses negative politeness
(interrogative form, the modal *would* and *please*).

4. You will eat your coleslaw honey won't you? (BNC KCH 6235)
5. Would you please bring your chairs and that table over here? (BNC
   FMC 8)

It is important to stress that such forms are culture specific. Features
of positive and negative politeness may be abundant in Present-day
English, but – as we will show – they are relatively recent in the history
of the English language.

Negative politeness can take two different forms. The form illustrated in (5) above is called 'non-imposition politeness' and it subsumes
all the linguistic elements that give the addressee an option, or at least
pretend to give the addressee an option. These elements are directly
addressed to the addressee's wish not to be imposed upon. A second
type of politeness that Brown and Levinson (1987) also subsumed
under negative politeness is called 'deference politeness' and includes
elements that express the speaker's humble submission and respect

towards the addressee. Prototypical examples are titles and honorifics, such as *Professor* or *Mr President.*

From these examples, we can see that Brown and Levinson's concept of positive and negative politeness covers only part of what we might wish to call polite behaviour. It is basically designed to account for situations in which the speaker's or the addressee's face is in some way threatened. Thus, it accounts for what we might want to call strategic politeness; that is to say, politeness that is used to soothe potentially tricky situations in interactions, to minimise the severity of impositions, or to minimise the risk of losing the addressee's appreciation.

Thus we need a term to describe behaviour that is polite without being strategic in the above sense. Two useful terms that have been suggested are 'discernment politeness' or 'politic behaviour'. This describes a type of behaviour that comes across as polite because it is appropriate in a given social and situational context. It is a base line which contrasts, on the one hand, with impolite behaviour and, on the other, with strategically polite behaviour.

Terms of address are an obvious example. Whether a person is addressed as *Mary, sweetheart* or *Dr Smith* depends largely on the speaker and their relationship with this particular individual. It is, of course, easy to imagine situations in which these choices are also used strategically. Parents have often been noted to change their terms of address to their children in the process of telling them off for some misdemeanour; for example, by switching from a term of endearment to the full first name and perhaps even to full first and last name. But in general, terms of address are chosen on the basis of the social and situational context without strategic implications. Many languages have an elaborate system of choices, where speakers must use the appropriate verb endings, for instance, or use particular lexical items depending on the social status of the interlocutor.

7.3 Old English: Mutual obligation, kinship loyalty, *caritas* and *humilitas*

Old English does not use such politeness-related terms as *courtesy, civility* or *politeness* itself. These only became part of the English vocabulary as a result of French influence in the Middle English period. But under the heading of 'courtesy' *The Historical Thesaurus of English* gives a number of Old English words that give a first impression of politeness or courtesy in Anglo-Saxon England. These include *manþwærnes* 'gentleness, courtesy, weakness', *wynsumnes* 'loveliness, pleasantness, rejoicing' or *swetnes* 'pleasantness; kindliness, goodness', *þeawfæstnes* 'adherence

to the rules of right conduct or method, discipline, obedience to rule'
and *þeawfæst* 'decorous, moral, virtuous, honourable, of good manners,
of well-ordered life; gentle'. They all refer to gentle, kind and obedient
behaviour that does not seem to be concerned with face-threat mitigation or face enhancement but rather with face maintenance and with
behaviour that conforms to social and contextual expectations; that is,
with discernment politeness. It is noteworthy that in the Old English
sections of the *Helsinki Corpus*, these words and their various case forms
are only used in religious contexts.

Anglo-Saxon England was a warlike and violent society that was
organised on strictly hierarchical principles within tribal networks. It
was characterised by frequent feuds between these tribal networks. As
a result, individuals had their fixed places in society. In fact this place
in society could even be given a monetary value, the so-called *wergild*,
i.e. the money that had to be paid as ransom if somebody was captured
by another tribe or as settlement in the case of manslaughter. In this
sense, it was a 'brutally commercial society' (Campbell 1991: 59). In
such a context, the personal wishes of a warrior, such as his wish to be
appreciated and liked by others, and his wish to remain unimpeded and
free from imposition, were not of primary importance. What counted
was his kin loyalty within his own tribe and his obedience to his
sovereign.

> In the tribal world of Germanic warriors, where mutual obligation and
> kin loyalty were prevalent, it was certainly most important to maintain
> friendly relationships within one's tribal network and to emphasise
> affectionate family relationships, but also to respect the fixed hierarchi-
> cal distinctions as manifested in the difference between lord and man.
> (Kohnen 2008c: 154)

Superimposed on these values of the Germanic warriors, Kohnen dis-
cerns the distinct values of Christianity.

> Within a Christian setting, the friendly or even affectionate relationship
> to one's fellow Christians is part of the basic Christian ideals of *humilitas*
> and *caritas*, which forbid you to place yourself on a higher level than your
> fellow Christian and order you to care for your neighbour. Complying
> with these guidelines can hardly be called face work. (Kohnen 2008c: 155)

This particular Anglo-Saxon blend of Germanic and Christian values
can also be discerned in the use of Old English terms of address, in
particular *leof* 'dear one', *broþor* 'brother' and *hlaford* 'lord' (see Kohnen
2008c). Such terms reflect the fixed positions of interlocutors in
Anglo-Saxon society and do not enhance the addressee's positive face

(endearment) or negative face (deference). Kohnen (2008c: 155), with reference to Watts (2003), argues that this 'could not be called politeness in the sense of face work but only in the sense of discernment or politic behaviour'.

Requests and other directives constitute, in Present-day terms, an imposition on the addressee who is asked to do something that he or she might not have done anyway. In Old English, typical constructions to perform requests were directive performatives, such as 'I ask you to . . .'; constructions involving a second-person pronoun plus *scealt/sculon* 'you shall'; constructions with *uton* 'let's' plus infinitive; and impersonal constructions with (*neod*)*þearf* 'it is necessary for x' (Kohnen 2008a). The authoritarian *þu scealt* construction was particularly common in secular or Germanic contexts. It does not show any concern for considerations of face (Kohnen 2008a: 40). For speakers in an authoritative position, the mitigation of face impositions does not seem to have been important. The *uton* and the (*neod*)*þearf* constructions, on the other hand, were more common in religious contexts. In this sphere, the speaker includes himself or herself in the required action or formulates it in an impersonal way.

> In the monastic world of humility and obedience there are (or there should be) only limited face wants since Christians are not allowed to assume a rank above their fellow Christians, and everybody is bound to follow the requirements of a Christian life. (Kohnen 2008a: 40)

The Old English constructions *ic wille* 'I want to' and *ic wolde* 'I would like to' appear to be early examples of expressing requests with negative politeness as personal wishes rather than as directives. However, Kohnen (2011) convincingly shows that a careful assessment of the extant examples reveals a rather more complex picture. Most of the instances of *ic wolde* are based on translations from Latin texts and therefore reflect Latin usages rather than genuinely Old English patterns of politeness. Constructions with *wille*, on the other hand, appeared mostly in vernacular genres (laws and charters) and reflect the authority of a king or lord, who 'simply specified his wishes and that was that. In all likelihood, no association with "impoliteness" or "inappropriateness" applied' (Kohnen 2011: 251).

The evidence that we have does not allow any far-reaching conclusions about politeness in the Anglo-Saxon period, but it provides some interesting hints about a particular type of politeness; that is, discernment politeness. In the areas of nominal terms of address and directives, there is no evidence of face-threat mitigation or face-enhancing politeness.

7.4 Middle English: *Curteisie*

In 1066, William the Conqueror, Duke of Normandy, defeated the British at the Battle of Hastings and became King of England, and within a generation the entire nobility including all the higher levels in the Church hierarchy was replaced by Normans. The effects on the English language are well known. In certain contexts, English was completely replaced by French; for example, as the language of the court, for official business and as a legal language. In the context of the church, Latin kept its strong position as a language of religion and learning. English underwent far-reaching changes over the next few centuries. In particular the vocabulary of English was massively affected by contact with French. The changes did not happen overnight but took several decades to have a real impact, and this is why the beginning of the Middle English period is usually set at around 1150, several generations after William the Conqueror. Middle English has always been seen as a kind of bridge between Old English and Early Modern English because it links Old English and Early Modern English on all levels, not just the level of vocabulary, but also on the level of phonology, morphology and syntax.

However, the linking function of Middle English on the level of pragmatics has so far not received the same degree of scholarly attention as the other levels. The evidence of the *Historical Thesaurus* affords a first overview. Under the headings of 'courtesy' and 'courteous' it lists a large range of terms with the dates of their first attestation in the English language. It turns out that it was in the thirteenth and early fourteenth centuries that we find the earliest appearance of some lexical items in the semantic field of courteous behaviour and courtesy. In fact, a search for these words with all their spelling variants in the *Helsinki Corpus* reveals that these terms make their first appearance in the second subperiod of Middle English that is dated from 1150 to 1250. The words *courtesy* and *courteous* themselves are first attested in texts from the thirteenth century. The *Oxford English Dictionary* gives the following definitions for the words *courtesy* and *courteous*:

> Courteous behaviour; courtly elegance and politeness of manners; graceful politeness or considerateness in intercourse with others. (OED, courtesy, *n.* 1.a.)
>
> Having such manners as befit the court of a prince; having the bearing of a courtly gentleman in intercourse with others; graciously polite and respectful of the position and feelings of others; kind and complaisant in conduct to others. (OED, courteous, *adj.* 1.a.)

The connection with behaviour that was expected at court is very obvious. The *Oxford English Dictionary* indicates that the word is borrowed from Old French. In the earliest quotations, this quality is ascribed to knights and their character. It is only in later quotations that the quality is also used to describe behaviour and even later still to describe ways of speaking.

Chaucer uses the term frequently to describe the characters in his *Canterbury Tales*. For the Knight, as a representative of the aristocracy, the designation seems particularly appropriate. In the General Prologue the narrator describes him in the following way:

> 6. A KNYGHT ther was, and that a worthy man,
>   That fro the tyme that he first bigan
>   To riden out, he loved chivalrie,
>   Trouthe and honour, fredom and curteisie. (GP I 43−6)[1]
> 'There was a Knight, a worthy man who loved chivalry, truth and honour, freedom and courtesy ever since he first began to ride out.'

Courtesy is here mentioned in a list of high courtly qualities that befit a member of the aristocracy. His son, the Squire, is also described with this term. However, Chaucer also uses it regularly for characters that belong to the clergy, and in these cases the term is often used with a touch of irony. The Prioress, for instance, is described in all the splendour of a courtly lady. She is carefully dressed, she has good table manners, she feels so compassionate about her lap dogs that she feeds them with the finest bread only and her greatest pleasure is in good manners ('In curteisie was set ful muchel hir lest', GP I 132). The narrator thus creates a picture of subtle irony in which these qualities contrast with what would be more appropriate praise for a nun; that is, her religious devotion or her compassion for her fellow human beings.

In the case of characters from lower classes, the term is again used in a slightly different way. It is often used in the speech of such characters when they address other characters using the phrase 'of (for) (your) curteisye', which Benson (1987: 1234) glosses as 'if you please'. As such, it could be taken as a mere formula without much meaning, but it appears that it is typically used in situations when the decorum of the situation is somehow threatened. In *The Miller's Tale*, for instance, Alison cries out 'Do wey youre handes, for youre curteisye!' (MilT I 3287) in her (very brief) mock resistance to the indecent advances of her lodger, Nicholas. And in the frame narrative the Summoner uses the following words to protest against what he sees as a slanderous tale told by the Friar:

7. 'Lordynges,' quod he, 'but o thyng I desire;
   I yow biseke that, of youre curteisye,
   Syn ye han herd this false Frere lye,
   As suffreth me I may my tale telle.' (SumP III 1668–71)
   'Gentlemen,' he said, 'I desire only one thing: I beseech you, for your cour-
   tesy and since you have heard this false Friar tell lies, allow me to tell my
   tale.'

Thus both Alison and the Summoner use the phrase 'for your curteisye'
in a situation where they perceive that the usual decorum of decent
behaviour is seriously challenged in order to remind their addressees
of the proper behaviour. The term 'curteisye', therefore, is used by
Chaucer to describe a high moral quality that aristocratic characters
possess or strive to possess. It is a quality that Chaucer also ascribes to
some members of the clergy, usually with a clear touch of irony. It is in
addition a quality that lower ranking individuals try to invoke in cases
where there is an immediate danger that the decorum of appropriate
behaviour is in danger or has already been violated.

It is also in the Middle English period that the use of the personal
pronouns changed. Starting in the thirteenth century under the influence of French, English writers started in certain situations to use the
second-person plural pronoun *ye* rather than the second person singular
pronoun *thou* to address a single addressee. It was used, for instance, to
address higher-ranking individuals in order to indicate a higher level of
respect. This development must be seen in connection with the more
general increase in awareness of social distinctions, and of the social
decorum of appropriate behaviour towards people of different social
classes, and thus it is part of the development of politeness in English.
Such developments were described in more detail in Chapter 5.

7.5 Early Modern English: Positive and negative politeness

Politeness in the Early Modern English period has been analysed
mainly from two perspectives. The earliest approaches were those by
Brown and Gilman (1989) and Kopytko (1995). They used Brown and
Levinson's model of positive and negative politeness and tried to apply
it to some of Shakespeare's plays. Ulrich Busse (2002) and Beatrix Busse
(2006) also used Shakespeare's work for their investigations, but they
looked at terms of address. This work has already been referred to in
Chapter 5 on terms of address. Here we will focus on the politeness
models proposed by Brown and Gilman and by Kopytko and the more
recent impoliteness model proposed by Culpeper (1996, 2005, 2011).

In their analysis of four plays by Shakespeare (the tragedies *Othello*, *Macbeth*, *King Lear* and *Hamlet*), Brown and Gilman (1989) proposed a taxonomy of positive and negative politeness strategies derived from the taxonomy initially outlined by Brown and Levinson (1987). Positive politeness strategies are those that enhance the positive face of the addressee, that is to say they make the addressee feel appreciated. Negative politeness strategies enhance the addressee's negative face, either by giving deference to the addressee or by suggesting that a face threat is non-imposing. Brown and Gilman maintain that these strategies cannot really be quantified in their data. They just give relevant examples of all the strategies in a qualitative analysis.

Kopytko (1995) extends Brown and Gilman's analysis. He adds four comedies (*The Taming of the Shrew*, *A Midsummer Night's Dream*, *The Merchant of Venice* and *Twelfth Night*) to the corpus used by Brown and Gilman and proposes a slightly modified taxonomy of sixteen different positive and ten negative politeness strategies. He also provides frequency figures for all the strategies in all eight plays of the corpus. In the following we illustrate these strategies with examples from *Romeo and Juliet*. The first example illustrates positive politeness strategies:

8. Benvolio: I pray thee, good Mercutio, let's retire:
   The day is hot, the Capels are abroad,
   And if we meet we shall not scape a brawl,
   For now, these hot days, is the mad blood stirring. (R&J 3. 1. 1–4)[2]

In this example Benvolio urges Mercutio to avoid an encounter with members of the Capulet family and he emphasises his request with several positive politeness strategies. He prefaces Mercutio's name with the epithet *good*, which counts as an instance of the positive politeness strategy 'notice admirable qualities, possessions, etc.' The formulation 'let's retire' can be seen as the strategy 'include both S and H in the activity'. The next three lines outline the reasons for his request and thus are an example of the strategy 'give reasons' (Kopytko 1995: 517–24).

9. Nurse: Gentlemen, can any of you tell me where I may find the young Romeo? (R&J 2. 4. 97–8)

In example (9) the Nurse approaches Romeo, whom she does not recognise, and two of his friends, Benvolio and Mercutio. She wants to know where she can find Romeo in order to deliver a message from her mistress, Juliet. In her request, two negative politeness strategies can be discerned. The address term 'Gentlemen' is an instance of the negative politeness strategy 'give deference'. The formulation 'can you tell me' can be seen as an instance of the negative politeness strategy 'be conventionally indirect', in the same way that 'can you pass the salt' is conventionally indirect. However, in the case of the salt, the speaker knows that the addressee is able to pass the salt. The interrogative format, therefore, is merely a pretence of giving the addressee the option of non-compliance. The utterance is seen as non-impositive and, therefore, as strategically preserving the addressee's negative face. The Nurse's question, however, may well be a real question. The gentlemen whom she accosts may not be able to give her the desired information. It is interesting that Romeo in his jocular response (extract 10) first answers the surface question about his ability to give her the information and only subsequently answers her implied request by revealing his identity:

10. Romeo: I can tell you, but young Romeo will be older when you have found him than he was when you sought him: I am the youngest of that name, for fault of a worse. (R&J 2. 4. 99–101)

Brown and Levinson listed the strategy 'Be conventionally indirect' as their first and most prominent strategy – but without any explicit claims that it is the most frequent one. In Shakespeare's plays, however, it is attested only very rarely. This stands in contrast to the conventionally indirect ways of issuing a request in Present-day English with formulations involving 'could you' or 'would it be possible' mentioned at the beginning of this chapter. In Shakespeare's plays, requests are very often issued as straight imperatives. The face threat involved in this action is reduced by other strategies and very often by positive politeness strategies.

On the basis of his frequency analysis of positive and negative politeness strategies, Kopytko (1995: 530–1) finds that the positive strategies clearly outnumber the negative strategies both in Shakespeare's comedies and tragedies and he concludes:

I tentatively assume that the high rate of occurrence of positive politeness strategies in Shakespeare's plays characterises the interactional style or 'ethos' of Elizabethan society. It should be stressed, however, that this assumption is valid for in-group politeness only. There is no reason to believe that Shakespeare created an 'artificial' society in his plays rather than reflected the one he belonged to. This is surprising, especially in view of popular claims about the interactional styles of modern British society which is associated instead with high *social distance* (D), i.e. negative politeness culture. (Kopytko 1995: 531–2)

In *Romeo and Juliet*, the characters are not always polite to each other: quite the contrary. One of the driving forces of the play is the enmity between the two houses of Montague (Romeo's family) and Capulet (Juliet's family). Culpeper (1996) has provided an early analytical framework to capture impoliteness strategies, a framework very closely modelled on Brown and Levinson's work. Impoliteness strategies are basically seen as mirror images of politeness strategies. Where politeness strategies are seen to enhance the addressee's face in order to minimise the risk of face loss, impoliteness strategies are used to intentionally attack the addressee's face.

In the crucial encounter between Tybalt and Romeo and their respective friends in the third act, the interaction is particularly hostile, except that Romeo, who is already secretly married to Tybalt's cousin, Juliet, wants to avoid any open confrontation.

> 11. Tybalt: Romeo, the love I bear thee can afford
> No better term than this: thou art a villain.
> Romeo: Tybalt, the reason that I have to love thee
> Doth much to excuse the appertaining rage
> To such a greeting. Villain am I none;
> Therefore farewell, I see thou knowest me not.
> Tybalt: Boy, this shall not excuse the injuries
> That thou hast done me, therefore turn and draw.
> Romeo: I do protest I never injuried thee,
> But love thee better than thou canst devise,
> Till thou shalt know the reason of my love;
> And so, good Capulet, which name I tender
> As dearly as mine own, be satisfied.
> Mercutio: O calm, dishonourable, vile submission!
> 'Alla stoccata' carries it away [*Draws.*]
> Tybalt, you rat-catcher, will you walk? (R&J 3. 1. 53–68)

This passage starts with some blatant impoliteness by Tybalt. He greets Romeo with the words 'thou art a villain'. The term *villain* is 'a very serious insult demanding reprisal, carrying not only the sense of "depraved scoundrel" but undertones of "low-born fellow" (= villein)' (Evans 2003: 137). This falls under Culpeper's (1996: 358) positive impoliteness strategy 'call the other names'. In addition, Tybalt uses the personal pronoun *thou*, which can be used either to signal intimacy or to insult (see Chapter 5). Tybalt uses it to insult (strategy: 'use inappropriate identity markers'). Romeo is at pains to defuse the situation and therefore ignores the insult, but takes the greeting as a mere description which does not apply to him. He is not a villain. The greeting, therefore, reveals that Tybalt does not know him. As a result, Tybalt steps up his insult. Whereas in the first utterance he called him 'Romeo' and now calls him 'boy', which is a term of contempt, appropriate for a servant but not for a member of a noble household. He sticks to the insulting pronoun *thou* and challenges Romeo to a duel, but Romeo still desists and tells Tybalt that he loves him even if he cannot tell him the reason for that love (i.e. his marriage to Juliet). Romeo also uses the pronoun *thou* for Tybalt, but in this case we may take it as a pronoun of intimacy for Tybalt, who – through Romeo's marriage with Juliet – is now his kinsman. Mercutio is outraged by what he sees as Romeo's submission to Tybalt's insults. He calls Tybalt 'Alla stoccata', which is an Italian fencing term that literally means 'at the thrust'. Mercutio despises this technique and therefore uses the term as an insult ('call the other names') for Tybalt (Evans 2003: 138). He also uses the term 'rat-catcher' for him, a metaphor that he continues later in this hostile conversation when he calls him 'Good King of Cats'. It is noteworthy that Mercutio in spite of his insults still uses the more polite (and more appropriate) personal pronoun *you* for Tybalt.

7.6 Present-day English

We have started this chapter with the observation that in Present-day English speakers often use indirect and non-imposing formulations for making requests. In fact, these formulations seem to be so prototypical that commentators often focus more or less exclusively on them when they describe aspects of politeness. The sociologist Kate Fox (2004: 97), for instance, claims that

> English rules of politeness are undeniably rather complex, and, in their
> tortuous attempts to deny or disguise the realities of status differences,
> clearly hypocritical. But then, surely all politeness is a form of hypocrisy.

However, our survey of a few aspects of politeness in the history of English reveals that rules of politeness have always been complex. Language is multi-functional and it is used to communicate on several levels. Speakers do not only exchange information, they also signal their awareness of the complex social relationships they have with their addressees and their awareness of the face-wants of all the participants in a communicative situation. The way in which this awareness manifests itself in language is both language specific and time specific. Each speech community develops its own forms of communicating in accordance with the social complexities of its society.

In Present-day English, there is a considerable amount of evidence that indirect and non-imposing forms of communication are often appropriate. Wierzbicka (2006: 45–8) lists a range of non-imposition politeness forms and claims that these forms are characteristic for Present-day English. Typical forms are 'whimperatives' such as *could you (do x)*, *will you (do x)*, *would you* (do x) or suggestory formulae such as *you might like to, you might consider, I would suggest, perhaps you could, I wonder if you could*. Examples (12) to (15) taken from the *British National Corpus* are relevant examples.

12. Perhaps you might like to investigate epilepsy in dogs and do an article on the subject. (BNC C8U 341)
13. I would suggest that you refer to the December 1990 edition of RUNNING Magazine in which the causes of groin pain are discussed. (BNC AR7 692)
14. Perhaps you could open the door, could you? (BNC APM 385)
15. I know you're very busy [. . .] but I wonder if you could help me? (BNC HYA 1987)

According to Wierzbicka these forms are typical for speakers of English. She stresses the fact that such strategies are not universal but very culture specific:

> Clearly, speakers of English are quite happy to identify some of their utterances as (mere) *suggestions* but are reluctant to identify any as attempts to *put pressure* on the addressee. For speakers of many other languages, for example, Russian or Italian, on the other hand, the opposite is true. (Wierzbicka 2006: 39)

Leech et al. (2009: 88–9) add a further piece of evidence in the form of a dramatic decline of the use of *must* in explicit requests in favour of *should* and *need to* in the second half of the twentieth century.

However, our knowledge of politeness phenomena in the history of English is still very limited. The research has only just begun and what we have are no more than snippets of relevant insights. They cannot even begin to compare with the level of knowledge that decades of research have revealed on the development of the phonology, morphology and syntax of the English language.

There are three limitations that weigh particularly heavily on our current knowledge of politeness in the history of English. They are theoretical, methodological and practical. On the theoretical level, politeness research has made some significant advances in recent years. Researchers have come to develop increasingly sophisticated analytical tools. They distinguish different types of politeness and impoliteness. They have increasingly moved away from the Brown and Levinson type of analysis, which concentrates on individual utterances and their impact on the addressee, in favour of models that adopt a more comprehensive point of view by analysing the way in which conversationalists discursively negotiate politeness and impoliteness in their interactions. However, such models have not yet been applied to historical data.

On the methodological level, historical politeness research suffers perhaps even more from the limitations of historical pragmatic research than other areas. As a secondary language function, features of politeness and impoliteness often cannot be searched for directly and more sophisticated search techniques have to be developed; for example, through lexical analysis.

Finally, the practical level refers to the fact that research in the history of politeness in English has only just started, and therefore a lot of work still needs to be done. The task of getting a comprehensive overview is daunting both because of the sheer amount of data that has survived from the Old English period to the present day and also because of the huge gaps in the material that has survived. Our necessary reliance on written material means that for the large illiterate sections of earlier societies we do not have any direct evidence at all. Finally, we cannot expect a linear and direct development from the earliest periods to the present day. The vast linguistic diversity of dialectal differences and differences of genres and text types means that even in the foreseeable future we are unlikely to be able to provide more than snapshots of selected periods and selected contexts.

Notes

1. Extracts from Chaucer are quoted from *The Riverside Chaucer*, Benson (1987). Benson (1987: 24) glosses *curteisie* here as 'refinement of manners'.
2. Quotations of Shakespeare's work follow the *New Cambridge Shakespeare* edition (Evans 2003).

Exercises

1. The following extract is part of a standard message that is used to invite expert scholars to read and assess an article that has been submitted for possible publication to an international journal. Such a request poses a considerable imposition on that scholar's time and therefore constitutes a face threat to the negative face of the scholar, i.e. his or her wish to remain free from imposition. What kinds of elements of positive and negative politeness has the author put into this standard message to mitigate this face threat?

As co-editor of the *Journal XY* I would like to ask you whether you could help us with a review. We have received a paper entitled xxxxxxx, for possible publication in our journal, and I wondered whether you would be willing to give us your expert opinion on its suitability and publishability. I would need to know whether the ms is in your opinion publishable as is, whether it requires revisions or whether it is not publishable or perhaps better suited for another journal. If you think that revisions are necessary it would be helpful to have specific suggestions. I would need your comments within about three weeks.

2. The following is a short extract from Shakespeare's *Romeo and Juliet* in which the characters talk explicitly about 'courtesy'. Mercutio and Benvolio have been waiting for Romeo, who had not returned home after falling in love with Juliet at the ball given by her father. Identify forms of politeness that you may find in this passage and discuss the characters' use of the term 'courtesy'.

> Mercutio: (…) Signior Romeo, 'bon jour'! there's a French salutation to your French slop. You gave us the counterfeit fairly last night.
> Romeo: Good morrow to you both. What counterfeit did I give you?
> Mercutio: The slip, sir, the slip, can you not conceive?
> Romeo: Pardon, good Mercutio, my business was great, and in such a case as mine a man may strain courtesy.
> Mercutio: That's as much as to say, such a case as yours constrains a man to bow in the hams.
> Romeo: Meaning to cur'sy.
> Mercutio: Thou hast most kindly hit it.
> Romeo: A most courteous exposition.
> Mercutio: Nay, I am the very pink of courtesy.
> Romeo: Pink for flower.
> Mercutio: Right.
> Romeo: Why then is my pump well flowered. (R&J 2. 4. 38–52)

Notes: *French slop*: Romeo is still in his masking costume of the previous evening. *Gave us the counterfeit*: deceived us. *Slip*: counterfeit coin. *Conceive*: understand (the pun). *Strain courtesy*: transgress good manners, but interpreted by Mercutio as *cur'sy*, i.e. make a bow because of the effects of a venereal disease. *Very pink*: flower, i.e. acme. *Pump*: light shoe.

3. Kate Fox (2004: 97) described politeness in English as follows:

> Our politenesses are all sham, pretence, dissimulation – an artificial veneer of harmony and parity masking quite different social realities.

With this she refers in particular to the indirect ways of making requests. Applying a historical perspective on politeness, do you agree or disagree with Kate Fox's assessment?

Further study

1. Use the *Historical Thesaurus of the Oxford English Dictionary* (www.oed. com) to find all the attested words in the semantic field of 'courtesy' and 'courteous' and note the first attested date of each of them. On the basis of this list, find out in which century the politeness vocabulary of the English language grew most.

Further reading

There is a wide and growing research interest in linguistic politeness and impoliteness with annual conferences and even a journal (*Journal of Politeness Research*). There are a number of textbooks that give a good introduction to politeness or impoliteness research. The classic in the field is still Brown and Levinson (1987, first published in 1978). In spite of continuing criticism, this book is still regularly referred to in the relevant literature. Eelen (2001) and Watts (2003) endeavour to present alternative frameworks. Bousfield (2008) and Culpeper (2011) are book-length studies of impoliteness research. However, there is still relatively little research on politeness and impoliteness in the history of English, or indeed of other languages, especially in the sense of attempts to cover the entire history and more than just one specific form of politeness. The only exceptions seem to be the two articles to which this chapter is most heavily indebted (Jucker 2008b and in particular Jucker 2012b). A classic study in the field is Brown and Gilman (1989), who applied Brown and Levinson's (1987) approach to four plays by Shakespeare. Kopytko (1995) extended this work in a more comprehensive and more systematic way. More specialised studies deal with speech acts that are particularly relevant for considerations of politeness; for example, directives (see Kohnen 2008a) or compliments (Taavitsainen and Jucker 2008) or expressives in general (Taavitsainen and Jucker 2010). Watts (1999) focuses on the ideology of politeness in eighteenth-century Britain and thus adopts a broader view of politeness, but only for a relatively narrow time period. Several scholars deal with issues of politeness in the context of terms of address; references to this work can be found in Chapter 5.

8 The pragmatics of language change: Grammaticalisation and pragmaticalisation

8.1 Can we find regularities in the way in which language changes?

The following extract is a brief interaction on a radio show broadcast in the United States in 2011, in which some newly-elected Representatives and Senators of the United States Congress discuss their arrival in the capital.

1. B: What's really amazing is the fact that just how normal the people you see, you know, like even Nancy Pelosi, just – you know, just a regular person when you see ...
   A: What did you think, she was the devil with horns?
   B: Well, you know, no, but, I mean, you see a totally different person, kind of like when we see you on TV. (COCA, This Week: 'The State of the Presidency', 2011)

Speaker B uses a range of discourse markers, such as *you know, well, I mean* and *like*, which we introduced in Chapter 4. In the way that they are used in B's utterances they do not have lexical meaning, or very little lexical meaning. This contrasts with the uses recorded in extracts (2) to (5). Here, these phrases have their full lexical meaning.

2. You know that I'm on the same side of the argument. (COCA, Changing the Way America Talks About Issues, 2011)
3. At some point he told them that he didn't feel well. (COCA, Nightline Investigates; Fatal Venture 2011)
4. That's what I mean. (COCA, NBC_Today, 1999)
5. Wow. That looks like fun. (COCA, Trigger Happy, 1993)

What is interesting for the historical linguist is that in all these cases the lexical use of the expression is older than the discourse marker use. Historically, discourse markers derived from lexical material. At a certain point in the history of the English language, these expressions developed an additional use, or rather, people started using these expressions in contexts in which they lost their original semantic meaning and adopted increasingly pragmatic functions. But at the same time the expressions could still be used with their original meaning. The expressions became ambiguous between their old, lexical meanings and new discourse marker meanings.

Such developments of lexical material into elements with primarily pragmatic functions are known as cases of 'pragmaticalisation', and they should be seen in the larger context of similar developments which are usually known under the heading 'grammaticalisation'. The term 'grammaticalisation' describes processes in which lexical material comes to serve grammatical functions. In the case of both grammaticalisation and pragmaticalisation, researchers try to find regularities in the diachronic processes. What kinds of elements are enlisted for which purposes? Are these developments unidirectional or can we also find the opposite direction of development? Can we perhaps find the motivations for such changes? In the following we will describe the processes of grammaticalisation and pragmaticalisation with some relevant case studies. It must be noted, however, that the terminology is controversial. Many researchers subsume what we call cases of pragmaticalisation under the general heading of grammaticalisation.

8.2 Grammaticalisation

The process of grammaticalisation, according to the often-cited definition by Hopper and Traugott (2003: 18), refers to 'the change whereby lexical items and constructions come in certain contexts to serve grammatical functions and, once grammaticalised, continue to develop new grammatical functions'. This is usually understood to be unidirectional, that is to say that such changes always lead from lexical to grammatical items and not vice versa. In addition, such changes are often seen to have pragmatic motivations. It is this second issue that we want to demonstrate with the following case studies.

In extract (6), the phrase *as long as* means 'for the duration', while in (7) and (8) the element of duration is less important. The phrase can be glossed by 'provided that'.

6. I'm not prepared to die. I want to live as long as I can and enjoy life and enjoy the companionship. (COCA, CNN_King, 1998)
7. TV is fine for kids as long as he or she is watching the right shows and watching in moderation (COCA, Newsweek, 2002)
8. His only distraction was the television and he didn't seem to care what he

watched – as long as it wasn't the news. (COCA, *Virginia Quarterly Review*, 1990)

In Old English, the phrase *as long as* could always have either the spatial meaning 'the same length as' or the temporal meaning 'for the duration'. Traugott and Dasher (2005: 36, examples (18) and (19) italics original, their translations) illustrate this with the following examples given in (9) and (10).

9. þa   het   Ælfred cyng timbran   lang scipu ongen ða
   then ordered Alfred king   build-INF long ships against those
   æscas;   þa   wæron fulneah tu   *swa lange swa* þa oðru.
   warships they were   nearly twice as long as   the others.
   'then King Alfred ordered long ships to be built to battle the warships; they were almost twice as long as the other ships.' (850–950 ChronA., p. 90)

10. wring þurh   linenne clað   on þæt eage *swa lange swa* him ðear sy
    wring through linen   cloth on that eye   as long as him need be-SUBJ
    'squeeze (the medication) through a linen cloth onto the eye as long as he needs.' (850–950 *Lacnunga*, p. 100)

In extract (9) the length of the new ships is compared to the length of the old ships. The phrase *swa lang swa* has clearly spatial meaning. In (10) the phrase can be paraphrased as 'for the duration'. The medication is to be applied for the length of time that it is needed and no longer. However, in this case the reader may also interpret the phrase with a conditional meaning, which can be paraphrased as 'provided that'. The medication is only to be applied on the condition that it is still needed. Traugott and Dasher (2005) call this an invited inference. The reader or listener is invited by the speaker/writer to draw the inference of conditionality, but the main meaning is still temporal. Such a reading is available whenever the verb refers to future events or generic events. Something will happen or would happen at the same time as, and provided that, something else happens. According to Traugott and Dasher (2005: 37) it is in Early Modern English that the first examples occur in which the conditional meaning predominates over the temporal meaning. In their words, the invited inference has been generalised from the original context to additional contexts and has become a generalised invited inference.

Traugott and Dasher (2005: 37) provide the following two examples:

11. 'Would you tell me, please, which way I ought to go from here?'
    'That depends a good deal on where you want to get to,' said the Cat.
    'I don't much care where – ' said Alice.

'Then it doesn't matter which way you go,' said the Cat.

'– *so long as* I get *somewhere*,' Alice added as an explanation.

(1865 Carroll, Chapter 6, p. 51; quoted by Traugott and Dasher 2005: 37, example (21a), italics original)

12. Galligan told the jury that it is proper for police to question a juvenile without a parent present *as long as* they made 'a reasonable effort' to notify the parent.

(9 August 1990, United Press Intl.; quoted by Traugott and Dasher 2005: 37, example (21b), italics original)

In these cases the phrase *so long as* or *as long as* must be paraphrased with 'provided that'. The temporal meaning is very much backgrounded.

Traugott and Dasher (2005) point out that similar constructions in other languages have led to other invited inferences and, therefore, have developed in slightly different ways. The development may be largely unidirectional but it is not deterministic. In French, for instance, the phrase *tandis que* developed from 'aussi longtemps que' to 'pendant que' and finally to 'au lieu que' or 'opposition dans la simultanéité', that is to say that speakers of French who used *tandis que* in certain contexts may have regularly invited the inference that there is a contrast between the two elements that are thus linked, and this inference then became generalised and semanticised. In English, speakers may also occasionally have invited the inference that there is a contrast between the two linked elements but this invited inference has never been generalised. Instead it was the inference 'provided that' which became generalised and semanticised, and which led to the polysemy in Present-day English, illustrated in examples (6) to (8) above. German *während* provides another example. It also started out as a temporal expression indicating co-temporaneity 'at the same time', and it took the same path as French *tandis que* by developing a concessive meaning alongside the temporal one.

In each case the speaker or writer innovatively exploits the potential of a coded meaning in order to invite a particular inference. In the course of time these utterance-token meanings may be conventionalised and lead to an utterance-type meaning (that is, a generalised invited inference). At the last stage of this development the utterance-type meaning is semanticised, that is to say it becomes a new coded meaning, which may exist in addition to the old meaning, which is also still available to speakers. The result is a polysemy in the language. The new meaning may, then, be the starting point of another cycle of invited inferences; that is, generalised invited inferences to a new coded meaning.

8.3 Pragmaticalisation

As we have pointed out at the beginning of this chapter, discourse markers may show a very similar history but in this case the result of the development is an element with a pragmatic function. Erman and Kotsinas (1993) draw a useful distinction between two paths of development in the change from lexical item to function word:

> one of them resulting in the creation of grammatical markers, functioning mainly sentence internally, the other resulting in discourse markers mainly serving as text structuring devices at different levels of discourse. We reserve the term *grammaticalisation* for the first of these two paths, while we propose the term *pragmaticalisation* for the second one. (Erman and Kotsinas 1993: 79, italics original)

The starting point for both developments is lexical material, usually a word with a specific lexical meaning. In the course of grammaticalisation, this element comes to serve increasingly grammatical functions as in the case of *as long as* illustrated above, which became a subordinating conjunction paraphrasable as 'provided that'.

8.3.1 Jesus: *From religious invocation to taboo expletive*

In the course of pragmaticalisation the lexical element also comes to be used in contexts where its original meaning is bleached, but in this case it adopts pragmatic rather than grammatical functions. A good example is the interjection *Jesus*, which has derived through repeated use of *Jesus* as an invocation in religious but also in non-religious contexts. In the following examples taken from the *Corpus of Contemporary American English*, the expression *Jesus* is used as a name in reference to the Christian Son of God, as in (13). In (14) it is used as an invocation to Jesus. The speaker addresses the religious being and asks for divine intervention. In (15) the expression has lost its referential function. It is used as a taboo expletive.

13. I went through the motions, but I still prayed to Jesus at night, still went to church. (COCA, ABC_20/20, 2010)
14. Oh, Jesus please bless her. Here goes another one, little lady. (COCA, CNN_King, 1997)
15. He flicks on the TV. Nothing. Goddamn box. Not even plugged in. Jesus. He can't be prowling around looking for a socket. Shit. (COCA, Gologorsky, Beverly. *The things we do to make it home*, 1999)

Expletives are elements that are typically relatively detached from the rest of the utterance. In extract (15), taken from a novel by Beverly

Gologorsky, the expletive *Jesus* is even set off by punctuation as an independent sentence. Taboo expletives have homonymic forms in other parts of speech with meanings in the domains of religion, sex or bodily excretion. Extract (15) contains two more taboo expressions; the adjective *goddam* and the expletive *shit*, and thus reinforces the interpretation of *Jesus* as an expletive. It is typical for expletives that they develop moderated phonetic forms, that is to say forms that sound similar to the original form and at the same time camouflage their origin, such as *gosh* or *goodness* for *God* and *gee* for *Jesus*.

In the *Helsinki Corpus*, *Jesus* as a proper noun is already attested in the Old English period, as for instance in extract (16) and in Early Middle English as in (17).

16. Iesus wæs gehaten ure Hælend on life.
    'Jesus was called Our Saviour during his life.' (HC O3, Aelfric: Aelfric's Letter to Sigeweard, 950–1050)
17. þat it was iesus þan wist i wel,
    'I knew well that it was Jesus.'
    (HC M2, *Cursor Mundi,* 1250–1350)

In these cases, *Jesus* is used as a referential expression to refer to the religious being. However, the proper name *Jesus* was also used as a term of address, an invocation in an appeal to Jesus in prayers, oaths, cursings and so on. Originally this happened only in a religious context, as in (18) and (19), but even in the Middle English period it is already attested outside of religious contexts, too, as in (20).

18. Ihesu cryst, god almyghty,
    Of þys folk haue þou mercy.
    'Jesus Christ, God Almighty,
    Have mercy on this people.'
    (HC M2, Mannyng, Robert: *Handlyng Synne,* 1250–1350)
19. and [he] cried vn-to
    oure Lord with lowde voyse, 'Vicisti, Galilee, vicisti –
    þou, Ihesu of Galilee, þou hast ouercome me.
    'and he cried to our Lord with a loud voice: 'You have conquered me, Jesus of Galilee, you have overcome me.'
    (HC M3, Anonymous: Sermon (MS Royal 18 B), 1350–1420)
20. Bi iesus, with here ieweles, howre iustices she shendeth.
    'By Jesus, with her jewels, she disgraces our justice.'
    OED, 1377, s.v. Jesus (quoted by Gehweiler 2008: 83)

In a religious context, the proper name *Jesus* used as an invocation is an appeal to somebody who is in a position to influence the speaker's fate. Such invocations form part of religious rituals and as such are highly conventionalised. In such contexts, Jesus still has the referential meaning to the religious being, but it is regularly associated with the pragmatic meaning, the invited inference, of an appeal to positively influence the speaker's personal fate. Gehweiler (2008: 83) argues that outside of religious contexts, the referential meaning of *Jesus* was backgrounded, and the pragmatic meaning, that is, the appeal to favourably influence the speaker's fate, was foregrounded, and as a result *Jesus* turned into a taboo expletive. In fact, the expression *bi iesus* in extract (20) is presumably already ambiguous between an invocation to the religious being and a taboo expletive indicating surprise and annoyance at a particular situation.

In extracts (21) to (23), however, from Late Middle and Early Modern English, *Jesus* is clearly used as an expletive.

21. Ihesu Lord! what thei were glad, When thei here noble leder had!
    'Jesus Lord! how glad they were, when they had their noble leader!'
    MED, a1425, s.v. Jēsŭs (quoted by Gehweiler 2008: 84)
22. Juliet: I would thou hadst my bones, and I thy news:
              Nay, come, I pray thee speak, good, good Nurse, speak.
    Nurse: Jesu, what haste! can you not stay a while?
              Do you not see that I am out of breath?
    (Shakespeare, *Rome and Juliet*, 2. 5. 27–30)
23. And why did'st thou tell so many Lyes then? Jesu God! that we should live to see any such Creatures among Mankind, nay, and among us too, to the Shame and Reproach be it spoken of our Nation and Religion
    (HC E3, *The Trial of Lady Alice Lisle*, 1640–1710)

For many occurrences it is difficult to decide whether the expression *Jesus* is part of a pious wish, a mild oath or an expletive. It often depends on the context in which it occurs. What is an honest, pious plea in a religious treatise may well be used as an expletive in a fabliau (see Taavitsainen 1997: 817). As a result it is not possible to date the emergence of the expletive precisely because many contexts are ambiguous, but the most likely period is Middle English (Gehweiler 2008: 82). With so many ambiguous uses, it is very plausible to assume invited inferencing as a source for the new pragmatic function of *Jesus*. The expression is regularly used with both the original meaning of religious invocation and the invited inference that the speaker also wants to communicate a certain amount of surprise and annoyance, and, therefore, the invited inference becomes part of the coded meaning of the expression, while the original meaning is increasingly backgrounded. Examples (14) and (15) above have shown that both these uses are still available in

Present-day English. In (14) *Jesus* is used in an earnest religious invocation for the help of the religious being. In (15) it is a taboo expletive that has lost its referential meaning. This is a typical situation. The old form co-exists with a new form that derived from the old one.

Gehweiler (2008: 84) also describes this development of the taboo expletive *Jesus* from the proper name *Jesus* as a case of 'subjectification in grammaticalisation' because a concrete, and in some sense 'objective' lexical element in the proper name *Jesus* becomes more pragmatic and more 'subjective', that is to say founded in the attitudes and beliefs of the speaker. The invocation with the religious name *Jesus* was originally restricted to specific pragmatic contexts, contexts of prayers, oaths, and curses, and it was in these specific contexts that ambiguities could arise between the objective lexical meaning and the more subjective pragmatic uses leading to the emergence of a taboo expletive. Another contributing factor in this case was the fact that the invocation tended to occur in sentence-initial position that was somewhat detached from the rest of the sentence. In this position it was particularly susceptible to a reinterpretation as an interjection.

> 'Subjectification in grammaticalisation' is, broadly speaking, the development of a grammatically identifiable expression of speaker belief or speaker attitude to what is said. It is a gradient phenomenon, whereby forms and constructions that at first express primarily concrete, lexical, and objective meanings come through repeated use in local syntactic contexts to serve increasingly abstract, pragmatic, interpersonal, and speaker-based functions. (Traugott 1995: 32)

It did not take long in the development of the taboo expletive *Jesus* for people to try to camouflage the origin of the expletive by pronouncing it in a slightly modified form. They wanted to use the expletive without causing offence. In the extracts from the *Corpus of Contemporary American English* given in (24) to (26), for instance, the expression has been modified phonetically and in the process it has lost its remaining semantic meaning. It has only a pragmatic function, which the *Oxford English Dictionary* defines as 'An exclamation of surprise or enthusiasm; also used simply for emphasis' (OED, 'gee, int.²').

24. And anyone looking at that system would say, gee, we ought to put a lot more resources into the process of generating these (COCA, CNN_ Talkback, 2000)

25. So I guess one male cast member went up and said, 'Gee, we don't seem to be getting paid very much in comparison, do we?' (COCA, Celebrity News – Live! Tabloid Journalists, Author Jackie Collins Talk About Celebrities, 1994)

26. Second of all, I just thought, gee, I wish I were there to meet her. She
seems like such a beautiful young woman. (COCA, NBC_Today, 2011)

These contexts are devoid of religious associations. *Gee* has become
a mere interjection which in all these examples is used to introduce
direct reported speech or thought, and in all cases the speakers seem
to indicate not only surprise and enthusism as suggested by the *Oxford
English Dictionary* but rather some perhaps slightly ironic distance to
the content of the reported speech. According to the *Oxford English
Dictionary*, *gee* is first attested in the late Victorian period in 1895. But the
Corpus of Historical American English has a number of earlier occurrences:

27. One by one the packages were unwrapped and, with each unwrapping,
the youngster's excitement rose. 'Gee!' he cried, as he sat in the middle of
the heap of toys and brown paper and looked about him. 'Gee! They're all
here; everything I wanted – but that air-gun. I don't care, though. Maybe
I'll get that next Christmas. (COHA, E. Prentiss: *Stepping Heavenward*,
1869)

Here, too, the religious connotations are missing in spite of the context
of Christmas and Christmas presents. The young boy receiving presents
does not invoke the name of the religious being Jesus, but he expresses
surprise and emphasis. According to Gehweiler (2008: 86) *gee* did not
evolve gradually, and it did not develop as a result of invited inferencing. It was the result of tabooistic distortion:

the emergence of *gee!* involved an abrupt semantic change, triggered
by the (abrupt) clipping of *Jesus!*, which yielded *gee!*, and because of which
the hearer no longer recognised the meaning intended by the speaker
– or rather the meaning the speaker intended to disguise, i.e. the taboo
meaning of *Jesus!* (Gehweiler 2008: 86)

8.3.2 Well: *From textual to interpersonal uses*

Discourse markers in Present-day English generally serve two different purposes. First they serve a textual function in which they indicate
boundaries between discourse units. Second they serve interpersonal
functions in which they express the speaker's attitude and evaluations
about the preceding or upcoming discourse (see also Chapter 4 on
discourse markers and interjections). The discourse marker *well*, for
instance, in Present-day English functions as a frame in extracts (28)
and (29) and as a qualifier or face-threat mitigator in extracts (30) and
(31). They are all taken from the spoken part of the *British National
Corpus*.

28. Well I'm afraid ladies and gentlemen we're going to have to stop now, rather reluctantly. (BNC D90 290)
29. So he said, well you won't tell mummy or daddy will you? (BNC H4C 839)
30. Chris   I don't want to go to Ibiza again
    Lynne   No, no, but I [said the]
    Chris   [it's such a] touristy place,
                 [I don't wanna, I don't wanna go to a touristy] place
    Lynne   [Everywhere's a touristy place]
             Well I can go without you
    (BNC KBM 1697–1702)
31. Ann   Sound more like a man I do.
            I do on the phone don't I?
    Stuart Don't know really.
            I've not really heard you much on the phone.
    Ann   Used to telephone didn't you?
    Stuart Well yeah but
    (BNC KB7 52–7)

Extract (28) is taken from a Museum Society meeting. The chairperson brings the interaction to an end. The discourse marker *well* indicates the boundary between the preceding discussion and the final part of the meeting. The speaker in (29) is a retired midwife, who takes part in an oral history project and tells anecdotes about her working life. In this extract she relates how a child told her a secret about his being sick. He had smoked one of his father's cigars. In this case, *well* marks the beginning of the direct reported speech. In the reported speech the deictic centre shifts. The pronoun *you* now refers to the story teller herself. In extracts (30) and (31), *well* has more than just a boundary marking function. In (30) a mother, Lynne, is talking to her son, Chris, about holiday plans. They argue about Ibiza as a holiday destination, and they disagree. The mother tells her son that if he doesn't like the holiday destination, she can go on her own. The discourse marker here functions on an interpersonal level. It qualifies her son's reservations about Ibiza and it mitigates the impending face-threat. In (31) the team leader Ann (aged 46) talks to the factory operative Stuart (aged 33) about her voice. She wants him to agree that her voice sounds like a man's voice on the telephone, but he is reluctant to concede. When she reminds him that he should have had enough opportunities to hear her voice on the telephone, he reluctantly agrees to this second point, but the discourse marker *well* makes it clear that this does not mean that he agrees on the more important point about her voice.

In the history of English, the textual uses illustrated in (28) and (29) above are the older uses. They go back to Middle English in which *well* first occurred in its modern form. There is a related form in Old English; that is, the emphatic interjection *wella* illustrated in extract (32):

32. þonne gemetgað him God, þa reðan wyrde ge on þisse weorulde ge on þære toweardan, swa swa hi eaðe adreogan magan.
    § IV x. Wella, wisan men, wel; gað ealle on þone weg ðe eow lærað þa foremæran bisna þara godena gumena
    'Then will God moderate to them the severe fortune, both in this world, and in that to come, so that they may easily bear it.
    § iv x. Well! O wise men, well! Proceed ye all in the way in which the illustrious examples of the good men . . .'
    (HC O2, 888, King Alfred's Old English Version of Boethius' *De consolatione philosophiae*.)

Old English *wella* is an attention-getting device similar to *hwæt*. It regularly appears at the beginning of a discourse unit and co-occurs with a vocative. In Middle English *well* occurs stereotypically at the beginning of direct reported speech. It is a frame marker, and it could be surmised that it was particularly useful at a time when texts were often transmitted orally or read out and when modern punctuation marks did not exist to indicate the beginning and end of reported speech. As in Old English *wella*, Middle English *well* regularly occurs with a reporting clause of the type *he cwæð*, *quod he* or *seyde the damesell*. Extracts (33) and (34) are taken from Thomas Malory's *Le Morte Darthur*, a Late Middle English text. In both extracts, *well* introduces direct reported speech.

33. 'Now, jantyll knyghte,' seyde the damesell, 'I requyre the to kysse me but onys.'
    'Nay,' seyde sir Launcelot, 'that God me forbede.'
    'Well, sir,' seyde she, 'and thou haddyst kyssed me thy lyff dayes had be done.'
    (HC M4 Malory, Thomas: *Le Morte Darthur*, 531–5)
    '"Now, gentle knight," the damsel said, "I ask you to kiss me but once."
    "No," said Sir Launcelot, "God forbids me to do that."
    "Well, sir," she said, "if you had kissed me, the days of your life would have been finished."'
34. 'What is your lordis name?' seyde sir Launcelot.
    'Sir,' she seyde, 'his name is sir Phelot, a knyght that longyth unto the kynge of North Galys.'
    'Well, fayre lady, syn that ye know my name and requyre me of knyghthode to helpe, I woll do what I may to gete youre hauke; and

yet God knowyth I am an evyll clymber, and the tre is passynge
hyghe, and fewe bowys to helpe me withall.'
(HC M4 Malory, Thomas: *Le Morte Darthur*, 584–90)
"'What is your lord's name?" said Sir Launcelot.
"Sir," she said, "his name is Sir Phelot, a knight who belongs to the king of
North Galys."
"Well, fair lady, since you know my name and ask me in the name of
knighthood to help, I will do what I can to get your hawk; and yet, God
knows that I am a bad climber, and the tree is very high, and there are
only few branches to help me."'

It is interesting that in both these cases, *well* co-occurs with a vocative in
the form 'well, sir' and 'well, fayre lady'. The relation to the spoken language is very clear in these examples and in all the other relevant examples from the *Helsinki Corpus*. In Middle English, the discourse marker
well functions mainly on the textual level as a frame marker, which indicates boundaries between discourse units. However, in these cases it may
often have some overtones of interpersonal uses. The quoted speaker
accepts a given situation that has been expressed by his or her interlocutor, and perhaps wishes to qualify it in some way. In (33) the lady of the
house tries to seduce Launcelot, but the Arthurian knight remains firm
and refuses to kiss the lady. With her utterance introduced by *well*, she
accepts the situation and also makes clear that he would have lost his life
had he given in to the temptation. In a similar way, Launcelot qualifies
the preceding discourse with his 'well, fayre lady'. He clearly accepts the
situation as it presents itself and draws his own conclusions.

The fact that *well* only occurs in the very restricted frame of introduc-
ing direct reported speech suggests that the textual function was very
much part of the coded meaning of *well* at this time. The interpersonal
element of accepting and possibly qualifying the preceding situation
must have been a regularly invited inference in the sense of Traugott
and Dasher (2005).

It is only in the Early Modern English period that the discourse
marker *well* is attested in additional contexts. In (35), for instance, it
occurs in the middle of a long sermon. It does not introduce direct
reported speech, but it clearly marks a boundary in the argumentation.
The preacher, Hugh Latimer, expounds on members of the clergy who
occupy themselves with all sorts of secular and profane offices, and
after having listed many examples of such offices he proceeds to ask
rhetorically whether they should be doing this. The boundary between
the list and the rhetorical questions, which is no doubt a particularly
important point of his argumentation, is marked by a double 'well, well'.

It is interesting that in the layout reproduced in the *Helsinki Corpus*, the double *well* appears at the end of the preceding paragraph rather than at the beginning of the new paragraph. In this case, it marks a particularly heavy and important boundary. It appears to be used as a device to mark a rhetorical culmination.

35. They are otherwyse occupyed, somme
    in the Kynges matters, some are ambassadoures, some
    of the pryuie counsell, some to furnyshe the courte,
    some are Lordes of the Parliamente, some are presidentes,
    and some comptroleres of myntes. Well, well.
       Is thys theyr duetye? Is thys theyr offyce? Is
    thys theyr callyng? should we haue ministers of the
    church to be comptrollers of the myntes? (HC E1 Latimer, Hugh: Sermon
    (on ploughers) & Sermon (before Edward VI), 200–7)

In extract (36) from the beginning of the sixteenth century, we are again dealing with direct reported speech. Thomas Mowntayne recalls an interaction after his imprisonment when a jailor appears and informs him of his impending execution, but is unable on Mowntayne's request to produce the appropriate documents with the death warrant and finally concludes that he must have been misinformed and, therefore, apologises to Mowntayne. Mowntayne then relates how he brushed the supposed charges aside with an utterance beginning with the discourse marker *well*. In this case, the textual function is presumably superseded by the interpersonal function. It qualifies and corrects the jailor's utterance.

36. 'Than, (sayed he,) I have been greatly myseynformyd.
    I crye yow marsy; for I hade thowghte that yow had
    been bothe araynyd, and also condemnyd to dye, beynge sent hether
    for to suffer yn thys plase, bycawse that yow were here agaynste the
    quene with the ducke of Northethomeberland.' 'Well, (sayed I,)
    thoos materes hathe bene alredye suffysyently answeryd before your
    betters'; (HC E1 Mowntayne, Thomas: *The Autobiography of Thomas
    Mowntayne* 42–8)

The last example is taken from Samuel Pepys' *Penny Merriments*, a collection of texts from the end of the seventeenth century. The extract is taken from a conversation between Tom, the tailor and his maid, Joan. The widowed Tom proposes to marry Joan but only under certain conditions that she must agree to:

37. *Tom.* Secondly, when I come home drunk a nights, you shall be
         diligent to make me unready and get me to bed, and if I chance
         to befoul my self, you are to make me clean without chiding me.

Ione. Why must I not keep a maid to do these things for me?
Tom. Yes, you must keep a Maid, but it is not fit she should
        know of her Masters privicies. I say you must do these things
        your self.
Ione. Well if it must be so, it must.
(HC E3 *Penny Merriments*, 371–8)

Joan finds this request hard to accept. She would rather employ a maid
to take care of her husband when he comes home drunk. But according
to Tom a maid is not supposed to see her master in such a state, and,
therefore, his wife will have to deliver these services. Joan accepts the
condition with her utterance, 'Well if it must be so, it must.' In this case
the qualifying, i.e. interpersonal, function has clearly superseded the
textual function. The discourse marker does not separate larger discourse units. It just qualifies the preceding utterance and expresses both
Joan's reluctance and her acceptance of the condition set by her future
husband.

8.4 Conclusions

The study of grammaticalisation and pragmaticalisation processes tries
to find general patterns of language change. In the process of grammaticalisation, lexical elements come to serve grammatical functions
and in the process lose their semantic meanings, and in the process of
pragmaticalisation, lexical elements adopt pragmatic meanings. The
case studies of *as long as*, *Jesus* and *well* have shown that in many cases
Traugott and Dasher's concept of invited inferences helps to explain
these changes. Expressions are regularly used in contexts in which they
invite a particular inference; that is to say, they express meanings which
are not explicitly communicated but which derive from the interaction of the utterance with the given context. In the course of time, such
expressions come to be used in situations in which the invited inference
is foregrounded and the original lexical meaning is backgrounded, and
thus new meanings and functions develop. But the old meanings regularly survive alongside the new uses. Ambiguous uses get the process
started until the two or more uses become separated and start to exist
side by side.

Exercises

1. The following extracts are all taken from the Early Modern English
    sections of the *Helsinki Corpus*, and they all contain the discourse

marker *well*. Decide for each case whether it is mainly used on a textual level as a frame marker or on an interpersonal level as a qualifier or face-threat mitigator. If it is a frame marker, indicate the discourse units that it separates. If it is a qualifier or face-threat mitigator, indicate what kind of attitude it expresses, how it qualifies the previous or upcoming context, and what kind of face-threat it might mitigate.

1. Moyses was a meruelous man, a good man. Moyses was a wonderful felowe, and dyd his dutie being a maried man. We lacke suche as Moyses was. Well, I woulde al men woulde loke to their dutie, as God hath called them, and then we shoulde haue a florishyng christian commune weale. (CESERM1B 1549)

2. After that I had told him many consideracions why he had no cause so to say: 'Well,' said he, 'I pray god, sonne Roper, some of vs live not till that day,' (CEBIO1 1556)

3. the man that had even with very ydlenes spent more than wold set furth 2 of thes viages doth now desyre to have a bad rowme hearin and can not be herd. See what it is to be good for nothing. Wel because we had no chasing [\driving\] wynd to stem the tyde we lay a hul at an anchor athwart al the flud. (CEDIAR2A 1582)

4. Hee taught her how she might bring her to confesse. Well, she followed his counsell, went home, caused her to be apprehended and caried before a Iustice of peace. (CEHAND2A 1593)

5. Alas poore soule, this reward she hath for her good will. I wis I wis, she is more your friend, then you are your owne. Well let her be what she will sayd her husband: but if shee come any more in my house, shee were as good no. (CEFICT2B 1619)

6. *L.C.J.*   Did you lie with them?
   Dunne   No, my Lord, I did not.
   L.C.J.   Well, I see thou wilt answer nothing ingenuously, therefore I will trouble my self no more with thee: (CETRI3B 1685)

Further study

1. A well-known case of grammaticalisation involves 'be going to', which originally referred to physical motion and in the course of time adopted the meaning of futurity. Search the *Corpus of Historical American English* (COHA) for occurrences of 'going to' and analyse samples from different periods (e.g. from 1810, 1910 and 2000). In which cases does the meaning of physical motion predominate, in which cases does it coexist with a strong sense of futurity, and in

which cases does the construction only refer to futurity without any possible sense of physical motion?

2. Use the *Corpus of Historical American English* and search for instances of *Jesus*. Look at individual decades across the two centuries covered by the corpus and reduce the sample of found hits to subsamples of 100. Is the phrase used as a referring expression as in (1), as an invocation as in (2), or as an expletive as in (3)?

1. It was as though we had a choice between a Catholic Jesus and a Lutheran Jesus (COHA, 2000)
2. 'Thank you, Jesus,' a crew member says when the actress finally nails it. (COHA, 2005)
3. 'Jesus, Nick, if I'd wanted to commit suicide I could think of more enjoyable ways than climbing onto this damn ledge.' (COHA, 2004)

3. Use the *Corpus of Historical American English* and search for instances of *gee*. Look at the frequency development across the two centuries covered by the corpus. Check sample decades in order to ascertain whether *gee* is always used with the intended force of a mild expletive. Note that it can also be used as a name ('the Rev. Mr. Gee') and as a command to horses to go faster ('Gee up, Dimond').

Further reading

There is a vast literature on the topics of this chapter. The recent handbook volume *Historical Pragmatics* (Jucker and Taavitsainen 2010) contains useful overview articles on the key issues. Traugott (2010) deals with grammaticalisation, López-Couso (2010) with subjectification and inter-subjectification and Claridge and Arnovick (2010) with pragmaticalisation and discursisation. The most comprehensive treatment of all aspects of grammaticalisation can be found in the recent *Oxford Handbook of Grammaticalization* (Narrog and Heine 2011). Book length studies of grammaticalisation can be found in Hopper and Traugott (2003) and Traugott and Dasher (2005). The volume edited by Stein and Wright (1995) contains a series of useful papers on subjectivity and subjectivisation. Brinton (1996) provides a historical overview of the development of pragmatic markers, which she sets in relation to grammaticalisation processes. For the history of the discourse marker *well* see Jucker (1997, 2002: 221–4); Defour (2008).

9 'Take a pounde of sugir and halfe a pounde of tendir roses lyues . . .': Genres and text types

9.1 Introduction

In the previous chapters we have dealt with smaller units of communication at the lexical and phrasal level. We shall now move on to the macrostructures of genre and discourse. Genres have an important meaning-making function, as they guide readers' interpretations and indicate the mode in which utterances should be understood, whether serious or ironical, for instance. We discussed this earlier in Chapter 4, where the exclamation 'Lo, which a greet thing is affeccioun!' (Chaucer, *The Miller's Tale* I (A) 3611) was pointed out as ironical in a fabliau context with carnivalistic values that reverse the accepted societal norms. The audience knew what to anticipate from the start, as the story begins 'Hwilom ther was dwellynge at Oxenford/ A riche gnof . . .' (MiT I 3187–8), which is the reverse of a typical beginning of a romance 'Hwilom, as olde stories tellen us,/ Ther was a duc . . .' (KnT I 859–60), which would usually be set in classical surroundings among noble people in the distant past. Echoing the same patterns, for present-day audiences, 'Once upon a time' creates expectations of a fairy tale, and 'Have you heard this?' prefaces a joke. But how do we know? How do genres work in communication? How and why do genre conventions change?

This chapter begins with a short history of genre studies, and a brief account of the terminology follows. Following this, we describe a model which has proved good for historical pragmatic studies of the development of genres and text types and their dynamics in a long diachronic perspective. We then deal with different models and methodologies of genre studies in modern linguistics, which all contain valuable methodological insights for historical genre scholars to make use of in their own research. Finally, we give examples of genre studies in a diachronic perspective and first deal with recipes, a genre that has remained fairly stable throughout the centuries, and then look at some genres of personal communication that have changed a great deal, not least because of the changing media.

9.2 Finding one's way through the maze

Genres are classifications of texts into different kinds according to either formal or functional criteria. They are cultural products and social forms of communication, conditioned by their time and social setting. They vary a great deal in their linguistic realisations and change in time when sociocultural factors change. The notion of 'genre' is central for both linguistics and literary studies and classifications have existed ever since Aristotle's *Poetics*. The importance of genres to both the production and the reception of texts is a point of common agreement, but definitions vary a great deal especially in linguistics; literary scholars are more in agreement. Ten years ago the field of genre studies in linguistics was called 'a terminological maze' in an introduction to a special issue devoted to the topic (Moessner 2001: 131). Genre as a theoretical notion was first recovered in literary theory and the interest in genre developments in linguistics was at least partly prompted by literary historians paying attention to genre dynamics (e.g. Fowler 1982, Bakhtin 1986 (originally published in 1953), Todorov 1990). In the last two decades of the twentieth century, genre studies developed to accommodate not only literary but non-literary texts of newly-discovered historical genres in text archives (e.g. Taavitsainen 1988), as well as texts of very recent origin in new media. Some of the most important linguistic approaches are discussed briefly in section 9.5.

Aristotle distinguished the genres of tragedy, comedy, and epic on the basis of the object and the mode of presentation. In present-day classifications, the different approaches to categorisation can often be recognised in the metaphorical language that is used for their description. It reveals how the boundaries between categories are perceived. Fowler (1982) pointed out the advantages of the prototype approach as seen in family resemblances (see Rosch and Mervis 1975). The texts of a genre may exhibit genre features to different extents, and it is the family resemblance that counts. This metaphor emphasises blurred edges and fuzzy boundaries: the 'nose' or the 'chin' of family members may be similar but otherwise the features may differ, and multiple membership in more than one family is acknowledged. Fowler also deals with the dynamics of genres, their changes and mutations, and the mechanisms of change. Genres show different realisations in different periods, but more prototypical features may remain constant in a long diachronic perspective, and genres differ in their rates of change.

The prototype approach is particularly well suited to the study of historical genres and applies to both literary and non-literary texts. In contrast, some scholars talk about genres as species, a term derived from biology. The term implies that we can distinguish between different species without difficulty – a bear is different from a wolf, or a swan from a duck – and there are clear boundaries. Genre labels like 'recipe', 'letter' and 'will', for example, can also be taken as a guideline for genre classification, and they have been used in genre inventories of historical periods. Genres are cultural products, and classification according to genre labels gives an interesting ethnographic overview of social practices as it reflects different kinds of language use and how contemporary people understood and mapped speech and writing.

9.3 A two-tier model

Genre classifications have become important in several branches of study, including folklore, linguistic anthropology, ethnography of speaking, conversation analysis, rhetoric, literary theory, sociology of language, and applied linguistics, but definitions of the term 'genre' vary according to the branch of study. Besides literary studies, the Bakhtinian idea of genres has been influential for linguistic approaches to genre and especially to the issue of how genres are connected with pragmatics. Bakhtin brings genres to centre stage with the claim that all language use is framed within genres, and that genres are essential for communication, for creating and interpreting texts. This line of thinking and genre dynamics in a historical perspective have gained ground in recent decades, and genre studies can be included as an important branch of historical pragmatics. The aim of genre studies in English historical pragmatics is to identify repertoires of genres and their features in the history of English. Another aim is to create a dynamic model of analysis that would account for synchronic generic variation as well as diachronic change, and that would be flexible enough to take into account stylistic shifts in the course of time. Furthermore, genre studies try to discover concrete evidence for theoretical claims and assumptions about the mechanisms of change. Such evidence can be found with studies on stylistic features and macrostructures of language use, and although detailed empirical evidence is difficult to come by, it is there to be detected.

We can approach genres as inherently dynamic cultural schemata used to organise knowledge and experience through language (Taavitsainen 2001: 139–40); for authors they act as guidelines and for readers they provide clues for interpretation. Such a definition places genres in their sociocultural context and refers to both parties of communication, but leaves the linguistic realisations of genres outside the definition. Writing conventions are, however, important, and it has proved useful to distinguish between genres and text types and ascribe the terms to classifications made on different bases. In this two-tier model the term 'genre' refers to classifications according to external sociocultural evidence and 'text type' according to internal linguistic features of a text (Biber 1988: 170). Both groupings are abstractions made on the basis of individual texts and the level of the text itself is taken as the point of departure for generalisations and conclusions, as genres vary in their linguistic features and they are more or less heterogeneous or homogeneous. A third relevant concept is register, usually defined as situational language use. Registers contain several genres, and the genre repertoire within a register may also change in the course of time (see Chapter 10 on medical writing). Text tradition provides yet another kind of approach, and here the emphasis is on the different ways writing conventions are used. Traditions are also connected with meaning-making practices, as meanings are derived through other texts. This model allows for the codifications of linguistic features in different ways and the mechanisms of change and the dynamics of genres can be revealed in a new way. For example, a genre defined by its function (sermon, research article, cookery recipe) or audience (children's literature) may include several text types. The advantage of keeping genres and text types apart is obvious as we can achieve a more analytical grid for tracing the developments in a historical perspective. Passages of different text types are often inserted within longer treatises that may consist of narrative, instructive, argumentative, expository and descriptive sections (see 9.3.1.and 9.5.3 below). This insight is particularly important for studies on narratives as they can serve different functions and be embedded in different genres (see Chapter 12).

9.3.1 Application of the model

The following extracts are taken from a sermon by John Donne, preached at the marriage of Margaret Washington at the church of St. Clement Danes, 30 May 1621. The sermon is addressed to the couple to be married and at the same time to the congregation that has gathered to witness the solemn occasion. The purpose of the sermon is to give religious instruction and advice to the couple and at the same time strengthen the congregation's religious devotion and commitment at an important turning point of the addressees' lives. This eloquent sermon can be regarded as a core representative of the sermon genre in the seventeenth century. Its point of departure is a quote from Hosea 2:19 'And I will mary thee unto me for ever', with the theme being built by means of biblical elaboration. A careful examination reveals that the text is a mosaic of different text types. The first passage is expository: it tells the structure of the sermon. It is in three parts, each divided further into three sections:

> ... Be pleased therefore to give me leave in this exercise, to shift the scene thrice, and to present to your religious considerations three objects, three subjects; first, a secular mariage in Paradise; secondly, a spirituall mariage in the Church; and thirdly, an eternall mariage in heaven. And in each of these three we shall present three circumstances; ... (pp. 241–2)

The second extract begins with a narrative passage in the past tense using the third person, with God as the subject. It tells us first what God did not do when creating the first man and the first woman. The passage continues with argumentation pointing out the consequences of building obstacles to God's institution:

> ... When God had made *Adam* and *Eve* in Paradise, though there were four rivers in paradise, God did not place *Adam* in a Monastery on one side, and *Eve* in a nunnery on the other, and so a River between them. They that build wals and cloysters to frustrate Gods institution of marriage, advance the Doctrine of Devils in forbidding mariage. The Devil hath advantages enow against us ... (p. 242)

The third extract is descriptive of the couple, giving their most important qualities for the occasion:

> ... The Persons are He and She, man and woman; they must be so much; he must be a man, she must be a woman; And they must be no more ... (p. 243)

The fourth extract is instructive. It gives advice, with the help of a metaphor, on how the couple to be married should behave towards one another for mutual benefit. This passage continues with a blessing and a prayer, examples of embedded genres within the sermon:

> ... *In medicinam*, but as his Physick, yet make her his cordiall Physick, take her to his heart, and fill his heart with her, let her dwell there, and dwell there alone, and so they will be mutuall Antidotes and Preservatives to one another ... And with this blessing, blesse thou, o Lord, these whom thou hast brought hither for this blessing: make all the days of their life like this day unto them; and as thy mercies are new every morning, make them so to one another ... (p. 244)

The above analysis shows how the model allows us to probe deeper into the realisation of genres by means of different text types. The example text of a sermon unfolds with variation in this respect, and it also contains an additional genre text, a prayer, embedded within it.

9.3.2 From synchronic assessments to a diachronic view

In this model, the classification according to external evidence and text function gives a framework of genres. Every culture, present or past, has its own range of genres and the dynamics of genres are best seen against a larger cultural background. Linguistic realisations of texts within genres change in time, and we can follow their development by combining several synchronic descriptions. By comparing texts of a specific genre at different points of time we can distinguish what is conventional and what is new and innovative at any point in time. In this way it is possible to gain a deeper insight into the functions of individual linguistic features and their co-occurrence patterns as well as into the functions of external categories. Both abstractions, genres and text types, rely on conventions, but they need not coincide. Text traditions are also important as texts build on previous ones in a diachronic sequence, and intertextuality is important especially in the earlier periods when copyright was not an issue and authors competed with one another in finding the best expressions to the shared ideas, like the spring motif in descriptions of nature.

9.4 Genres as communication

Genres are created for the needs of discourse communities defined as groups of people who share cultural codes and contexts (Swales 1990). The notion was developed for modern applied linguistics, but it can be adapted to historical circumstances as far back as medieval times. Discourse communities are then defined more broadly to encompass people who have texts and practices in common, or use the same texts even if for different purposes (Jones 2004: 24). In a historical perspective, genres change according to the needs of discourse communities, and cultural and sociohistorical anchoring provides the wider context against which to evaluate texts. Reasons for change can be found in text-external factors and circumstances, such as better transport connections with the outside world or changing media of communication. The change from manuscript to print in the late medieval and early modern periods did not change much at first, but gradually new practices were established; in contrast, recent changes with electronic communication have had a profound influence on language use in a very short time span. The audience parameter is important as it provides explanations for the variability of texts (see below). There are educational differences and the capacities and understandings of audiences vary.

Sociohistorical background facts on authors and audiences help us gain insights into special qualities of texts and their linguistic features. A detailed analysis can show how texts were adapted to different audiences to be more easily understood. The following two passages (discussed in more detail in Taavitsainen 2005) deal with the same topic, the physiology of the nose, but the texts are targeted at different audiences, which shows in their linguistic features:

> De proprietatibus nasy. Capitulum 13m.
> Isidir seiþ þat þe nose is þe instrument of smelling, and haþ þe name of þe noseþrilles ... Constantinus seiþ þat þe nose haþ tweye holes þat ben departed atwynne by maner of grustelbone ... instrumentis of smelling ben tweye holowz ... So seiþ Constantyn. Constantinus seiþ þat þe nose is needful to drawe in aier temperatlyche, to clense and purge þe brayn ... And þerfore libro 12⁰ Aristotel seiþ ... As Constantinus seiþ, þe nose-thrilles ben isette ... And also super Cantica Galyen seiþ þat þe nose hyzteþ moste þe face ... (Trevisa, ed. Seymour et al. 1975: 192-4)
> 'Isidor says that the nose is the instrument of smelling and has the name of nostrils ... Constantin says that the nose has two holes that are parted by the cribriform ... instruments of smelling are two hollows ... So says Constantin. Constantin says that the nose is needful to breath in air temperately, to cleanse and purge the brain ... And therefore Aristotle says in book 12 ... As Constantin says, the nostrils are set ... And also Galen says in Cantica that the nose beautifies the face most ... .. (our translation)

The above text extract is taken from one of the highest achievements of medieval learning, an encyclopedic treatise written in Latin and translated into English at the end of the fourteenth century. According to scholasticism, authorities are referred to and their sayings are discussed in accordance with the conventions of the learned genre of commentaries. The same topic is treated in a popular 'encyclopedia' belonging to the genre of scientific questions in an anonymous pseudo-Aristotelian collection of questions and answers called the *Masterpiece*:

> Q: Why doth the Nose stand out farther than other parts of the Body?
> A: There are two Answers: The First, because the Nose is as it were the sink of the Brain, by which the flegm of brain is purged; and therefore it doth stand forth, lest the other parts should be defiled. The second (according to *Constant*) is because the Nose is the beauty of the Face, and therefore it doth shew itself, and shine ... (*Aristotle's Book of Problems*, 26th edition, 1749, pp. 20–1)

The topic is the same but the second passage is limited to two points only: 'purging' the brain and beautifying the face. The original version refers to the sense of smelling and breathing through the nose, but the simplified version focuses on bodily fluids and explains that the nose stands out in order to prevent us from defiling ourselves. The reference to Constantin has been preserved to lend authority to the text long after the heyday of scholasticism. The passage has been rendered without specialised vocabulary and Latinate constructions with fairly simple but emphatic language.

9.5 Shopping for an eclectic methodology for historical studies

There are several valid and useful approaches to genre studies in modern linguistics. In the following survey, we shall discuss linguistic approaches to genres and text types paying attention to what can be of use for historical pragmatics in which the communicative aspect of language use is enhanced and both the authors and their audiences are taken into account.

9.5.1 Systemic-functional linguistics

Genre studies have long received attention in systemic-functional linguistics as part of relating language use to its social context. The realisation of texts varies conventionally in relation to situational variables of 'field' (subject matter), 'tenor' (participants in interaction) and 'mode' (spoken or written). An article by Eggins and Martin (1997) shows how different genres unfold in different ways for different audiences and how different stages can be distinguished: the beginnings of texts are different from the middle part and the end. Researchers pay attention to the sequences of stages as a generic structure potential, with obligatory and optional components. In systemic-functional studies linguistic features are used for genre definitions as well as the functions of the genres, and in this respect the approach differs from what we suggest for historical genre studies. Similarities are also found, for instance, in the important issue of adaptation according to the audience parameter. The following example shows two very different but comparable modern texts on the same topic, postmodernism in art, illuminating the issue of audience adaptation that was discussed above on the basis of historical texts. The text for experts begins:

> Although the term postmodern had been in cultural circulation since the 1870s, it is only in the 1960s that we see the beginnings of what is now understood as postmodernism . . . (Eggins and Martin 1997: 230)

In contrast, the author of the second text begins:

> Most of this stuff I can't really comment on because I don't understand a word of it. If I understand 2 % I think I'm doing pretty well ... (ibid.)

The genres are different: the former sentence is probably taken from a textbook, the latter could be from a newspaper or magazine column for general readership. Differences are found in textual formality; for example, full syntax versus contractions, and in expressions of attitude, as intensifying adverbs are used sparsely in the first example, while the second abounds in them. The difference in the assumed knowledge or common ground is reflected in technical terms with specialised meanings in the first passage versus everyday vocabulary in the second.

9.5.2 Multidimensional studies

One of the most influential linguistic studies in the past decades has been Biber's (1988) multidimensional corpus linguistic study on the styles of contemporary written and spoken English. His material comprised over 481 text extracts of 23 different genres, and he charted the co-occurrences of 67 linguistic features whose functions had been identified in previous studies. The underlying dimensions of variation were identified by an advanced statistical computer program applying factor analysis, which gave the co-occurrence patterns of linguistic features. The communicative functions of these patterns were interpreted: the most important was the 'involved versus detached' dimension, followed by 'elaborated versus situation-dependent reference' and 'abstract versus non-abstract style'. In another study (Biber and Finegan 1989), the same method revealed patterns of variation in fiction, essays and letters across four centuries. The results showed how they all underwent a 'drift' towards a more oral direction and became more involved, less elaborate and less abstract in style. Explanations were sought in sociohistorical changes with a firm anchoring in external circumstances of production and cultural developments in the relevant periods. With this contextualisation the study is very much in accordance with recent trends in historical pragmatics which take societal concerns into consideration. In some consequent studies another statistical computer program applying cluster analysis was used to define linguistically based text types. These studies confirm that core texts exhibit a high concentration of particular linguistic features typical of that text type and more peripheral texts have lower densities of these features. These explorations have been influential as a model for a number of other studies. More recently,

Biber (2004) has developed the multidimensional method for mapping expressions of stance across genres showing that fine-tuned descriptions of styles of stance are possible. In all these studies, styles have been defined in terms of joint effects of multiple features and co-occurrence patterns.

9.5.3 Text linguistics

There are at least two useful approaches to genres and text types in text linguistics. The first has already been referred to, namely Werlich's model with five basic text types: descriptive, narrative, expository, argumentative and instructive. Texts seldom exhibit these text types in a pure form, but combine several. Werlich (1982: 28–9) gives proto-typical realisations for each, and these sentence patterns provide useful guidelines for identification. Description is concerned with phenomena in space and existential sentences are frequent in this text type, for example, 'Thousands of glasses were on the tables'. The narrative text base can be reduced to action-recording sentences, for example, 'The passengers landed in New York in the middle of the night'. The expository text base can be found in phenomenon-identifying sentences with the verb *be* in the present tense and a nominal group, as in 'One part of the brain is the cortex or rind', or with *have* in the present tense and a nominal group, as in 'The brain has ten million neurones'. The argumentative text base is realised with quality-attributing sentences: 'The obsession with durability in arts is not permanent'. Perhaps the easiest to recognise is the instructive text base with action-demanding sentences like 'Stop!' and 'Don't move!'. The above scheme is very useful for qualitative studies, but it also helps to define search strings for corpus linguistic studies as, for example, third-person pronouns or existential clause patterns provide operative units as a point of departure for electronic searches.

The second approach is through text strategies, defined as the underlying communicative principles in the large-scale disposition of texts, involving decisions and adjustments of goals to resources and vice versa (Enkvist 1987). The functions that texts perform in society are important: guidebooks employ the locative text strategy realised by lexical items like *to the left, above, in the next room* and the strategy is based on place and sight. A Cambridge guide, for instance, states 'King's College Chapel is the most famous building in Cambridge. Outside, the best views of the chapel are from King's Parade and Queen's Road, and from its entrance via Senate House Passage or Trinity Lane.' Chronicles follow the chronological sequence, and so do most narratives. Cookery recipes employ an iconic time sequence, as the ingredients have to be added in a certain order for the concoction to succeed. A biography is an agent-dominated text with temporal arrangement, which is not necessarily chronological, but the text may also contain guidebook-like descriptions of important locations. Thus in addition to a single strategy, texts may have dual or even multiple strategies (cf. text types above).

9.5.4 The cognitive approach: Frames and horizons of expectation

One way of defining genre is to see it as a mental frame in people's minds, which is realised in texts for a certain purpose in a particular cultural context. Genres are based on conventions, and they have become institutionalised so that they can function at the same time as 'horizons of expectation' for readers to know what to expect and models for authors to follow. By analysing sociohistorical and cultural factors, we can understand and perhaps explain the reasons for the linguistic realisations of genres and their changes in a larger frame. The term 'horizons of expectation' was coined by Jauss (1979). *Hwilom* has already been mentioned as a trigger of genre expectations. In the electronic *Middle English Compendium* it is encountered 461 times in 31 records in a variety of genres from saints' legends to chronicles, from Chaucer and Lydgate to Gower and Hoccleve. The association with romances is very strong; for example, Gower writes: 'Ther was *whilom* be daies olde/ A worthi knyht . . .' and Hoccleve: 'How many a gentilman may men nowe se/ þat *whilom* in þe were olde of frauce,/ Honured were . . .' Likewise, the occurrences in saints' legends were in contexts that referred to the noble ancestries in the distant past. *The Life of St Edmund* by John Lydgate (1433) begins: 'In Saxone *whilom* ther was a kyng/ called Alkmond, of excellent noblesse . . .' and there are many other similar examples. Thus 'Oxenford' and 'gnof' in *The Miller's Tale* reverse the default value set by the first words, and they must have caused laughter and merriment in the audience.

9.6 Case studies of genres

A communicative view of genres emphasises the link between forms of communication and the sociocultural contexts that gave rise to them. Genres are very different in their realisation patterns: some are homogeneous so that the same linguistic features pertain throughout the centuries, while some others show a great deal of variation. In the following, both ends of the scale are treated.

9.6.1 Recipes

A genre that has retained its prototypical features over the centuries is recipes. There two principle kinds, medical and culinary, which are partly overlapping as our examples show. The function of the genre has remained the same in the history of English; the texts are written to instruct in making medicine or preparing food. Accordingly, the text type is instructive: the opening has been conventionalised so much that the form 'Take', mostly used as an imperative form, gave 2,475 hits in the two-million-word *Early Modern English Medical Texts* (EMEMT) corpus. Another search for the string 'Take a' points even more clearly to an imperative form at the opening of a recipe, and it produced 487 finds in 48 texts in the recipes category of the corpus. The structure that follows is also fairly regular with compulsory components shared by both medical and culinary recipes. Both begin with a title or rubric, and ingredients and instructions for preparations follow. In addition, medical texts indicate the ailment for which the recipe provides a cure as well as advice for application. Optional components include efficacy phrases at the end of medical recipes or instructions on how to serve the dish in culinary recipes.

> To clense the heed/ the brest/ yᵉ stomake/ & to make one to haue good appetyte
> Take .iii. handfull of Centory & sethe it in a galon of water vnto a potell/ & than clense it & put therto a pynte of clarified Hony & sethe it softly to a quarte & drynke therof .ii. spone full at ones/ erly in yᵉ mornynge & late in the euenynge. (EMEMT: Anon. (1552), *Antidotharius*)

> For to make one slender. Take Fennell, and seethe it in water, a very good quantitie, and wring out the iuyce therof when it is sod, and drinke it firste and lest and it shal swage either him or her. (EMEMT: Dawson, Thomas (1596), *The good huswifes Iewell.* London: Edward White)

> To make Almond cakes. Take one pound of Almonds blanchet in cold water beat them in Rose water take a pound of double refined Sugar beaten and Searcht, 8 spoonfuls of fine flower 8 new laid eggs both whites and yolkes Some Chorriander Seed prepared, butter your plats and Shake some double refined sugar on them. (H. W. Lewer (ed.) *A Book of Simples* (1750), London: Sampson Low, Marston and Co. Ltd, 1908)

The above texts have a regular structure and typical text type features. The titles are short and to the point, expressing purpose with an infinitive. The body texts begin with the imperative form *take*, followed by the ingredients and instructions what to do with them, how to prepare the target substance. The verbs are simple, and so are the clauses. The middle example finishes with a promise, but the optional components are missing from two others.

9.6.2 Personal communication in the written form

In contrast to recipes, the conventions of private communication between friends or relatives in the written form have changed radically in recent decades with the arrival of new media. The first private letters in English are extant from the late medieval period. Letters were delivered by hand and the gap between writing and receiving the message could be months. Postal systems became more reliable in the early modern period and regular weekly services were created in the seventeenth century along six main roads to different parts of the country. With the improved circumstances and literacy, letter writing became more common. In the early periods it was customary to adhere to fixed formula, recommended in handbooks, at the beginning and end of a letter. In the middle, the style was freer and speech quotations and other more spontaneous passages can be found. The following opening line is by Anne Clifton Westmorland (who probably dictated it) from the year 1518: 'To my ryght wrychypfull brod*yre* s*yr* harre eh clyfforthe be the byll byll delyuyryd in haste'.[1] In the modern world 'in haste' would be a genuine description of the production circumstances, but in the early modern period it was a set phrase added to any letter, perhaps by way of an apology for possible errors. The letter begins in a conventional way: 'Ryght wyrchypfull brod*yre* I hartely recowmawnd me vn to ʒow besechyng ʒow ...' The subscription lines were also formulaic. The same letter ends with the phrases 'By ʒowr loffyng syst*yr* Ane clifton'. Similar address and subscription formula and almost identical opening lines are common. They remained in use for centuries, but in due course became simplified; there are still strict rules for address and subscription lines, for example in business letters and in letters addressed to people who are not known personally to the writer. The revolution in letter-writing conventions in personal communication is only recent.

Electronic communication began a couple of decades ago with personal computers and easy access to the internet. Changes are now taking place with accelerated speed. The development suggests that the personal letter genre has split into multiple kinds in the new electronic communication, and the linguistic features used in conveying messages

[1] The quotations are from the edition by Cusack 1998: 224–5.

online have changed. The following authentic email messages from 2012 were written by a second-year doctoral student at a British university whom we shall call Ashley. Originally she is from Australia. A short email to her partner, who had just returned from a short trip reads: 'Hello you, welcome home! :-) Still good for dins tonight? Xxx'. She wrote the following Facebook message to a male friend from London, using mock 'ghetto' English (*yo* and the *hood*): 'yo eevs, when are you back in the cam hood?'. A message to multiple recipients, to several girlfriends by email in this case, is another recent development in 'letter-writing'. She wrote: 'chickadees, do we want to go see that rubbish movie w george clooney in it tonight at eight thirts? followed by a drink in the bar? X'. The following sample text comes from her Facebook message in response to a formal wedding invitation from a good friend. She uses slang and abbreviations throughout, but includes the phrase 'I shall be attending your wedding' as a tongue-in-cheek mock formal response to the traditional hard-copy invitation she had received. The abbreviated word *brng* is probably just a typo that slipped in, but *anyhoo* is probably intentional:

> hi darl plz consider this my rsvp – i shall be attending your wedding! but tom cant make it though sadly, for obvious reasons. (though maybe i will brng my sister as my plus 1 – or would you like to use tom's place for someone else?). anyhoo i think I'd like to stay at hotel that night but I'm not sure if I'll be with my sis or alone, and i spose there aren't really any single rooms (or are there?) . . . also, when do u leave for the honeymoon? does this mean i can't do my traditional crash at your place for my sydney visit? ta tas!

The above examples show how modern media have also brought some new features to personal correspondence. The sender's personality is allowed to show especially in playful and humorous touches, the more innovative the funnier, and the close interrelations of text participants are maintained with playful written messages. In all, there is a greater diversity of styles. Thus private messages today are in sharp contrast with more formal and conventional business correspondence, which in general resembles early letter writing.

Exercises

1. The genre conventions of private messages can be analysed from the point of view of interpersonal relations within the frame of sociohistorical developments in family relations. They have changed a great deal in the course of time. We have selected two messages between

nuclear family members. Both are from students who are studying at university away from home and are writing to their parents.

Discuss these texts in terms of their discourse features and linguistic realisations, paying attention to letter-writing conventions and their breakdown in email messages.

The first sample text is a letter by Henry Fleming in 1678 to his father:

> Oxford Sep. 28. 78.
> S^r,
>   Yours I received and am very sory to heare of ye sad fall
> that my brother Roger gott. According to your last letter, I
> lett you know all my study here. My tutor reads to me once for
> ye most part every day, and sometimes twice, in Sandersons
> logick which booke is all he reads to me as yet, where in I haue
> read two of ye first bookes, and part of ye third. And in
> spaire hours from logick I read Lucius Florus, Sallus and such
> histories out of which I write collections. And for excercise
> I make none yet but such as all ye scholars makes, which is
> verses every Saturday during ye terme, and sometimes declames.
> I think I shall goe into ye hall ye beginning of this next
> terme to ye disputations, which is ye 10 of ye next month.
> My cousen Henry makes ye same excercise y^t I doe, and M^r
> Dixon reads ye same booke to him y^the reads to me but not
> soe often. Soe with my duty to your selfe and my love to my
> brothers and sisters, I rest
> Sr Your dutifull son
>   Henry Fleming.
> My cousen Henry praesents his service to you.
>   For Daniel Fleming Esq^{ir} at Rydal-hall near Kendal These
>   forward 3
>   Post paid to London 2^d. (CEEC)

The second is an email message sent by Ashley to her mother in February 2012:

> Hey ma!
> Yep I know, lots going on! Yesterday went to see Billy Elliot the musical in London, it was sooooooooo good! really funny, great acting/singing/dancing etc (more my cup of tea than the opera ;-) And tomorrow is England vs Holland at Wembley! We're 5 people going, so we're just trying to figure out now if we should train it or hire a car (traffic is bad, car wise, but that would be heaps cheaper [use of 'heaps' here =

Australianism!] than the train and also the trains don't come back to Cambridge during the night, so we'd have to take a bus tour all around England . . .). The pics you saw on facebook were of the provost sheppard formal at king's, prov. Sheppard was some old guy who left all his money for the drinks at an annual formal rather than for scholarships or anything useful, so once a year we get to eat/drink on him, haha ;-) no pics of the masquerade ball up yet but they are coming! That was a fun night but since they didn't manage to sell all the tickets they culled the massage room where you get a free massage and a goodie bag with creams and smelly stuff, not impressed!

Just finished the anna funder book you got me from the book depository, was very good! now on the other one, 23 things they don't tell you about capitalism (I'm only on Thing 1 so far: there's no such thing as a free market (apparently)...

Our football final was postponed until the 10th, so the day before I leave for KL! [=Kuala Lumpur, where the author's sister lives and her family is planning to meet up the following week] Lucky timing. Was postponed because of the frost, but now it's all cleared up and we reached a balmy 17 degrees the other day! Good thing it was postponed though because one of my friends emma, who is one of our good players (as opposed to the rest of us, who are not really players at all ;-) had a drunken bike accident the night of the provost sheppard formal and somehow managed to get her foot STUCK in her bike chain and all cut up. So now she's recuperating and not allowed near bikes again (alcohol's still ok though, haha). ;-)

What else . . . last Friday I gave a talk in the king's lunchtime seminar series, which is where grad students present their work to the other phd students, all of them in different fields so it has to be really basic and it's supposed to be funny etc. mine was called 'good English is proper English and other fallacies' ;-) went well but I woke up that morning feeling like I was getting a cold, but had to ignore it till after the presentation then went home and crashed in bed! Still have a sniffy nose and croaky voice but feeling better now . . . not cool about the rash pre-holiday! Has it cleared up now??

Oh yeah, got a new phone now because I discovered that with [service provider] you can get unlimited texts for 5 pounds a month on a pay as you go sim, so I just decided to do that (still didn't sort out the contract thing, but I think this will be better . . . I only ever text and rarely call anyone, and 5 pounds a month is pretty cheap!). so that's why the new number, I guess you got my msg then ;-)

. . .

Anyway that's all for now, looking forward to KL, place that jenny [=sister] booked looks nice! Not long now, less than 2 weeks till arrival! Looking forward to seeing all! till soon! Xoxox

2. *The Anglo-Saxon Chronicle* is one of the most important documents surviving from Old English, originally compiled c. 890 AD, and subsequently added to until the middle of the twelfth century. These annual recordings were initiated by the order of King Alfred the Great. The following translation into Present-day English is by Rev. James Ingram (London, 1823). Analyse the following passage from the point of view of its text strategy: single, dual, or multiple?

> **A.D. 1066.** This year came King Harold from York to Westminster, on the Easter succeeding the midwinter when the king (Edward) died. Easter was then on the sixteenth day before the calends of May. Then was over all England such a token seen as no man ever saw before. Some men said that it was the comet-star, which others denominate the long-hair'd star. It appeared first on the eve called "Litania major", that is, on the eighth before the calends off May; and so shone all the week. Soon after this came in Earl Tosty from beyond sea into the Isle of Wight, with as large a fleet as he could get; and he was there supplied with money and provisions. Thence he proceeded, and committed outrages everywhere by the sea-coast where he could land, until he came to Sandwich. When it was told King Harold, who was in London, that his brother Tosty was come to Sandwich, he gathered so large a force, naval and military, as no king before collected in this land; for it was credibly reported that Earl William from Normandy, King Edward's cousin, would come hither and gain this land; just as it afterwards happened . . .

3. How would you analyse the structure of the following recipes? The first is a medical recipe from the year 1700, 'A Remedy to stay the Vomiting', the second is culinary from the year 2011, but they serve the same instructive purpose. What are the compulsory and what are the optional components? Does the following modern recipe conform to the long-standing conventions of recipe writing? What has changed and what has remained constant?

> Take two handfuls of Spear Mint, the like of Wormwood, Red-Rose Leaves dried, some Rye Bread grated, boyl all these in two quarts of Red-rose Water and Vinegar; till the Herbs are tender, then put them in a bag and lay them to the Stomach as hot as you can endure it, and it boyls heat it again, three or four times with the Liquor boyling: *Probatum est.*
> (EMEMT: Woolley, Hannah, *Supplement to the compleat servant maid.*)
>
> **Almond cake**
> This moist-textured cake is best the day after it is made. Serve with whipped cream or fruit, perhaps a berry compote.

Ingredients
  5 egg whites (at room temperature)
  pinch of salt
  75g/3oz caster sugar
  175g/6oz ground almonds
  1 orange, zest only, grated
  1 tbsp orange liqueur (optional)
  25g/1oz slivered almonds

Preparation method (preparation techniques shown by video clips)
  1. Preheat the oven to 190C/375F/Gas 5.
  2. Grease and line a 20cm/8in springform cake tin.
  3. Whisk the egg whites with the salt until they stand in soft peaks. Whisking constantly, add the sugar a little at a time. Continue whisking until the mixture is firm, shiny and very thick.
  4. Fold in the ground almonds, orange zest and the liqueur, if using, with a metal spoon. Pour the mixture into the cake tin and sprinkle the slivered almonds over the top.
  5. Bake for 30 minutes or until a skewer inserted into the centre comes out clean.
  6. Allow to stand in the tin for 10 minutes, then loosen, turn out and leave to cool on a wire rack.

(Source: http://www.bbc.co.uk/food/recipes/almondcake_74644; Dec. 2011)

Further reading

Brian Paltridge (1997) has a comprehensive overview of approaches to genres. Alastair Fowler (1982) discusses genres and their changes from a more literary point of view, but much of the theory is applicable to non-literary genres as well. George Lakoff's (1987) *Women, Fire and Dangerous Things* gives a comprehensive account of categorisation principles in linguistics. For genre theory and applications, see also the Special issue of the *European Journal of English Studies* (EJES) from 2001. For more recent discussions see Biber and Conrad (2009) and Claridge (2012).

10 'I pray thee friend Humfrey, what is phisicke?': Scientific and medical discourse

> *Ioh.* I pray thee friend Humfrey, what is phisicke? I would bee glad to learne some of thy knowledge, for thou hast a good order in talking, and seeme to be grounded of authority. (Bullein, *The Gouernayle of Health,* 1595: 4)

10.1 Introduction

The beginning of Bullein's teaching dialogue builds on conflict (see the qualitative analysis in Chapter 3). Once it is resolved, John becomes an attentive and polite student, eager to learn about 'phisicke' and healthy lifestyles. The text is targeted at a general audience and lays down principles of medicine based on humoral theory. The author was a learned medical doctor, William Bullein, who had the skill to present his teaching in an appealing and amusing guise. Popular texts like this were important for the dissemination of knowledge for wider audiences.

In this chapter we will continue to deal with macrolevel phenomena, illuminating the dissemination of knowledge and the development of discourse in the prestigious domain of scientific and medical writing from the pragmatic point of view. The register of scientific writing is unique in English as it has now reached the *lingua franca* position in professional science and has a global spread; all other languages in the world are put to more national and local uses in this domain. The earlier *lingua franca*, Latin, prevailed for almost a millennium in England; 1700 usually being given as the watershed after which the majority of scientific writings were in English. The history of English as a *lingua franca* goes back only about five decades as the rival languages, German and French, were still competing in the mid-twentieth century (Taavitsainen 2006). The development has been rapid, and without exaggeration we can say that at present all new knowledge in medicine is communicated fast in electronic form all over the world in English, and it is published in highly specialised journal articles that exhibit conventionalised language use with regular structure and fixed phrases (see exercise 1). The advantage is that the way of writing is fairly easy to master by non-native members of the worldwide discourse community. The majority of texts in English on medical and scientific topics are written by non-native language users.[1] Popularisation of science takes place in English as in other languages.

The present situation is very new, and there is a continuum of about 700 years from the first emergence of English in learned medical writing, with the vernacularisation boom from the shadows of Latin in the late medieval period to its present-day position as the medium of communication within the global discourse community.

In this chapter we shall pursue the historical developments and explain how the domain evolved in the course of time. The pragmatic point of view offers an interesting angle to the dissemination of scientific knowledge from local to global and from elite practices to popularised knowledge for mass consumption. We have already discussed the role of genres in meaning-making practices, and we shall continue the theme here. The pragmatic angle focuses on people by examining scientific writing as communication between writers and readers, authors and their audiences, as both participants of the communicative situation have an active role in the meaning-making process. We shall begin with the question of what constitutes science as it is crucial for determining what counts as scientific writing. It varies from one period to another, and relates to the dynamics in this register. The formation of genre conventions is a central topic of (written) communication. Medicine was the spearhead of science even in earlier times, and it is perhaps the most thoroughly researched discipline so far. The spectrum of genres and the inventories of their linguistic features change over time in response to the needs of the discourse communities. The language of science and the dissemination and appropriation of knowledge will be discussed in relation to the sociocultural context, discourse communities and lay audiences. In a long diachronic perspective, the author's position in the text and whether personal or impersonal expressions are favoured provides an intriguing pattern of changing practices from the scholastic prescriptive mode of writing to more personal author-centred texts of the Royal Society. Pragmatic principles in conveying and

---

[1] The development is not without problems. It has caused an unusual situation where discourse communities of some smaller vernacular languages (like the Scandinavian languages and Finnish) face the risk of losing the prestigious register of writing original science in their own language. As a remedy they have adopted a conscious policy to maintain scientific writing in their own languages as well.

negotiating meaning as well as attitudes to language use, also receive attention.

10.2 Science and pseudo-science

We shall begin by defining and demonstrating what science is, as it varies in different periods. A prognosticatory text from the fifteenth century gives advice for appropriate times of actions:

> Nowe yt ys to wytte what gude or herm maye betyde whene the mone ys in ony of the signes
> When the Mone is in Aries, yt ys gude to speke wythe grete lordis of myghty men, as kynges, erlis, barons, knyghtes, popis, princes, ... and for to gange ['go'] to fyght in batell aganys thy foys ['enemies'], and for to take vyages into the estward, ... Also, yt ys gude for ... to deyll wyth golde, and to wyrke all maner of werkes that ys wroght wyth ffyer, ... and for to do all maner of werkes that thowe walde haue hastely done, for this is a hasty signe.
> Bot yt ys yll and perilus to do oght ['anything'] tyll a manys hede, as to wesche or to keme yt or to schaue, or to do ony medicyne therto, or arise ony blode that be any maner of wyse, or to blede at the nesse ...
> (MEMT: *When the Mone is in Aries.* MS: BL Egerton 2572, ff. 58–61. ed. Taavitsainen, 1994: 293)

The above citation comes from a moon prognostication. Such texts are practical applications of scientific doctrines and they were consulted for advice on issues of everyday life. The basic principle was simple: all acts should be in accordance with the characteristics of the time. Aries is a sign connected with fire, and the time is favourable for business with mighty men, dealing with gold, and so on. Aries had dominion over the head as seen in the medical advice: the head had to be left untouched. The above text is included in a strictly professional medical display volume, the *Guild-book of the Barber Surgeons of York*, from 1486, but the tone is exceptionally light, even jocular. The effect is achieved by cumulative lists that go on *ad infinitum*, and by somewhat surprising juxtapositions of things that had a similar grounding in astrology. All these details are prefixed by the serious and didactic opening phrase *it is to wit* that derives from learned scholastic treatises (see below) and ultimately from Latin (*sciendum est*). Here it is used to convince the reader of the truthfulness and authoritative origins of the text. The writer seems to have extended the lists of applications according to his own will, as similar lists are not found in other texts, though moon prognostications are extant in great numbers in manuscripts and handbooks of the late medieval period. The *homo signorum* principle, explaining how the various body parts are ruled by the signs of the zodiac, formed a standard component in medical texts of the early periods. Similar advice is given even today in almanac lore where dissemination of knowledge has reached the widest possible audience but become downgraded to pseudo-science and superstitious lore, as the basis of this knowledge is outdated.

The above example shows that the modern perspective is not reliable and that historically the borderline between science and pseudo-science is fuzzy. In the late medieval and early modern periods, astrology was not separated from astronomy but together they formed a progressive mainstream branch of science with practical applications. In the Renaissance, nativity prognostications were cast for the future of a child according to the positions of skies at the precise moment of birth. It was a standard practice among the upper classes of society, but most people had to be satisfied with approximations. Medical astrology defined correct times for taking medicine and undergoing operations. The owners of moon prognostications for miscellaneous actions range from John Argentine (died 1507), Provost of King's College, Cambridge, to rural empirical practitioner John Crophill of Wix, Suffolk, who illuminated his text with amateurish sketches of appropriate farm tools, even a thief sneaking away with a money bag is depicted. Prognostications had a wide appeal, as witnessed by the number of extant manuscripts in verse and prose in various vernaculars and in Latin from all over Europe. Another example of science becoming pseudo-science is provided by alchemy, the predecessor of modern chemistry. It was a central scientific pursuit in several European courts for centuries, as it was believed that alchemy could produce gold and riches as well as health and longevity (see Taavitsainen 2000). Even later spearhead scientists like Newton and Boyle are known to have had alchemical interests, and alchemists' furnaces are extant from the nineteenth century. From the modern perspective, alchemy is a pseudo-science as its premises are faulty: base metals cannot be transmuted into gold.

Such paradigm shifts prompt a broad definition of science in a historical perspective, as what constitutes science varies in different periods and consequently what is to be included in scientific writing also varies. Modern classifications limit science to modern notions, but a broad view is more in line with how people in the past understood science and how it affected their lives. Accordingly science includes knowledge of the order of the world, natural phenomena and laws that govern human life. It is a fundamental aspect of culture, reflected in extant literary and non-literary written works.

10.3 Science and the changing world view

At the turn of the medieval and early modern periods, the world view changed, and it influenced the concept of how knowledge was obtained. It has been stated that in c. 1500 all scholars believed that knowledge was contained in old books and texts by ancient authorities. The discovery of new continents contributed to the change in attitudes as eyewitness reports of nature, plants, trees and animals reached Europe. The premise of the knowledge base was shaken, as there was new empirical evidence of the physical world which showed that plants and animals were not like the inherited pictures that were printed and reprinted in books. This fundamental change in thinking took place gradually between 1550 and 1650 at the educated level (Grafton et al., 1992: 1–5). According to the old Ptolemaic world view, man was the centrepiece of the universe, as expressed in the *homo signorum* doctrine. His humoral composition, physiological character and complexion were determined by celestial influences, but the new Copernican view taught otherwise. Voices casting doubt on received truths began to be heard in sixteenth-century literature:

> The nauigations in these latter yeeres made by the Portingales into the east Indians, and by the Spaniards into the west Indians, hath made manifest to vs, how greatly the old authors, I meane Dioscordes, Galen, Plinie, Auicenna, Serapio, and other writers of the former time were deceived . . . For first, all the ancient writers in their monuments haue deliuered to vs . . . But by the nauigations of the Portingals, and of the Spaniards into those countries, in which these pepper trees do growe, it is euident and well knowen, that . . . (1588, Bailey, f. A5–5v)

In the early modern period, it was still believed that perfect knowledge had existed in Paradise and was derived from Antiquity in a corrupt form, but by studying books it could be revived. The idea of uncorrupt and perfect knowledge proved problematic and in need of rethinking when new instruments opened up new avenues for science. Henry Power, the author of *Experimental Philosophy* in 1664, dedicates some thought to this development in the Preface to his work:

> . . . our Primitive father *Adam* might be more quick & perspicacious in Apprehension, than those of our lapsed selves; yet certainly the Constitution of *Adam*'s Organs was not divers from ours, nor different from those of his Fallen Self, so that he could never discern those distant, or minute objects by Natural Vision, as we do by the Artificial advantages of the *Telescope* and *Microscope*. So that certainly the secondary Planets of

Saturn and *Jupiter*... were as obscure to him as unknown to his Posterity;
... And as those remote objects were beyond the reach of his natural
Opticks, so doubtless the Minute Atoms and Particles of matter, were as
unknown to him, as they are yet unseen by us ... (Power, 1664: a 5–6)

In the early modern period the idea of how knowledge was obtained
changed: observation became a more important mode of knowing than
hearsay. The new way of thinking diffused slowly through layers of
scientific writing, working within the old frame, but combining with
the new modes of thought. New instruments such as the microscope
inspired people to new explorations of nature. They could also give the
scientist ecstatic moments of joy when exploring something new (see
exercise 2).

10.4 From the shadows of Latin to the Royal Society

The process of the vernacularisation of science started on a broad front
in the late medieval period and included a power struggle between Latin
and the vernacular. It is not yet fully known what happened when scientific writing emerged as a new linguistic register. Writers of vernacular
treatises had to cope with the problem of communicating abstract ideas
in a language that did not have the linguistic resources or conventions
for presenting them. Latin had established ways of expressing syntactic
constructions of complex causal relationships, whereas the first attempts
in English show muddled passages (Pahta and Taavitsainen 2010).
The creation of scientific terminology in the vernacular has semantic-
pragmatic aspects, and, for example, medical texts provide evidence of
ongoing processes in the vernacular from the adoption and incorpora-
tion of Latin terms by glossing with near-synonymous words or phrases,
like 'metacentesyn, i.e. evyn drawing' and 'inveterate, i.e. old' in the
following example. However, English versions of learned texts were not
attached to particular institutions as universities used only Latin texts.
Presumably the readership widened to people who were not literate in
Latin, but evidence from the earlier periods is scarce.

The following text extract comes from the first phase of vernacularisation and shows how Latin scholastic style was transferred into English:

> The purpos forsoth of þis present besynes yt ys forto tret shortly in which
> maner sekenes flebotomie ys competent and of which veynis. Þerfor it is
> to wyt that some minision is made or done by metacentesyn, i.e., evyn
> drawyng, some by antepasyn. . . . It ys to wyt forsoþ yf the body be plec-
> toryk or replete, minucion owth to be done by antepasyn, elles forsoþe
> by methasentasyn. . . . But here resith a dut, if þe body be plectoric and

the passion old, minucion owth to be by the fyrst comandment done
by antepasyn, by the last comandment by methasentesyn. (MEMT:
Phlebotomy, p. 37)
'Truly the purpose of this present activity is to treat shortly in what kind
of sickness bloodletting is effective and of which veins. Therefore it is to
know that some bloodletting is done by metacentesyn or even letting and
some by antepasyn. It is truly to know if the body is swollen, bloodletting
should be done by antepasyn, or else by methasentasyn. . . . But a doubt
comes up here, if the body is swollen and the passion old, bloodletting should in the first order be done by antepasyn, by the last order by
metacentesyn.'

This text of academic origin is one of the first of its kind, translated
from Latin into English at the end of the fourteenth century. It represents the highest level of learning. We do not know who the author
or the translator were, and we do not know the target audience. All
we have is the text itself and its Latin original, which is rare. The text
demonstrates how features of learned academic discourse were being
transferred into English, perhaps for the first time, and how they stand
in sharp contrast to the better-known Royal Society style of writing
(see below). In accordance with the source text, the passive voice predominates, while active sentences are few, and stand out as emphatic:
But here resith a dut. The scholastic phrase *it is to wit* occurs twice, *forsoth*
'truly' is also found twice even in this short extract. These phrases had
an afterlife in other genres, as discussed above. The text is a translation,
but several other kinds of processes were involved in other texts: they
could be modified, adapted or compiled into larger wholes, and there
is a great deal that we do not know. The influence of the underlying
Graeco-Roman style of writing is pervasive, as it set the model from
vocabulary to syntactic structures, discourse types, argumentation
patterns, and genres (see Taavitsainen and Pahta 2004). As a result of
the first wave, authors had some vernacular models to rely on in the
mid-fifteenth century. Medieval conventions continued as early printed
books drew much of their material from earlier manuscripts till c. 1550.
The next period of 150 years, 1550–1700, can be considered the third
phase of vernacularisation, and the time when the number of texts composed in English began to increase. Paradoxically, the cause of English
was promoted by the revival of Greek learning and the renewed interest in Latin, as people became more conscious of the styles of writing
in the vernacular (Blake 1996). The growth of science and technology
pointed out the insufficiency of English, but at the same time language
developed to meet the new challenges of the scientific register. Authors

published in both languages, as illustrated by some milestones of science: Francis Bacon's *The Advancement of Learning* (1605) was in English, but his *Novum Organum* (1620) was in Latin; William Harvey's treatise on the circulation of blood (1628) was in Latin. Newton's *Principia* (1687) was in Latin, but his later works were in English, including *Optics* (1704). Latin continued as the *lingua franca* at universities and in higher learning in England even in the following centuries.

Genre change and mutability was discussed in Chapter 9, but there are interesting developments in scientific and medical writing that deserve to be pointed out here. In historical genre analysis, a central position is occupied by the creation of genre conventions, changes of genre features over time in response to the needs of the discourse communities, and how authors chose to communicate scientific ideas to various audiences for various purposes; for example, how they instruct people in making medicine (recipes), healing sicknesses or maintaining health throughout the centuries. The core genres of the late medieval period included commentaries, compilations, encyclopedic treatises, questions-and-answers and pedagogical dialogues. At the end of the early modern period the map of science had already become very different (see Taavitsainen 2010).

In recent literature, medical historians have adopted the metaphor of a medical marketplace to describe the multitude of therapeutic practices and their connections with various social and economic networks (Jenner and Wallis 2007, Mikkeli and Marttila 2010). The idea has been extended to the study of the exchange, acquisition and evaluation of medical information through various channels and in various circumstances in institutions and households, which were the primary places of treatment. The late medieval medical profession included both literate and illiterate people, practitioners at various levels and from different backgrounds, from university-educated physicians and surgeons, to barber-surgeons, barbers, midwives, itinerant specialists like bonesetters and oculists, herbalists, apothecaries, wise-women and other mixed groups. The picture changes radically in the Royal Society period, when we know much more of the sociohistorical background. The available information increases the nearer we come to our own time. Professionalisation is first encountered in the early modern period in the sixteenth century when texts cease to be anonymous at all other levels except the most popular. Specialisation is a later phenomenon, and even more recently, during the last few decades, local practices have given way to global discourse communities.

The first scientific journal, The *Philosophical Transactions* was founded in the 1660s, and with it the new style of writing became the norm in spearhead experimental science (Gotti 2001). As an example we quote a passage written by 'the Inquisitive Mr. Edmund King', a member of the Royal Society, who reported on his scientific experiment in 1666, in which other members of the discourse community looked on. After a description of his unsuccessful efforts to isolate blood vessels (see exercise 3), he dwells on his own feelings and thoughts in an inner monologue, which is in sharp contrast to the scholastic style of earlier spearhead writing. The new insights are reported tentatively in the first-person singular (*I began to think with my self, That it was not impossible . . .*), hedges (*probably, which seem'd*), subjective thoughts (*came into my mind*), modesty formula and almost humiliative discourse (*Yet I durst not be so presumptuous as to indulge my self too much*). The principle of the scientific method is mentioned at the beginning and the end of the passage below, as experiments should be replicable with the same results.

> For I saw (and so must any, that will attemp this work) in my endeavouring to preserve one Vessel of a traceable magnitude, I spoiled an infinite number of others less discernable, which were as truly Vessels, as the other, differing only in size and figure (as to appearance.) Then reviewing what mischief I had done in every place, quite through the whole Tract of my Fingers, Knife, &c. I began to think with my self, That it was not impossible for these parts to consist wholly of Vessels curiously wrought and interwoven (probably for more Uses, than is yet known;) And the consideration, which came into my mind, of a piece of fine Cloth (which consists of so many several minute Hairs, call'd Wool) was no discouragement to this opinion. Yet I durst not be so presumptuous as to indulge my self too much in it; much less to venter presently to speak of a thing, which seem'd to contradict so many Learned Men's belief. But being restless, till I might receive more satisfaction in the thing, I iterated experiments over and over; (1666 PT, vol. 1, num. 18, p. 316)

The *Philosophical Transactions* was founded for institutional communication of the Royal Society, which included people from several branches of science, and architects and mathematicians eagerly took part in medical discussions as equals. Radical changes took place at the top level of scientific writing with the introduction of a new way of reporting on experiments. As shown above, the style became more subjective, involved and author-centred as the emphasis shifted to observation of nature and its processes, about which one could not be quite sure. The experimental report represents the spearhead of scientific discourse during the last decades of the seventeenth century. In contrast, the old commentary style was retained in surgical treatises and textbooks mediating established learning with absolute certainty. There seems to be a dynamic movement of downgrading the old scholastic way of writing. Some central features of learned treatises, namely references to ancient authorities and prescriptive phrases, gain new metafunctions and become devices for lending an aura of learning to texts for more heterogeneous and popular audiences (Taavitsainen 2010).

10.5 Attitudes to the vernacular

For learned doctors, the use of English needed justification (see McConchie 1997). John Caius is a case in point: he wrote in Latin for the learned readership, but he wrote about the sweating sickness (1552) in English. He finds several unfavourable aspects about writing in English:

> ... neuer more to write in the Englishe tongue, partly because the comod-itie of that which is so written, passeth not the compasse of Englande, but remaineth enclosed within the seas, and partly because I thought that labours so taken should be halfe loste among them whiche sette not by learnyng. Thirdly for that I thought it beste to auoide the iudgment of the multitude, from whome in maters of learnyng a man shalbe forced to dissente, in disprouyng that whiche they most approue, & approuyng that whiche they moste disalowe. Fourthly for that the common settyng furthe and printing of euery foolishe thyng in englishe, both of phisicke vnperfectly, and other matters vndiscretly diminishe the grace of thynges learned set furth in the same. (Caius 1552: A4r–A4v)
>
> '... never again to write in English, partly because the usefulness of a text so written will not extend outside England but remains within the island, and partly because I thought that the pains taken would be half-wasted among the less educated. Thirdly, because I thought it best to avoid the judgement of the masses, with whom a man is forced to disagree in matters of learning, disapproving that which they most approve of, and approving that which they most detest. Fourthly, because the spreading and printing of all foolish things in English, both of medical knowledge imperfectly and other matters indiscreetly, diminishes the grace of things learned expressed in the same [language].' (our translation)

The fourth argument against the use of English refers to the readership of vernacular books, which were available for a broader range of people than Latin texts. In addition to learned men, women and less literate readers had access to them. Lay readers of scientific treatises increase in time.

A clearly condescending attitude can be seen in Nicholas Culpeper's text from 1652. Writing to both professional and lay readers, he showed no respect to the latter:

> First to the Vulgar: Kind souls I am sorry it hath been your hard mishap
> to have been so long trained in such Egyptian darkness, even darkness
> which to your sorrows may be felt; the vulgar road of Physick is not my
> practice, and I am therefore the more unfit to give you advice ... You
> must not think (curtaeous People) that I can spend time to give you
> examples of all Diseases, these are enough to let you see so much light
> as you without Art are able to receive, If I should set you look upon the
> Sun I should dazle your euyes and make you blind. (Culpeper 1652: 242)

Culpeper is not alone in placing himself above the multitudes. Henry
Powell has the same polarised view of educated versus uneducated, and
even university students come in for criticism. He writes in the preface
to his 1664 book:

> To the generous VIRTUOSI, and Lovers of Experimental Philosophy
> CErtainly this World was made not onely to be Inhabited, but Studied
> and Contemplated by Man: and, How few are there in the World that
> perform this homage due to their Creator? Who, though he hath dis-
> claimed all Brutal, yet still accepts of a Rational Sacrifice; 'tis a Tribute
> we ought to pay him for being men, for it is Reason that transpeciates
> our Natures, and makes us little lower than the Angels: Without the right
> management of this Faculty, we do not so much in our kind as Beasts do
> in theirs ... But, alas, How many Souls are there, that never come to act
> beyond ...
> *Pugs* and *Baboons* may claim a Traduction from *Adam* as well as these, and
> have as great a share of Reason to justifie their Parentage.
> But it is not this numerous piece of Monstrosity (the Multitude onely)
> that are enemies to themselves and Learning; ... For, instead of solid and
> Experimental Philosophy, it has been held accomplishment enough to
> graduate a Student, if he could but stiffly wrangle out a vexatious dispute
> of some odd Peripatetick qualities, or the like; which (if translated into
> *English*) signified no more than a Heat 'twixt two Oyster-wives in *Billings-*
> Gate. (Power 1664: 183–4)

10.6 Dissemination and appropriation of scientific knowledge

The sociohistorical backgrounds of people involved in writing science,
and their attitudes to their audiences and to the language of writing,
change in the course of time. Texts in this field span wide both dia-
chronically and synchronically as the levels vary from expertise in
disciplinary knowledge to a shallow understanding of the common
knowledge. Information on the readership and attitudes to learning
can be gleaned from the prefatory materials of scientific writings, even

though these statements need to be reviewed critically both against the treatises themselves and on book historical evidence. Prefatory materials to medical texts often mention that the leading motif for writing in English was to make medical advice available to 'the poor' and to improve their condition by giving them access to useful knowledge. Such ascriptions have been attributed to social decorum as these texts rarely reached the illiterate (Slack 1979, Taavitsainen 2005). It is, however, possible that they were read aloud. The following preface is from an early printed book from 1530 of a medieval scientific encyclopedia for as wide an audience as possible:

> Than is this book necessary to al men for it exhortyth to wysdome, good maners, ensamples hystoryis ... Than I counsayle euery man to rede this boke, or that cannot rede to geue dylygent eere to the reder for they shal fynde therin great frute bothe to the soule and body in its various manifestations. (*Sidrak and Bokkus*, 1530, CUL, Peterborough Sp. 27, p. ii)

From the late medieval times onwards, the scope of potential readers widened with the aspirations of the middle classes, as merchants, lawyers and other middling groups were eager to learn about useful matters. The production of new translations and compositions was financed by patronage, and we have an abundance of prefatory materials in praise of the patron. Changing sociohistorical conditions in the sixteenth and seventeenth centuries led to increasing prosperity, allowing upper-middle-class men to devote time to scientific pursuits and form new types of discourse communities.

The audience parameter is crucial for discourse features, and choices of linguistic items begin to vary according to the target audiences even in the early periods; diversification of styles is not a recent phenomenon. In medieval times, prose was sophisticated and intended for learned audiences. Manifestations of the popular mode are fairly simple: verse and especially rhyming couplets were used to disseminate popular knowledge and, for example in *Sidrak and Bokkus*, the question-and-answer format made the contents more easily digestible. An early printed book from 1530 is annotated by underlining, marginal notes and manicula of pointing fingers. Scientific questions are interspersed with moral and religious topics. The questions of reproduction seem to have been particularly interesting to the user of the book, and the basic schemes of nature are also singled out by underlining: 'Tell me now aftr thy wyt/ The frute in erth who norysshys yt ...', 'The erthe sustayneth whan he to hym taketh/ the ayre norysheth and it maketh ...' (not foliated). In the early modern period, the most heterogeneous widening readership was reached by almanacs printed in millions of copies, and next in scale are pamphlets adapted to appeal to the masses. Almanacs and other popular texts were also read by learned people and by the upper levels of society, but the lowest social group of readers remains a matter of speculation. The question of literacy is important in the early periods and the potential audience for vernacular scientific, medical and utilitarian writings included all those who could read, but degrees of literacy and reading practices varied (see Jones 2011), and the issue is complex.

The dissemination of knowledge is an intriguing phenomenon. The following rhymes from 1607 were enormously influential and lived on for centuries. The textual form continues the medieval tradition, as medical advice was commonly given in verse for the more heterogeneous audiences:

> The Salerne Schoole doth by these lines impart,
> All health to Englands king, and doth aduise
> From care his head to keepe, from wrath his harte.
> Drinke not much wine, sup light, and soone arise,
> When meat is gone long sitting breedeth smart:
> And after noone still waking keepe your eies,
> When mou'd you find your selfe to Nature's Need
> Forbeare them not, for that much danger breeds,
> Vse three Physitians still, first doctor Quiet,
> Next doctor Mery-man, and doctor Dyet
> (EMEMT: Mediolano, Joannes de, *School of Salerne*, p. 125)

The rhymes echo inherited knowledge recorded in, for example, William Bullein's *Government of Health* (1558: 50[V]): 'I should not staye my selfe vpon the opinion of any one phisicion, but rather vpon three ... The first was called doctor diet, the seconde doctor quiet, the thirde doctor mery man.' References to the same three doctors are found in *Polite Conversation* (II. 154) by Jonathan Swift from 1738: 'The best Doctors in the World, are Doctor Dyet, Doctor Quiet, and Doctor Merryman'. Much later a quote in *The Spectator* of 30 January 1909 mentions that a proverb prescribes for sickness Dr Diet, Dr Quiet, and Dr Merryman.

At the popular end of scientific and medical writing, pseudo-Aristotelian books provided popularised scientific and medical reading for centuries, and show how knowledge disseminated to the widest possible audiences. The Preface to the Reader in *Aristotle's Book of Problems* (28th edition, 1775) claims a universal need for what was contained in the book. Notice the reference to the medieval concept of man as the centrepiece of the universe:

The Matter it contains is necessary for all People to know; and, as Man is said to be a *Microcosm*, (or little World) and in him the Almighty has imprinted his own Image so livelily, that no Power whatsoever is able to blot out, so this Image and Similitude are the Soul and Understanding. (A2)

The target group of the 1776 edition of *Aristotle's Last Legacy* is also addressed to the widest possible circles, and it, along with *Aristotle's Masterpiece*, were considered the most popular sex guides in Britain for centuries. The passage discussing a delicate subject states its motifs in the following guise:

> In describing the Organs of Generation in Women, I shall use all possible Plainness and Perspicuity; and shall not be afraid (since I design nothing but the Instruction of the Ignorant for their own good Safety) to speak so as I may be understood by the meanest Capacity, and say with the Motto of the Royal Garter, *Honi soit qui mal y pense*. (*Aristotle's Last Legacy* 1776: Chapter II, 15–16)

More specialised medical journals were established at the beginning of the eighteenth century containing research articles, book reviews and medical news for professional audiences, paving the way to the modern practice of publishing original research in journals. In the eighteenth century the audience parameter becomes even more important as the first mass media developed and the spectrum widened. Lay people were reached by new mass media: newspapers, pamphlets, broadsides and almanacs. New publications like *The Gentleman's Magazine* provided channels for the distribution of medical knowledge for non-professional members of 'polite society' (Porter 1985). England was undergoing major social and cultural change, and with upward social mobility politeness played a key role. The characteristics of eighteenth-century scientific writing have not been studied yet, but it is certain that texts for different audiences exhibit different features, and that the old style lived on in some layers of writing. The new style in medical and scientific writing in pamphlets and other treatises for a wider audience is an understudied area. At the other end of the scale, texts with inherited knowledge prevail and remain fairly stable, and almanac lore changes even less. Medical writing was also influenced by the period style as seen, for example, in the new magazines, in phrases like 'if you please you may . . .'. The following text comes from a patient's own report published as a letter to the Editor in *The Gentleman's Magazine* in 1761:

Mr Urban,
HOwever great at Vienna, and elsewhere the success may have been

from the use of Hemlock, it has not, as I am informed, been equal to the expectations of practitioners here. I therefore send you, and if you please you may lay it before the public, thro' the means of your Magazine, the success of its administration in my own case.

Having for many years been corpulent, and being obliged to sit many hours every day, occasioned, several years since, my legs to swell, and frequently to become very hard and painful. At times, for these four years, this has encreased, and several ulcers have broke out in both my legs, . . . Since Christmas last, my complaints grew worse, . . . My sorrows did not end here . . .

In this state I was in the beginning of May last, . . .Under these circumstances, and be-lieving myself to be in a great degree dropsical, I consulted Dr Watson, who, after having weighed all the particulars, was of a contrary opinion . . . ; he also prescribed that I should have my legs fomented every night and morning with a decoction of hemlock for half an hour, . . .

I must here observe, that as other plants are much like, and had in other instances been used for hemlock, the Dr was so obliging as to examine the herb I made use of, not only to satisfy him-self of the identity of the herb, but likewise of its condition . . .

Not to be too tedious in my recital, I must inform you, that at the end of a month, every ulcer in both my legs was entirely filled up and healed . . . and I never was in better health in my life.

. . . I used nothing but the fomentation and poultice of hemlock, as beforementioned. I cannot but attribute my cure principally to the virtues of the hemlock, which I think in my case were very remarkable; & as far as one instance will go, are a strong argument of its excellent effects. I pretend not to determine how far it has been useful in other cases, and under other direction; and I cannot here suppress my gratitude to Dr Watson for his humanity and kind attention to me during the continuance of my illness. Your's, &c. (Michell, Henry, Letter, *The Gentleman's Magazine*, October 1761; 31)

This is a rare case study because of its viewpoint. Texts like this are included in the broad view of medical texts as witnesses of the dissemination and appropriation of medical knowledge in society. Passages that illuminate the lay side of medicine can be found in diaries and letters, but on the whole they are rare.

10.7 Conclusions

Historical pragmatic studies on scientific writing is a rapidly growing area of research, but there is plenty of scope for more, both in synchronic studies examining scientific texts in particular past periods, and in diachronic research investigating long lines of development. For example, the Late Modern English needs more attention, but the situation is being remedied by a forthcoming corpus *Late Modern English Medical Texts* (Taavitsainen et al.) and studies based on it. Even within genre and discourse studies, the scope can widen and novel points of departure can be adopted and interdisciplinary approaches enhanced. On the one hand, the cross-fertilisation of linguistic studies with cultural history and the history of science can provide new angles for contextualising past practices of language use. On the other hand, a wider scope of pragmatic theories should be taken as the point of departure as they could yield new insights. This chapter outlines the earlier phases of this register from the historical pragmatics point of view, but our knowledge of pragmatic conventions of scientific writing and meaning-making practices is far from complete in any historical period, and in some periods pragmatically-oriented research is still completely lacking.

Exercises

1. Case studies are usually reported by doctors. The genre has continued through seven centuries, but the function changes from core teaching to curious cases in the present-day medical literature. The language changes too, and becomes highly conventionalised in medical case studies of today. Analyse the linguistic features of the following case studies, paying attention to the position of the author and his or her self-representation. Do any features remain stable?

> 1. I, Iohn Arderne fro the first pestilence that was in the 3ere of oure lord 1349 duellid in Newerk in Notyngham-shire vnto the 3ere of oure lord 1370, and ther I helid many men of fistula in ano. Of whiche the first was Sire Adam Eueryngham ... ; whiche Sire Adam, forsoth, ... The forsaid sir Adam, forsoth, suffrand fistulam in ano, made for to aske counsel at all the leche3 and cirurgien3 that he my3t fynde in Gascone, at Burdeux, at Briggerac, Tolows, and Neyrbon, and Peyters, and many other places. And all forsoke hym for vncurable; ...
>
> At last I, forseid Iohn Arderne ... come to hym and did my cure to hym and, oure lord beyng mene ['Our Lord granting'], I helid hym perfitely within half a 3ere; and aftirward, hole and sounde, he ledde a glad lif by 30 3ere and more, ffor whiche cure I gatte myche honour and louyng þur3 al ynglond. And the forseid duke of lancastre and many othir gentile3 wondred ther-of. (MEMT, Arderne, p. 2; late 14th century)

2. [}OBSERV. I.}]
THE Countess of Northampton, aged 44. on March the 6th, 1622. as she was walking in her Bed-chamber, suddenly fell into a swoon, without either sense or motion for half an hour, she fell with her face on the frame of a Table, which caused a Wound with contusion, whence arose Inflammation, as also a great and troublesom Flux of Rheum, which distilling from her eyes, excoriated the whole face with exulcerations; the habit of her Body was Scorbutick and Cacochymick: her residence then was at Ludlow-Castle: To whom being called, I cured perfectly, by God's assistance . . . (EMEMT, Hall 1657: 2)

3. A 31-year-old male patient had a history of hypertension, gout, and . . . Laboratory tests showed that both white blood cell and platelet counts were within the normal range. He was examined with abdominal sonography in our hospital. The abdominal sonographic examination was initially performed in the supine position and showed splenomegaly in the left upper abdomen (Figure 1A). When the patient switched to the right decubitus position (right side down), the spleen migrated into the midline . . . (Figure 1B). Colour Doppler sonography showed . . . On the basis of sonographic findings . . . a diagnosis of a noncomplicated wandering spleen with splenomegaly was made. Abdominal MRI was subsequently performed . . . At a 5-year follow-up, he was doing well . . . (Chen et al. *Ultrasound in Medicine*, March 2012: 484)

2. The style of writing could become elevated with rhetorical questions and personal affect features. How does it differ from modern descriptions of butterflies? Compare the following seventeenth-century text with the Wikipedia description from 2012.

Observation
The Butter Fly
This animal might well deserve our Observation without the assistance of a *Microscope*; for who does not admire the variegated diversity of colours in her expansed wings? which do not onely out-vye the peacock in all his pride, but does as far out-go the strip'd bravery of the Tulip, as that did *Salomon* in all his glory. But view them in the *Microscope*, and you may see the very streaks of the celestial pencil that drew them. For the wings of the Butterfly seem like a great plume of feathers, with glistering splendor exceedingly pleasant to behold, especially if the wings be strip'd with several colours; yea, that small meal and dust of their wings (which sticks to your fingers when you catch them) is all small little feathers, which grow out of their wings; and you may plainly see the twills by which

they stick to the wings, and the holes in the wings, out of which they are plucked. (Power 1664: 7)

Butterfly

A **butterfly** is a mainly day-flying insect of the order Lepidoptera, which includes the butterflies and moths. Like other holometabolous insects, the butterfly's life cycle consists of four parts: egg, larva, pupa and adult. Most species are diurnal. Butterflies have large, often brightly coloured wings, and conspicuous, fluttering flight. Butterflies comprise the *true butterflies* (superfamily Papilionoidea), the *skippers* (superfamily Hesperioidea) and the *moth-butterflies* (superfamily Hedyloidea). All the many other families within the Lepidoptera are referred to as moths. The earliest known butterfly fossils date to the mid Eocene epoch, between 40–50 million years ago.[1]

Butterflies exhibit polymorphism, mimicry and aposematism. Some, like the Monarch, will migrate over long distances. Some butterflies have evolved symbiotic and parasitic relationships with social insects such as ants. Some species are pests because in their larval stages they can damage domestic crops or trees; however, some species are agents of pollination of some plants, and caterpillars of a few butterflies (e.g., Harvesters) eat harmful insects. Culturally, butterflies are a popular motif in the visual and literary arts. (http://en.wikipedia.org/wiki/Butterfly, accessed 17 March 2012)

3. The following passage is also by Edmund King from *The Philosophical Transactions* in 1666. How does the subjective point of view come out here? What is the author's position in the text?

    Some Considerations Concerning the Parenchymous parts of the Body.
    . . .
    But having many years endeavoured to excarnate several parts of the Body, . . . and being very desirous to make a Scheme of the Vessels of any of these, what ever they were, I fixt upon; I found, notwithstanding all my care to preserve the Vessels, when I was freeing them, as heedfully as I could, from the supposed Parenchyma, that in every breach, I made, either with my fingers or otherwise, all my endeavours were destructive to my purpose; and, upon examination of those bits, much of which is called Parenchyma, I met in them more Vessels, than I had preserved in the parts whence they came: And though the Portion were never so small, yet my bare eye could make this discovery; much more could I, when assisted by a Microscope, perceive, I had destroyed more Vessels, than preserved, in despight of the exactest care, I was capable to use. And being not a little concern'd, that I should undertake to preserve the

Vessels by such a Cause, as I saw plainly to be their destruction (were the part never so big, or never so small) I was both confounded and tired.

Further reading

See the bibliography in the overview of scientific and medical writing from the historical pragmatics point of view (Pahta and Taavitsainen 2010). Medical writing in a historical perspective in late medieval and early modern England is discussed, for example, in Taavitsainen and Pahta (eds) 2004, 2010, and 2011; see also Taavitsainen 2009b. The history of case studies is outlined in Taavitsainen and Pahta 2000.

11 'By letters from Riga we have advice': Historical news discourse

11.1 Introduction

In recent years, the ways in which we are informed about the news of the world and the news of our local communities have changed quite drastically. Not so long ago, we had to rely on newspapers, radio and television, and we were used to regular intervals of news publication. Newspapers generally appeared once a day, and if something important happened in the world, readers had to wait until the next issue became available. On radio and television, these intervals were shorter, but apart from the very occasional breaking news that was important enough to interrupt other programmes, the audience also had to wait for the next news bulletin for an update of the news. These traditional formats still exist, of course, and this also applies to the new format of free papers that are distributed in the morning or in the evening to the masses of commuters on trains or on the underground. However, with the advent of the internet and smart phones, entirely new patterns have developed alongside. It is now possible to get more or less continuous news updates. We no longer have to wait for the next news bulletin or the next issue of a daily newspaper. We can receive up-to-the minute news whenever and wherever we like. If we like, we can even get our smart phones or computers to acoustically alert us to the arrival of some breaking news. In this situation where we can observe changes in the patterns of the dissemination of the news within just a few years, it is interesting to situate these changes within the larger picture of how such dissemination patterns have changed over the last several hundred years.

Mass media obviously depend on ways in which messages can be distributed from one sender to a mass audience. Before the invention of the printing press such ways did not exist, or only to a very limited extent; for example, in the form of billboards posted in public places or town criers, who announced their messages to village populations.

It was simply not possible to communicate with more than a very limited number of people at the same time. With the printing press this changed. Messages could be duplicated in great numbers and distributed to a diverse audience, and thus mass media communication became possible. In an important sense, therefore, the printing press made the distinction between public and private possible. News that is distributed to hundreds, thousands or even millions of people is public.

It is interesting that we are now, some five and a half centuries after the invention of the printing press, at a point where the distinction between public and private is starting to get blurred once again, albeit in a very different way. The internet offers countless ways for private individuals to post messages to a mass audience, and in many spheres of life it is no longer clear how to draw the line between public and private.

In the following we shall give a brief outline of the history of news discourse from the early days of printing up until today, and in fact even a little further, by gazing into a crystal ball and venturing some predictions as to which of the current changes are most likely to have an impact on the further development of the dissemination patterns of news. The story will obviously have to be selective. It will focus on some of the communicative patterns whose developments can be discerned most easily, it will try to focus on those aspects that are particularly promising for further research by historical pragmaticists, and it will mainly follow those aspects that so far have received most attention from scholars in this field.

11.2 Early beginnings: The revolution of the printing press

Johannes Gutenberg invented the art of printing with movable types in the middle of the fifteenth century in the German town of Mainz. This invention had an enormous influence on the dissemination of information and it was this invention that made mass media in the modern sense possible. It made books cheaper and more accessible to a wider range of the population and, thus, led to markedly increased literacy levels. In 1476, William Caxton, who had learnt how to print books on the Continent, installed his printing press in Westminster, but it was almost four decades later when Richard Faques, in 1513, produced what came to be known as the first 'newspaper' in England (Griffiths 2006: 2–3). It gave an eye-witness account of the Battle of Flodden that had been fought in northern England between an invading Scottish army under James IV and an English army. The news pamphlet bears the heading:

Hereafter ensue the trewe encountre of Batayle lately don betwene Englade and Scotlande. In whiche batayle the Scottishe Kynge was Slayne.

This is followed by a woodcut showing part of the English army and its leader, the Earl of Surrey preparing for battle. The text itself gives a detailed account of the battle including the outcome with a list of casualties and a list of knighthoods awarded to military leaders in the English army. However, news pamphlets were only produced in response to bigger and more important events. In general, people still had to rely on ballad singers and town criers in order to keep up to date with current events. Street ballads were verse narratives, often on some current events, and ballad singers sang the texts to chance audiences on markets or in alehouses in order to sell cheap prints of the ballads (Würzbach 1990: 13). Town criers were court officials who had the task of making public pronouncements.

For the first 200 years of printing the production of news reports in England was controlled by censorship. Journalists had to accommodate themselves to the requirements of the day, and many English language pamphlets were produced on the Continent. Foreign news was generally considered safest for publication and appeared in London or elsewhere in England. Such publications varied in length. They could be just a single sheet or newsbooks of 100 pages or more. It is a matter of definition what is still to be counted as a 'pamphlet', and usually an upper limit of pages is imposed by scholars interested in such publications. Brownlees (2011: 1), for instance, considers only publications of no more than twenty-eight pages, because 'longer publications contain features more typical of extended essays or monographs'. Suhr (2011: 55), on the other hand, uses an upper limit of forty-eight pages for her definition of a pamphlet.

News pamphlets were produced in increasing numbers. They were usually headed by words such as 'newes' or 'relations' or indeed both.

Figure 11.1 gives the title page of a news pamphlet that was translated from Spanish into English and was published only a few years after the first news pamphlet mentioned above.

This pamphlet consists of sixteen pages and an added illustrated title page and contains several woodcuts. The added title page depicts a flooded port with several shipwrecks and people clinging to wreckage to keep afloat. Additional woodcuts in the pamphlet show rain falling on a village with rising floods and an area of flooded land with animals and people in anguish in the water. The text itself gives an account of the severe weather conditions and the resulting floods on several Spanish

A
TRVE RELATION
OF THE LAMENTABLE
Accidents, caused by the Inun-
dation and rising of *Ebro, Lobregat,
Cinca* and *Segre*, Riuers of
SPAINE.

Together with
A Narration of a fearefull Storme,
which happened the third of *Nouember,*
in the yeare 1617, in the Hauen and
Port of BARCELONA.
Written originally in Spanish by V. Rejaule *the*
Kings Aduocate.
Printed by Authoritie at Valentia, and now
Translated into English

Figure 11.1 A true relation, London 1618 (*Early English Books Online*)

rivers and how different towns were affected. It also tells of the endeavours of the people by prayers and processions to stop what was seen as
God's punishment.

This pamphlet may be taken as fairly typical for its time at the very
beginning of the seventeenth century. It was an occasional publication
relating an extraordinary event that was likely to find an interested
audience willing to pay a small price to read it and to look at the accompanying pictures. It was a piece of foreign news, which was generally
much safer than home news, depending on the current censorship
situation. It reflects the fact that by this time international travel had
become easier. News travelled from one country to another in more
regular fashion, but it still took several months from the time of these
events until the published account appeared in a London bookshop.
The related events were couched, moreover, in a religious or moral
context. The author of the pamphlet gives an extended explanation for
this exceptional flood and the storm that destroyed Barcelona's harbour.
It ends with the words:

> God grant that these chastisements and warnings which hee giues vs, may
> cause vs to cast from vs all vices, that from henceforward wee may serue
> him with more truth and sinceritie, that so his holy name may be praised
> for euer. Amen. FINIS. (A true relation, London 1618, *Early English Books
> Online*)

For the historical pragmaticist it is interesting to note how the dissemination of information was thus dependent on and influenced by

technological innovations and social conditions. The printing press made it possible to produce sufficient numbers of copies of the same text, and it also led to an audience that could read and was prepared to pay money to learn more about strange events in foreign countries. Travelling merchants provided appropriate contents for these publications and censorship in England regulated what could be published at any given time.

11.3 The newspaper revolution in the seventeenth century

In the seventeenth century, the dissemination of news saw an important change, and with hindsight it turned out to be a revolutionary change. News was no longer produced on an occasional basis, but in regular cycles; first weekly, then twice weekly, and at the very beginning of the eighteenth century, for the first time on a daily basis. As a result, producers of mass-media publications no longer waited for a newsworthy event to occur in order to produce a publication, but they actively sought to collect enough news in order to fill each new issue of a periodical publication.

The first periodical newspapers in English appeared in 1620 (Brownlees 2011: 25) but it was printed in the Netherlands not in England, and it was a translation from a Dutch copy. It was only in September 1621 that the first periodical newspapers were actually printed in England, but they were still translations of Dutch copies. A typical example from the year 1621, for instance has the title 'Corant or weekly newes from Italy, Germany, Hungaria, Polonia, Bohemia, France, and the Low-Countries'. Like all other early newspapers of this particular size it was called 'coranto'. It consisted of two pages with fourteen dispatches from correspondents in places such as Rome, Vienna, France, Prague, Bergstrasse and Upper Palatinate. The dispatches bear dates between 17 September and 5 October, in no apparent order. The last line on the second page indicates that this coranto was printed in London, on 11 October 1621, 'out of the Low Dutch Coppy'. The first dispatch from Rome relates the death of a cardinal. Most other dispatches are concerned with events that are related to the Thirty Years' War that had just started at that time. Reports from Vienna tell of war preparations and of the movements and negotiations between military leaders.

This was typical of early newspapers. They were mainly collections of dispatches received from correspondents from their postings. There was no other organisational principle in the newspapers except for the headings for each individual correspondent.

For scholars of early English newspapers, the *Zurich English Newspaper*

Berlin, May 7.

The Baron *d'Hostel*, Envoye from the Prince of *Parma*, Governor of the *Spanish Netherlands* (whose Errand, as we are informed, is to complain of the Proceedings of the French in the Countrey of *Luxemburg*) arrived here the fourth Instant, and had yesterday his first Audience of the Elector and Electress; it is believed he will not make any long stay here.

Our last Letters from *Poland* give an Account, that the Negotiation between the Poles and the Moscovites, concerning the Defensive Alliance, advanced not, for that the latter would not proceed therein till they had an answer from the Czar (...).

By Letters from *Riga* in *Livonia* we have Advice, that the Czar lay desperately sick, and that it was believed, the next Post would give an account of his death, which if so, may make a great alteration in Affairs.

Amsterdam, May 15.

The Brandenburg Frigats, which after they had taken the Spanish Ship in the Road of *Ostend*, went for the *West-Indies* to pursue the same design, and to make what Prizes they could upon the *Spaniards*, are come back, having taken two Spanish Ships and a Galiot, but nothing near so richly laden as was at first reported.

These proceedings will, it's feared, still keep open the Differences between that Crown and his Electoral Highness, and render the Endeavours that are used for an amicable composure of Matters, ineffectual.

The Minister which the Prince of *Parma* sent to the Princess of *Germany*, to complain of the proceedings of the *French* in *Luxemburg*, has been likewise at *Berlin*, but he made a very short stay there, and it's believed had no very satisfactory Answer; though for the rest he was very kindly received.

Figure 11.2 Foreign news. *London Gazette*, 1681 (ZEN: 1681lgz01615)

corpus (ZEN) is a very useful tool. It consists of thirteen samples collected at ten-year intervals between 1671 and 1791 and amounts to some 1.6 million words. The extract in Figure 11.2 is taken from ZEN. It is from the *London Gazette* of 1681, at a time when newspapers had already been well established, but censorship was still in force and as a result newspapers published mainly foreign news.

This extract reports a range of events that are part of longer and ongoing actions or dealings. In this respect, it is more similar to modern newspapers than to the incidental news of the news pamphlets of the sixteenth century. The first dispatch is from Berlin and reports political negotiations between a diplomat serving the Duke of Parma and the Elector and Electress of Brandenburg and similar negotiations between Poles and Russians. It also expresses fears that the Tsar, who is seriously ill, might die very soon. The dispatch from Amsterdam concerns a conflict between Brandenburg and Spain, and then also mentions the visit of the Duke of Parma's diplomat in Berlin and his negotiations there. This indicates that the newspaper publisher in London did not merge the contents of the two dispatches. They must have been reproduced in exactly the form in which they had been received.

The extract is illustrative of several stylistic features of early English newspapers. The content is embedded in dispatches from correspondents who write from the places of their postings. The extract reproduces a dispatch from Berlin, dated 7 May, and a dispatch from Amsterdam, dated 15 May. However, the dispatches do not only report events that took place in Berlin and Amsterdam, they also relate reports that these correspondents must have received from further afield. The headings, therefore, do not seem particularly helpful in structuring the news for the reader. Apart from these headings, there are no headlines as a guide to the contents of the article. Newspaper readers were evidently expected to read the entire newspaper. For a modern reader it is difficult to guess which of these items were particularly newsworthy and to what extent the correspondents could rely on the readers' previous knowledge of the people who are mentioned in these reports, but neither the newsworthiness nor the presumed familiarity with the news actors seems to play a part in the ordering of the individual dispatches.

Particularly noteworthy in these reports are the distancing devices. Many reports appear in indirect speech. The newsworthy content is carried in the reported speech while the reporting clause gives the source of the information: 'Our last Letters from *Poland* give an Account, that . . .', 'By Letters from *Riga* in *Livonia* we have Advice, that . . .'. These phrases authenticate the news content and make it trustworthy. In addition, there are many parenthetical devices that fulfil a similar function; 'as we are informed', 'it is believed', 'it's feared' and so on. In these cases, the source remains unspecified, and the reader does not learn whether it is only a single individual who informed the correspondent, or who believed or feared, or whether we are dealing with widespread public rumours.

Modern newspapers still rely heavily on reported speech to carry their messages, but the function of this stylistic device seems to have shifted somewhat. In the extract above, which is typical for seventeenth-century news reporting, reported speech was used to give the content the appearance of objective reporting. The 'journalist' did not intervene and alter the content. His only job was to collect the news as he received it and pass it on to the newspaper audience. In modern newspapers, reported speech can still be used as an authenticating and distancing device, which shifts the responsibility for the content to the quoted sources. However, while seventeenth-century newspapers relied almost entirely on indirect speech reporting, modern newspapers, especially the downmarket press, also rely on direct speech or a mixture of direct and indirect speech. This allows the journalist to include interesting 'soundbites' and get the audience more involved in the actual speech of whoever is quoted.

Seventeenth-century newspapers also differ from modern newspapers in terms of the people who are mentioned. In this respect, the above extract is also typical. The only people that are mentioned are members of the nobility and high-ranking diplomats. Only political, military or church leaders are considered to be newsmakers. Today the range of people who make an appearance in newspapers has very much broadened. Newspapers also report widely on celebrities, sports personalities, business people, scientists, experts, spokespersons and so on, although ordinary citizens are also interviewed on their opinions about some events of the day or, for example, about a neighbour who became a perpetrator or a victim of some crime. Thus, modern newspapers have a much broader notion of newsmakers as a direct result of the broadening notion of what actually constitutes news, and they also report voices of people who are not newsmakers.

11.4 Structuring the news

At the end of the seventeenth century the censorship laws were no longer renewed, and as a result newspapers began to change. They shifted their attention to home news and increasingly they also included what today would be called human-interest stories. In 1786, *The Times*, which had started publication just a year earlier, published the article reproduced in Figure 11.3.

This article differs markedly from the earlier style of news reporting. First of all, it is preceded by a headline. Headlines had become quite common in the eighteenth century, and they appeared in different formats and different functions. In this article the headline is marked off from the main text in that it uses only capital letters and appears on a separate line above the text, it is centred and the characters are printed with some extra spacing between them. In contrast to the headings of the earliest newspapers, this headline does not indicate the geographical source of the news item but it indicates its topic. It is a thematic headline (Studer 2003: 32).

The story itself concerns a minor incident on a boat sailing on the River Thames from London to Staines, which, after a collision with another boat lost a man overboard. However, the man was saved and apparently did not suffer any serious injuries. Thus, the title of the story – at least from today's perspective – might seem a little exaggerated. The story is told from the point of view of an omniscient narrator. There are no distancing features which mark the story or any of its details as derived from some other source or from hearsay. It is a factual account, narrated in strictly chronological order. We hear of the preparations

UNIVERSAL REGISTER

A DISASTER.

Wednesday morning a barge belonging to one of the
Worshipful Companies of the City of London, having
taken in twenty-four hours provisions, and completed
her lading of Common-Councilmen, sailed for Staines
with a fair wind. Their voyage was as prosperous as
they could wish, till they came opposite to Chiswick,
when lo! a west country *dung* barge, sympathetic
vessel, under full sail, ran *foul* of its city brother,
and from the violence of the concussion soused Mr.
Deputy – who was smoking his pipe on the stern
– into the river. The Deputy, who has an *alacrity* at
sinking, immediately disappeared, but soon after fortu-
nately emerged, owing to his having drank an unusual
quantity of old hock, impregnated with Seltzer water.
He was instantly laid hold of with a boat hook, and
hoisted on board, where he lay for some time spraul-
ing like a turtle. After disgorging a gallon of Thames
water, he recovered, so far as to be able to proceed to
Staines, where he made a warm attack on a haunch
of venison, and returned to town in the evening in
his usual health and spirits. (*Times Digital Archive. The
Times*, Friday, 18 August 1786; p. 4; Issue 517; col A,
Universal Register, A Disaster.)

Figure 11.3 A Disaster, *The Times*, 18 August 1786 (Times Digital Archive)

for the sailing and of the initial progress of the vessel on the Thames
before the accident happened. At this point in the narrative, the narrator
marks the turn in events with an interjection, 'lo!' creating some suspense for the reader who is likely to expect the revelation of the disaster
announced by the headline of the article. Eventually the reader learns of
the misadventure, the rescue and the speedy recovery of the gentleman.
The narrator even takes time to comment on some incidental details,
such as the pipe that the unfortunate gentleman was smoking when the
accident happened, the meal that helped him in the speedy recovery, and
the healthy appetite with which the meal was consumed. The headline
of the news item does not give away very much of the story, except that
it might warn the reader that the unspectacular situation described in the
first few sentences is only the background to some unhappy events. But
the reader needs to read to the very end of this short article in order to
find out that the 'disaster' announced in the title was not a very severe
disaster after all. Thus the story is told in strictly chronological fashion
like a personal narrative. It starts with an introduction that gives the
background of the story and it describes the location of the events and

RAILWAY ACCIDENT IN
SCOTLAND.

A fireman lost his life and considerable damage was
done by an accident which occurred last night at
Newton Stewart Station on the Port Patrick and
Wigtownshire Junction Railway.

The 5.15 p.m. goods train from Stranraer left
Kirkcowan after shunting some wagons there, and
proceeded on its way to Newton Stewart. The train
consisted of 15 wagons and guard's van. It is thought
the couplings of the sixth wagon gave way at a steep
decline about three miles from Kirkcowan. The driver
was not aware of anything wrong, and proceeded
to Newton Stewart with the engine and six wagons.
Arriving there, he as usual drew up at the end of the
platform at a water tank. While the fireman was on
the tender of the engine adjusting the water apparatus, and before the signalman could give warning,
the remainder of the train ran into the rear of the
first portion. The fireman was knocked between the
tender and the first wagon and was killed. His name
is William Currie, and he lived at Gasstown, near
Dumfries. The driver was badly shaken, and the guard
was thrown with great force against the side of his van,
sustaining severe shock and injuries to his chest.
Considerable damage was done to the rollingstock,
some of the wagons being smashed.

Figure 11.4 Railway Accident in Scotland. *The Times*, 10 February 1910
(Times Digital Archive)

the main actors before it continues to the main point of the story – the
accident – and finally relates the outcome of the story.

At the beginning of the twentieth century, newspaper articles were
written quite differently. Apparently it was no longer assumed that the
reader would read the entire article, and as a result the most important
points are given first in the headline and then in a lead paragraph, as in
the article reproduced in Figure 11.4, which appeared in *The Times* on
10 February 1910.

In this article the headline gives a precise indication of the content of
the article, and the first paragraph, the lead, provides a succinct summary
of the entire article. A reader who might decide to stop reading after the
first paragraph already knows the main point of the story. The remainder
of the article is then devoted to some background to the story. It adds to
a better understanding because it gives an elaborated version of the accident summarised in the first paragraph. This is the so-called top-down

strategy of news presentation. Ungerer (2002: 91) dates the introduction of this principle in the British press to around 1900, i.e. some ten years before the publication of the article in Figure 11.4.

The top-down principle is now well established in newspaper reporting and is adopted in many news items. The principle has the advantage of allowing the busy reader to quickly read just the headline and the beginning of an article for a brief outline of the news. It also has the added advantage that in the production process the article can be cut from the end if it turns out that it does not quite fit into the available space of the newspaper.

Table 11.1 gives an outline of a somewhat more complex example of an article that appeared in *The Times* in 1920. The headline of the article has three decks; that is, a headline and two subheadlines. The first paragraph, the lead, is given in full. The remaining paragraphs are briefly summarised because the article is too long to be represented in full (879 words). The layout is partly borrowed from Ungerer (2002: 99) and partly from Bell (1998: 81). The timeline in the last column indicates the order in which the events took place in reality with the main news event given as the point of reference.

The main headline of this story reads 'Another Dublin murder'. The first subheadline specifies who was killed and how he was killed. The second subheadline refers to unrest in the south. The story later reveals that this unrest took place before the shooting. The lead paragraph summarises the killing first in one single sentence and then – still in the same paragraph – in some more detail. The rest of the article is concerned with the background of the killing; that is, with events that had taken place before the killing, but it also briefly relates two incidents after the killing. In the timeline in the last column the killing is given as the main event at time 0. The eyewitness in paragraph 3 obviously gave his account of what he had seen at some time after the crime, i.e. at a time +1. The killing of the police constable was the second murder. The first murder had taken place on the previous night, at a time -3. This incident is described in detail in paragraph 8. As a result of this first murder, soldiers and policemen protested violently (paragraph 6, at a time −2). The British Labour Mission promised to investigate the troubles and the Labour party issued a statement (paragraphs 7 and 9, certainly after the protests and presumably before the second killing). The brief flashback to the second murder-victim's life, who earlier in the year had been appointed to his present position in the police force, constitutes the earliest event that is recorded in this article (time −4). In the final paragraph a government spokesman promises that the government will look into the issues and decide on future policies (time +2).

Table 11.1 Another Dublin Murder. Police Commissioner Shot. *The Times*, 22 January 1920 (Times Digital Archive)

Paragraph	Content	Structural element	Timeline
	ANOTHER DUBLIN MURDER.	Main headline	0
	POLICE COMMISSIONER SHOT.	Subheadline	0
	UNREST IN THE SOUTH. (FROM OUR OWN CORRESPONDENT.) DUBLIN, JAN. 21.	Subheadline By-line Place and date	−2
1	A terrible crime was committed in Dublin this evening.	Lead	0
	Between 6 and 7 o'clock, as Mr. W. C. F. Redmond, Deputy Assistant-Commissioner of the Dublin Metropolitan Police, was walking to his hotel in Harcourt-street, one of the main streets of the city, two shots were fired at him, and he fell on the pathway. One bullet entered the jaw and came out the other side of the head. He was carried into a house on the other side of the street and died in a few minutes. The body was afterwards taken to the Meath Hospital.	Main event	0
2	Three suspects seen at scene of crime	Details	0
3	An eyewitness recalls crime scene		+1
4	Mr. Redmond's appointment earlier this year		−4
	POLICE ANGER.	Subheadline	
6	British Labour Mission taken by surprise; soldiers and policemen enraged by another shooting the previous night	Background	−2
7	British Labour Mission will investigate		−1
8	Details of yesterday's shooting		−3
	BOMB-THROWING	Subheadline	
9	Labour Party statement on yesterday's shooting	Follow-up	−1
10	Interview statement of a government spokesman about future policies	Future	+2

11.5 Recent trends: The internet revolution

In the last decade of the twentieth and the first decade of the twenty-first century, the internet drastically changed the dissemination patterns of news once again. In fact, it seems to be no exaggeration to say that the internet has had an equally revolutionary effect on communication patterns as the printing press had back in the fifteenth century, except that this time it does not take decades for the new technology to have a real impact. In the fifteenth and early sixteenth century it took some time for the production of pamphlets to pick up and to become an important medium of mass communication. At present these changes are much more rapid and it is almost impossible to give an up-to-date picture of mass media communication because of the complexity of the situation and the speed with which it develops. We would therefore like to comment on some of the trends that can be observed at the moment. The focus will be on the way in which the development of technology has had an impact on communicative patterns, and in this case the patterns of mass media communication.

First of all, we can observe a significant diversification of news channels. As we pointed out in the previous section, the invention of new technology generally does not immediately make the old patterns of communication obsolete. The printed newspaper did not die out because of the invention of radio and television but it had to redefine its position in the overall inventory of news channels. It had to adopt a somewhat modified role. In the same way, internet-based forms of mass communication will not immediately make either the printed newspaper or the traditional electronic channels of mass media, i.e. radio and television, obsolete. It is to be expected that the repositioning of individual channels of mass-media communication will continue, and, in fact, there will be an increasing number of mergers of the different channels.

In the early days of the internet, traditional newspapers, television and radio stations started providing themselves with their own home-pages, but in general the individual media channels stayed true to their parent publications. Newspapers published texts and pictures, radio stations soon started to produce lifestream outputs on the internet, and television stations provided some video clips of their regular broadcasting. Even for the very beginning of the internet era, this is a somewhat idealised picture, but in the course of time it became less and less obvious what kind of traditional media channel was behind a particular mass-media website. They all increasingly produce content in the different modalities.

Moreover, news is disseminated in many more forms on the internet. The dissemination of news, and this is just one significant aspect of the revolution, no longer depends on an institutional or professional context, such as a commercial newspaper or a radio or television station. Private individuals can now produce news content in the form of blogs or contributions to social networks, such as Twitter or Facebook. Blogs are often accessible for whoever has access to a computer with an internet connection and happens to search in the right place or with the right kind of key words. Tweets on Twitter or status updates on Facebook can generally be read by what are called friends (if they have to be acknowledged as a member of the audience by the author) or followers (if they can self-select to read messages by a particular author). Such status updates and tweets are often of a private nature, but they are also used to convey issues of broader significance. Journalists are no longer the gatekeepers who decide on the flow of information that reaches the individual recipient of news content, but the recipient can choose from an ever-growing wealth and diversity of news content via the different channels.

Another significant aspect of technological innovation concerns the life cycle of information and its chunking into smaller and smaller units. Traditional printed newspapers are published once a day and whenever a new issue appears the old one becomes obsolete. It may still be kept in some library archive but it is no longer freely available. Thus the life cycle is twenty-four hours both in terms of the frequency of news updates and in terms of the general availability of the news content. In the traditional electronic media, this life cycle is often very much shorter with gaps of just a few hours between news updates in the form of new bulletins. On the internet, however, the news cycle is further speeded up as articles can be updated at very short intervals. News tickers and live text commentaries take this even further. The news is updated almost continuously, but in contrast to a traditional update in the form of a new issue of a newspaper, the old content does not become obsolete and more or less inaccessible with each new update. It often lives on in the form of searchable news archives and thus remains easily accessible.

Finally, and perhaps most significantly, internet news content is characterised by a fluidity that is entirely new. Ever since the invention of the printing press, the act of printing creates a fixed and stable text. There may, of course, be handwritten scribbles in a written text, or there may be further editions with a modified text, but each printing creates a tangible product that cannot easily be altered, if at all. Electronic texts, however, do not have this kind of fixity. A news update can be published and only minutes later some of the text may be changed again. This often happens with breaking news. A newspaper hurriedly publishes an article almost immediately after the event and regularly updates it as the event unfolds.

11.6 Outlook

The previous section has taken the story of the patterns of the dissemination of news right up to today. It is perhaps not the task of a historian to describe developments any further because that involves peering into a crystal ball, but in this case some predictions seem to be possible. They derive from the developments that are already underway. Here are some of the trends that are likely to continue in the near future.

First, the channels in which news is distributed have diversified. Not so long ago, there were, basically, newspapers, radio and television. Today, news is also distributed via computers, smart phones, tablet computers, and so on.

Second, modalities will merge even further. Print media and electronic media are no longer separate entities. On the computer and a range of hand-held electronic devices, these formats merge. Written texts include video sequences. Podcasts can be downloaded to MP3 players, and so on.

Third, with the advent of the internet, journalists have lost their traditional role as gatekeepers. They no longer control the flow of information that reaches the consumer. Everybody can access an ever-increasing amount of news content.

Fourth, the clear-cut separation of roles into news producers and news consumers is breaking down and it will continue to disappear; for example, comments to newspaper articles, blogs, Twitter, status updates on Facebook, Wikis, and so on.

Finally, the boundaries between public and private will continue to blur.

Exercises

1. Consider this text from *The London Post* of 1701:

> Amsterdam, Jan. 25.
> They Write from Coningsberg, That the Pomp and Magnificence with which his Electoral Highness was to be Crowned King of Prussia, was to be extraordinary Great: That every one endeavoured to Invent something in Honour to their Prince, and to add to the publick Rejoycings:

That the Burgers were to appear under their Arms, all in their best Cloaths; and after the Coronation, were to reconduct his Majesty; That a great many triumphant Arches were erected, through which his Majesty was to pass: That the Concourse of People from all Parts, to see the Ceremony was extraordinary great; and that, among others, most of the chief Burgers of Dantzick were arrived there: From Riga they tell us, That great Preparations were making there, to receive the King of Sweden, who was expected in a few days, with part of his Army.

From Lithuania, That the Animosities and Differences there, rather Increase than Decrease.

From Liban, That some Polish Troops were marching towards Warsaw, to force the King to conclude a Peace with Sweden.

From Moscow, of the 19th of December, That his Czarish Majesty was arrived there in good Health; but these Letters make not the least mention of the Battle that happened near Narva; from which place we have Letters, of the 19th past, Importing, That several days had been already spent, in bringing the Booty out of the Russian Camp, into that City; and that it would yet Imploy them 8 days, before they should be able to bring all in. (ZEN: 1701lpt00255)

The text reproduced above records the letter of a correspondent from Amsterdam, who for his part must have put together messages that he had received from other countries. Discuss the differences between these reports and a modern newspaper. Focus in particular on the content, the structure and the format of these news items.

2. The next text appeared in the *MailOnline* of 4 August 2011. Contrast its content, structure and format with the text above. The text reproduces the title plus the first five paragraphs of a much longer article. It was accompanied by several pictures that show the famous actress Blake Lively making a call on her cell phone or carrying it around on board a luxury yacht. Also note the four lines after the by-line of the article (underlined words are links in the original). What do they say about the life cycle of news and the interactivity of online newspapers?

Missing someone? Gossip Girl Blake Lively sneaks off set to make call after being forced to part from Leo DiCaprio

By Daily Mail Reporter
Last updated at 9:37 AM on 4th August 2011
Comments (3)
Add to My Stories
Share

It's terrible to be parted when in the first heady throes of love at the best of times, but when you're dating Leonardo DiCaprio, that feeling must multiply tenfold.

Blake Lively, 23, is Leo's current squeeze and just spent a heady weekend in New York with her 36-year-old beau.

The twosome rode around the city as if they were leading lovers in a French film, but on Monday it was back to work for Blake.

And despite the fact that 'work' consists of performing scenes on a yacht in Long Beach, California with Ed Westwick and Chace Crawford, the beautiful blonde seemed to be pained about something.

So it's no surprise to see she snuck away during a break to make a phone call, and we can all probably guess successfully at the recipient.

(MailOnline, 4 August 2011, http://bit.ly/prUhTS)

(Long link: http://www.dailymail.co.uk/tvshowbiz/article-2022235/Gossip-Girl-Blake-Lively-sneaks-set-make-forced-Leo-DiCaprio.html#ixzz1U5ckY1MB)

Further reading

There are many detailed histories of news publications in England. Griffiths (2006), for instance, tells the story of 500 years of the British press from the time when Caxton's apprentice, Wynkyn de Worde, set up his printing press in Fleet Street. This famous street was the main road connecting the commercial centre of the City of London with Westminster, the residence of the monarch, up to the end of the twentieth century. Historical accounts that focus in particular on the language of these publications are less numerous. Facchinetti et al. (2012) trace the development of the language of newspapers across the four centuries from their beginnings in the early seventeenth century to the present day. Conboy (2010) provides a brief and very accessible overview of the entire story of the language of newspapers from their earliest beginnings to the present day. He takes a sociohistorical perspective and shows how newspapers helped to shape social, political and historical events, and how these events in turn shaped the newspapers and their development. Raymond (2003) provides a good introduction to pamphlets and pamphleteering in early modern Britain, and Brownlees (2011) tells the story of periodical news in seventeenth-century England.

There are also several volumes that combine articles dealing with various aspects of the development of English language newspapers from a pragmatic perspective; for example, the volumes from the Conference on Historical English News Discourse (CHINED), i.e. Brownlees (2006) and Jucker (2009b).

12 'Fire! Help! Sir Walter has studied till his Head's on fire': Narrative patterns and historical pragmatics

12.1 What are narratives and how are they relevant to historical pragmatics?

In its simplest form, the definition of a narrative is that it tells a story. A prototypical narrative sequence in a nutshell has been presented with the sentence 'The *king died*, and then the queen *died*' (Forster 1927: 60), and the famous example continues with 'of grief', which gives us a plot. A definition by a scholar at the interface between language and literature gives a narrative as 'a perceived sequence of non-randomly connected events, typically involving, as the experiencing agonist, humans or quasi-humans, or other sentient beings, from whose experience we humans can "learn"' Toolan (2001: 8). This definition is particularly appropriate for historical pragmatic concerns as it mentions the learning aspect and is not limited to literary texts. Narratives are acknowledged to have an ability to teach and entertain at the same time, *docere et delectare*. This characteristic has raised narratives to a culturally significant position and they are commonly employed for didactic ends, particularly for religious and moral teaching, but they have other uses as well. From the pragmatic angle, narratives are seen as one means by which speakers make sense of and position themselves in relation to others and to the world in general (Page 2010: 283). The wider cultural context has been especially pronounced in narrative studies, as both texts and readers are framed by cultural assumptions as to what is significant and salient (Toolan 2001: 27). At first, pragmatic analyses of narratives focused on oral stories of personal experience told at family gatherings at mealtimes and peer group meetings, but with the broadening of accepted data written narratives have received increasing attention and include a much broader scope, with, for example, medical discourse and law courts, and other areas which are of interest to historical pragmaticists too. Narratives can also be found embedded in a wide range of genres, or they can act as frames for other types of writing. At present, the cognitive approach to narratives has proved dynamic and productive and has led to new types of questions being asked (Fludernik and Olson 2011: 3, 5). The interface between language and literature is broad and multifaceted, offering new challenges to historical pragmaticists. Narratives form a trait that runs through the history of English from the Anglo-Saxon period to the present day.

In this chapter we shall discuss some of the aspects that have made narratives so central and we shall demonstrate some useful approaches to analysing them. Empirical studies on narratives can combine discourse perspectives with text-linguistics and stylistics and make use of corpus-linguistic studies as well. A point of special interest is how narratives are constructed and what regularities occur in their linguistic realisations. Other features of interest include how turning-points of the plot are marked and what linguistic devices provide dramatic effects to capture the reader's attention. The issues are connected with the larger frame of diachronic developments of genres and styles of writing and how narratives are embedded in non-narrative discourse and what functions they fulfil.

12.2 Fairy tales and their analysis

Little Red Riding-hood is an example of a classic fairy tale with an appeal that has lasted for centuries and attracted new generations of readers and listeners. The first well-known written version of the story is found in Perrault's manuscript of 1695. It was published in 1697 in the first printed collection of fairy tales, *Histoires ou Contes du temps passé* (Opie and Opie 1974: 119), but it had been in circulation before that at least in France and Italy. The tale has a dramatic plot, with suspense building up as the story proceeds. The main plot is well known by nearly all children and adults in the Western world, but actually the story has a number of different endings, though in all versions the climax is reached along a similar plot path. In Perrault's version the wolf eats the grandmother and the little girl, while in the better-known Grimm's story a huntsman rescues the victims, and in another variant a happy ending is provided by a *deus ex machina* solution in the form of a bee that stings the Wolf's nose at the decisive moment. In his morphology of fairy tales, Vladimir Propp (1968/1928), the pioneer analyst of story structure, identified a set of thirty-one key actions. The storyline of our example follows Propp's outline in the following way (as presented in Toolan 2001: 17): a member of a family is absent from home; a villain receives information about his victim; a villain attempts to deceive his victim in attempt to take possession of him; the victim submits to deception; and the villain causes harm to a member of the family.

But how is the magic of lasting enchantment achieved? The story is fairly simple and even scary, and there must be something in the way the story is told that appeals to the audience from generation to generation. We shall take a closer look at the discourse features of Perrault's version, analysing how the narrative unfolds from various viewpoints and different methodologies, relating the issues to previous chapters of this book.

The story[1] begins with a fixed formula 'once upon a time' that signals the genre and creates a horizon of expectation of a fairy tale (see Chapter 9). The main characters are introduced with hyperbolic positive notions in superlatives 'the prettiest', 'ever', 'beyond reason', 'excessively', 'yet much more', and 'so very pretty'. The description of the heroine as 'a country girl' has connotations of innocence, and the adjective 'good' is given as an epithet of the grandmother. Personal relations between the family members are presented as warm and loving, and the 'etymology' of the heroine's nickname is explained:

> There was once upon a time a little country girl, born in a village, the prettiest little creature that ever was seen. Her mother was beyond reason excessively fond of her, and her grandmother yet much more. This good woman caused to be made for her a little red Riding-Hood; which made her look so very pretty, that every body call'd her, *The little red Riding-Hood*.

This concise description serves as the point of departure with the story time, and the initial location is the safety of home. The action line begins with a temporal signpost 'One day.' Events are set rolling by a direct quote, including an endearment as an address term 'my dear Biddy' (see Chapter 5), and repetition of the distal deictic (away from the speaker) dynamic verb 'go'. The presents that the heroine should take to grandmother, a custard (pie) and a pot of butter, are mentioned for the first time. The girl sets out immediately, which is a further sign of her goodness. The dramatic moment of meeting with the Wolf is presented in the simple past: 'she met', framed with the progressive 'as she was going through a wood'. The wood is perceived as a dangerous place away from home (see above). The omniscient narrator steps in

---

[1] The text we use (given by Opie and Opie 1974, 122–5) is the English translation of Charles Perrault's *Histoires ou Contes du temps passé* (1697). The translator was Robert Samber and it appears in *Histories or Tales of Past Times* (1729). This was the first time that the story was printed in English.

and reveals the bad intentions of the Wolf right away, but there is an obstacle in the way and the little girl is saved this time.

> One day, her mother having made some custards, said to her, Go my little *Biddy*, for her cristian name was *Biddy*, go and see how your grandmother does, for I hear she has been very ill, carry her a custard, and this little pot of butter. *The little red Riding-Hood* sets out immediately to go to her grandmother, who lived in another village. As she was going through the wood, she met with *Gossop Wolfe*, who had a good mind to eat her up, but he did not dare, because of some faggot makers that were in the forrest.

The Wolf's first question is presented in indirect speech, but the important turning point of the plot is told in direct speech quotations and the narrator interprets the action line with the emotive adjectives 'poor' and 'how dangerous', which anticipate calamity. The little girl's explanation of where and why she is going picks up her mother's words and the exact wording is repeated several times in the story. Such repeated elements have a special function in building up suspense. The Wolf asks a short direct follow-up question, 'Does she live far off?' The girl's answer is prefaced with 'Oh! ay', perhaps to emphasise her credulity and her readiness to give away the information that the villain wants. The deictic 'on the other side of the mill below yonder' introduces vividness as the reader can complement it with a pointing gesture, and deictic elements are further enhanced by 'the first house in the village'. The Wolf's last turn in this scene begins with the discourse marker 'well'; the reader has the impression that the Wolf is making up his mind concerning his future actions, condensing his resolution and bad intentions in one word, in accordance with the conventions of fictional language use (see Chapter 4 and further readings). The deictic elaboration of taking different ways by 'this' and 'that' and the dynamic verb 'go' combined with deictic locative elements create strong mental images. The mock competition 'who will be there soonest' also contributes to the suspense concerning the coming events.

> He asked of her whither she was going: The poor child, who did not know how dangerous a thing it is to stay and hear a Wolf talk, said to him, I am going to see my grandmamma, and carry her a custard pye, and a little pot of butter my mamma sends her. Does she live far off? said the Wolfe. Oh! ay, said *the little red Riding-Hood*, on the other side of the mill below yonder, at the first house in the village. Well, said the Wolfe, and I'll go and see her too; I'll go this way, and go you that, and we shall see who will be there soonest.

The contrasts continue with 'the shortest' and 'the longest' ways, and how the villain and the victim proceed. The Wolf is motivated by greed and hunger to make haste and run fast. The heroine is diverted and takes her time by gathering nuts, running after butterflies and picking flowers, which are actions that express the joy of life. The Wolf's story is told using a straightforward chronological action line with a shift of locative deixis to proximal dynamic 'he came to the grandmother's house, he knocked *toc toc*'. The imitation of the sounds creates suspense, and the subsequent dramatic pauses make for a vivid reading. Grandmother's question is short and direct. The Wolf's answer is given promptly without a comment clause and it echoes the girl's earlier words imitating her voice and repeating her mother's speech, as well as the heroine's answer to the Wolf in the forest.

> The Wolfe began to run as fast as he was able, the shortest way; and the little girl went the longest, diverting her self in gathering nuts, running after butterflies, and making nose-gays of all little flowers she met with. The Wolfe was not long before he came to the grandmother's house; he knocked at the door *toc toc*. Who's there? Your grand-daughter, *The little red Riding-Hood,* said the Wolfe, counterfeiting her voice, who has brought you a custard pye, and a little pot of butter mamma sends you.

The focus changes to the grandmother and her answer explaining how to come in, and again the same words are repeated in the action line. The adjective *good* in the first sentence is given as an attribute to the grandmother for the second time, and repeated in the 'good woman'. Grandmother's words are significant as they initiate later expectations; we know what the Wolf as grandmother will say. The omniscient narrator steps in again, giving reasons for the Wolf's great appetite expressed in a hyperbolic way, 'eat her up in the tenth part of a moment', and the reason is given as well.

> The good grandmother, who was in bed, because she found herself somewhat ill, cried out, Pull the bobbin, and the latch will go up. The Wolfe pull'd the bobbin, and the door open'd; upon which he fell upon the good woman, and eat her up in the tenth part of a moment; for he had eaten nothing for above three days before.

After this, the parts change and the Wolf impersonates the grandmother. The scene repeats the events and wordings of the previous episode. The narrator describes the Wolf's actions, and reveals the heroine's feelings and train of thought. The exact same words are used by the grandmother and by the Wolf disguised as her. The personal deixis is somewhat more complicated in this passage than in the rest of the story. The little girl addresses the fake grandmother with 'you', but instead of the first person singular, she talks about herself in the third person as children sometimes do; yet 'mamma' implies the first person possessive 'my'. 'The door opened' is a prototypical transfer which leads to the scene ending with the story's climax.

> After that he shut the door, and went into grandmother's bed, expecting *the little red Riding-Hood* who came some time afterwards, and knock'd at the door *toc toc*, Who's there? *The little red Riding-Hood*, who hearing the big voice of the Wolfe, was at first afraid; but believing her grandmother had got a cold, and was grown hoarse, said it is your grand-daughter, *The little red Riding-Hood*, who has brought you a custard pye, and a little pot of butter mamma sends you. The Wolfe cried out to her, softening his voice as much as he could, Pull the bobbin, and the latch will go up. The *little red Riding-Hood* pull'd the bobbin, and the door opened.

The use of the personal pronouns changes in the next scene, as inter-action takes place between the first and the second person with impera-tive forms and proximal deictic 'come', bringing immediacy to the scene. The narrator describes the heroine's feelings as 'astonished' and the dialogue begins. The last scene has a cumulative list of exclamations with a strong resemblance to interrogatives, and they serve as questions that the little girl poses to the Wolf, still thinking that it is the grand-mother but altered in a strange way. There are four different items, each in the same form. These exclamatory clauses regularly begin with an address term 'Grandmamma', 'what' serves as an intensifying deter-miner indicating a remarkable degree of size, and the exclamatory com-ponent gives the utterances a strongly subjective quality, expressing the speaker's strong emotional involvement in the situation (Huddleston and Pullum 2002: 918–22). The answer that 'this wicked Wolfe' (notice the proximal deixis) gives to the last question about his teeth. 'it is to eat thee up', has dramatic force. After it the story is rounded up with a fairly blunt statement.

> The Wolfe seeing her come in, said to her, hiding himself under the clothes, Put the custard, and the little pot of butter upon the stool, and come into bed to me. *The little red Riding-Hood* undressed her self, and went into bed, where she was very much astonished to see how her grandmother looked in her night-cloaths: So she said to her, *Grandmamma, what great arms you have got!* It is the better to embrace thee my pretty child. *Grandmamma, what great legs you have got!* it is to run the better my child. *Grandmamma, what great ears you have got!* It is to hear the better my child. *Grandmamma, what great eyes you have got!* It is to see the better my child.

Grandmamma, what great teeth you have got! It is to eat thee up. And upon saying these words, this wicked Wolfe fell upon *the little red Riding-Hood,* and eat her up.

This extended exclamation and response sequence is the most memorable part of the story, and it is essential to remember the exact words when telling it. Repetition here is the core element, raising expectations and then fulfilling them. The dialogue has resemblance to verbal contests in rituals. Such scenes are usually presented with a pattern of claim and counterclaim, often with boasts and insults addressed to the opposite party, but here the pattern is somewhat different. The dialogue has been linked with a long tradition of heroic poetry and folk tales. Similarities are found, for example, with *Elder Edda* of the thirteenth century, which contains a scene where Loki explains to the giant Thrym why his bride, Thor in disguise, possesses unladylike characteristics (Opie and Opie 1974: 119–20). The passage reads:

> 'I have never seen a bride eat so much and drink so much' remarks Thrym, when 'she' has tucked into an ox and eight salmon. 'It is because she has had such a longing to see you, she has not eaten for eight days.' explains Loki. 'Why are Freyja's eyes so ghastly?' asks Thrym, catching a glimpse of them beneath her veil. 'It is because she has had such a longing to see you.' replies Loki, 'she has had no sleep for eight nights.' (Opie and Opie 1974: 119–20)

Such similarity is an important proof of the depth of cultural connotations and long storytelling traditions that find expression in heroic poetry and fairy tales. It is no doubt the carefully built-in suspense of repeated elements, subtle uses and shifts in the deictic elements, and the ritualistic ending with cumulative elements leading to a climax and release of suspense that work together and contribute to the success of the narrative.

The above analysis of this well-known fairy tale demonstrates a stylistic qualitative analysis, but the same narrative can serve as a testing ground for some text linguistic instruments in our analytical toolkit. Speech and thought presentation has proved a useful approach to narratives. In principle, narratives include direct speech quotations, or they can employ more indirect ways of expressing verbal actions and thoughts. In the above story, indirect speech occurs only at the beginning of the action line and primarily as a framing function. Direct quotes are, however, the main device of taking the narrative forward, and they lend immediacy and vividness to the story. The narrator mediates the inner feelings of the protagonist to the reader, and has an important role

in this tale, explaining the intentions of the Wolf and the heroine's innocence to the young audience, thus making the didactic warning explicit.

In Chapter 9 we discussed genres and text types, and suggested a two-
tier model for analysis. The basic text type of the fairy tale is narrative,
though occasional descriptive elements are also found, for example, in
the adjectives 'good', 'big' and 'little'. According to Werlich (1982), narratives proceed in action-recording sentences with verbs of change in the
past tense, and with adverbials of time and place to specify the settings.
Corroboration of Werlich's model has been obtained by Biber's large
corpus-linguistic study (1988) across a wide variety of genres of speech
and writing in English. He established Narrative versus Non-narrative
concerns as the second most important dimension in its power to explain
variation in texts. Biber's study on a large computerised database defined
narrative functions of linguistic features on an empirical basis. Those
that had the highest scores overlapped with Werlich's text-type features
of narratives, including past tense verb forms and third-person pronouns.
Such sentences form the backbone of the storyline ('her mother . . . said
to her', 'she met with', 'he asked her', etc.). The present tense occurs occasionally, and such instances of the historical present brings the events
nearer to the reader ('*The little red Riding-Hood* sets out immediately . . .'),
though their use is irregular in the above example.

Another text-linguistic approach to narrative analysis (also discussed
in Chapter 9) was coined by Enkvist (1987), who assessed guiding
principles of text production and suggested 'text strategies' as a way of
describing texts. Such strategies involve decision-making and adjustments to the goals, and they can be single, dual or multiple. The above
folk tale has a very clear chronological sequence so that we can talk
about a temporal text strategy. The iconic chronological order of events
is prominent, but another strategy of locative deictic expressions is also
important for the plot: home – wood – village – grandmother's house.
Deictic expressions with a distal function 'go' forming a pair with 'come'
and 'yonder' with both proximal and distal demonstrative pronouns
create a locative image. A third guiding principle seems to be the contrast between good and bad, as a recurring conflict in the storyline. It is
likely that the unhappy ending of the Wolf eating up the good characters was too pessimistic, and therefore alternate endings were composed
in which the good were rescued.

12.3 Natural narratives and prototypical story-telling structures

The main incentive for broadening linguists' interests in narratives
came from sociolinguistic analysis of the patterns of 'natural narratives';

that is, oral narratives of the personal experience of ordinary speakers. In a groundbreaking empirical study, Labov and Waletzky (1967) used the sociolinguistic interview method to assess regularities in oral storytelling. They asked their informants to tell about life-threatening events when they had been confronted with death and relate their own story in their own words. The accounts were recorded and analysed, with attention being paid to recurring structural elements. Their study revealed that the overall narrative structure had a regular pattern and parts of the narratives performed specific functions. The stories follow the iconic order of events and preserve the temporal sequence of the original experience. Natural narratives have been discussed in several subsequent studies and the model has been developed and applied to various kinds of texts. Toolan (1988/2001: 148) gives a very useful sequence of questions by which the Labov and Waletzky model (1967) can easily be applied to narrative texts of different kinds. The following scheme links simple questions to the structural components of natural narratives and helps to identify its parts:

> **Abstract:** what, in a nutshell, is the story about?
> **Orientation:** who, when, where?
> **Complicating action:** What happened and then what happened?
> **Evaluation:** So what? How or why is this interesting?
> **Result or resolution:** What finally happened?
> **Coda:** That's it. I've finished and I'm bridging back to the present situation. (Toolan 2001: 148, emphasis original)

Inspired by the Labov and Waletzky model, Fludernik (1996, 2007) applied the natural narrative model to written data of saints' lives and letters in the late medieval and early modern periods and she also connected the model with the cognitive approach. Early vernacular genres display an episodic structure, which is the same as that operating in conversational storytelling today, with discourse markers playing an important role as signals marking structural regularities. She interpreted early narratives to reflect prototypical human experience and, according to her, mental frames provide the means for interpreting the shared cultural experience (Fludernik 1996:12, 2007). Fludernik also formulated a number of new questions to be asked and answered about late medieval and early modern narratives. Two of them are of particular interest for historical pragmatics. The first is concerned with changes within genres and across genres and their timing. Are developments chronological or genre-specific, i.e. do they occur in all genres at the same time or earlier/later in some genres? The second question is about developments in verse and prose. Such developments are relevant to assessments from the point of view of the audience function, as they were intended for different people. In the late medieval period, verse was more pedestrian and for a broad readership, while prose was more sophisticated and written for learned readers. Verse often had the simple form of rhyming couplets (see below), while prose followed Latinate models and was more elaborate.

The natural narrative model can be fruitfully applied to many other kinds of texts. Our examples below come from different genres of writing in accordance with previous scholarship, and they show how fundamental the scheme is. The first example is taken from a learned medical treatise from the fifteenth century and follows the pattern of a natural narrative. It begins with an orientation (a young man), followed by an abstract (infected and cured). The events proceed in chronological order, and the middle of the story contains an emphatic direct quote in which the patient expresses his gratitude and joy at regaining his health. At the end there is an evaluation, explaining why the story is told and why it is significant. A special efficacy statement is provided by the additional qualification 'the connyngest man' ('the wisest man'), which increases the significance of the cure as the community regained its best worker. In general, direct speech quotations are exceptional and give additional weight to the story. In the example, the storyline is told in bold, while the temporal text strategy is marked with italics.

A yonge man of xxx yere age flegmatic of complection ... was infected & in this wise cured ... he was enionid ['prescribed'] to exercese ... **his mete was degestible** as yong moton ... *The day folowing* **I gave** to hym. [Recipe] ... *that same nyght* **was gevyn** a clister laxatif and *after that* this pouder folowing thus. [Recipe] *this taken after half a nowre* **he slept** *tyll the morow. this done* ... *The next day folowing* **he toke** this syrop [Recipe] *and this toke* ... *ther upon at iij o the clok* **was ioynid** to a stew ['bath'] ...

he sayde to his phisician Syr I thanke good I am hole and delyvered of my grete grevans and weygt ['heavyness'] ffor now I may lyft my armis to myn hed and I may cast stonis and allso walke withowte a staffe. what sholde I doo more. *then* **the fysycion sayde** use styll thy diet ...

The sonday **he toke** his syrop ... *This completed* **all his pustules** ['inflammatory sores'] **were anoynted** ... [Recipe] ...

The vij day ... **delyverd of all maner of spotts or pokkis and soo whole and went to his labur**. and this was the connyngest man of byldyng of howsys that was in all rome. **yet ther was injoind to hym to take certayne days a pill ... that it shulde never come agayn**. (MEMT, Torrella, 15th century)

Conversational narratives are characterised by framing devices which set them off from the surrounding discourse. In naturally occurring situations storytellers are awarded turns which they attempt to hold. Narratives are almost always announced or invited to ensure that the audience will yield the floor for an adequate length of time. There are recognisable patterns for initiating conversational narratives, for example 'Have you heard ...' prefaces jokes and anecdotes. Time limitations make speakers attempt to get to the point soon, postponing background information, and the significance of the story is often evaluated and its point is made explicit. Thus there are similarities with the natural narrative patterns explained above: the plotline includes the initial orientation, the story episodes and the final result and evaluation, and an off-plotline level of the story combines embedded orientation and evaluative or explicatory commentary (Fludernik 1996: 63–4). Naturally occurring narratives are told in interpersonal situations, and there is interaction between the interlocutors. Listeners signal their interest by backchannelling and other 'pragmatic noise' (see Chapter 4), or by nodding and other gestures.

Jokes and anecdotes occur in the written data as well. An anecdote about the early years of tobacco in England illustrates the power of the natural narrative pattern. The story begins with a prototypical narrative sentence. A complicating action is that Raleigh took care to smoke in private. The action (who, where, when) is introduced next, followed by what happened and what happened next. The climax of the story is given in a direct quote with short exclamations *Fire! Help!* and an interpretation of what the man has seen, ignorant of the real cause of the smoke. The story continues with an evaluation and final resolution.

> [Tobacco] was brought into *England* by Sir *Francis Drake's* Seamen, but first into repute by Sir *W. Rawleigh*. By the caution he took in smoking it privately, he did not intend it should be copied. But sitting one day in a deep Meditation with a Pipe in his Mouth, inadvertently call'd to his Man to bring him an Tankard of small Ale; the Fellow coming into the Room, threw all the Liquor in his Master's Face, and running down stairs, bawld out *Fire! Help! Sir* Walter *has studied till his Head's on fire, and the smoak bursts out of his Mouth and Nose.* After this Sir *Walter* made it no secret, and took two Pipes just before he went to be beheaded. (*Gentleman's Magazine,* Sept. 1737, p. 384)

The plot of the story is typical of anecdotes and jokes, based on appearances and misunderstandings. The short exclamations echo Chaucer's devices in marking the turning points of the plot (see Chapter 4).

Short anecdotes can be found embedded in longer texts, as is the case with the following example. It comes from a herbal, the prose treatise of *Rosemary*, originally translated from Latin into English by Friar Henry Daniel in the mid-fourteenth century. The function of the anecdote is clear: it tells us about the protective power of the plant, in accordance with the generic core function of the virtues of herbs. The story begins with an 'inclusive we' involving the audience, and continues with the emphatic 'no man soo' to emphasise the intensity of fear that the Emperor felt during thunder. The narrative part is very short, consisting of one action-recording sentence in the third person.

> We redyn þat Tiberie þe Emperowre of rome dredde thonder no man soo and because þerof he dede maken a gardeyn all of lorer and eueri thonder þere he hydde hym Also þe flowris of rosemaryn kepyn clothis fro mowthes 3if it be leyd þer among Also don his brawnchys & his lewys
> ... (Daniel, *Rosemary*, p. 319; fifteenth century; ed. Mäkinen 2002: 319)
>
> 'We read that Tiberius the Emperor of Rome was more afraid of thunder than anybody, and because of this fear he had a laurel garden made where he hid himself. Also the flowers of rosemary keep clothes from moths if sprinkled between them, and so do the branches and leaves...'

12.4 Culturally salient underlying influences

Narratives are often stories of experience from which we draw lessons. The use of narratives in various genres is among the features transferred from classical sources, which are adapted and imitated in vernacular writing. Biblical stories provided a major source of inspiration in the Western imaginative tradition and in English literature from the Anglo-Saxon period until the present day, giving evidence of the spread of religious instruction among the common people. There are several Bible translations into English, beginning with extracts in Old English and the Wycliffite Bible. The 'Authorized Version' of 1611 is perhaps the most important as it set a stylistic model which had a fundamental influence on the following centuries. The Bible builds on recurring images that can be used as a point of reference to almost anything and have become archetypes in Western literature. Biblical narratives have versatile functions, as can be seen in the examples below. The Bible begins with the Creation when time begins, surveys human history till the end, and records narratives that are formative to our experience (Frye 1982).

In the medieval period, biblical stories were inserted into texts as they were familiar to the audiences in some form and could thus provide 'resting places' in texts of instruction, for example. Inserted narratives play an important role in moon prognostications, a genre mentioned earlier (in Chapter 9), as a biblical motif is assigned for each day of the moon. Some of them are narratives, some are short references to a biblical person's birthday that served as reminders of the relevant life story. Most narratives are very short 'nutshell' versions, but some are more comprehensive; for example, the narrative of Moses leading his people through the Red Sea is told in vivid terms:

> þe xxvj day of þe mone/ Alle þyng is good to done,/ I telle þe ful wel,
> þat day lad Moyses/ Ihesu Cryst withoute les / Thurweoute Israell.
> þe Rede Se Moyses can passe /Thurw help of Ihesu Crystes grace/ Fful redy way he fonde.
> And Kyng Pharo wyth hys host/ Sewyd han wyth grete bost/To done han shame and shonde.
> He wente haue sewyd han ouer þe se,/But þerin drenchyd he/ And hys men ichon. (lines 625–39, ed. Taavitsainen 1987)

> 'The fourteenth day of the moon, all things are good to do, I tell you full well.
> That day Moses led Jesus Christ through Israel, without lie,
> He passed the Red Sea. Through Jesus Christ's grace he found a ready way.
> And King Pharaoh with his troops followed him with great boast in order to shame and harm him. He thought to follow him over the sea, but he and all his men drowned in it.'

Even more widely spread is the story of Adam and Eve, one of the narrative commonplaces which recur in all kinds of texts. The *Authorized Version* from 1611 tells the story in prose (line numbers omitted):

> And the LORD God formed man *of* the dust of the ground, and breathed into his nostrils the breath of life; and man became a living soul. And the LORD God planted a garden eastward in Eden; and there he put the man whom he had formed. And the LORD God said, *It is* not good that the man should be alone; I will make him an help meet for him. And the LORD God caused a deep sleep to fall upon Adam, and he slept: and he took one of his ribs, and closed up the flesh instead thereof; And the rib, which the LORD God had taken from man, made he a woman, and brought her unto the man. (Genesis 2:7)

The story has been used in various ways. In the medieval lunary, Adam was born on the first day, Eve on the second. In a marriage sermon, John Donne (quoted in Chapter 9) takes the biblical narrative and elaborates on it. An early example of the story is also found in an encyclopaedic

work, *Sidrak and Bokkus*, in simple rhyming couplets for the widest possible audience. The biblical reference is inserted to provide common
ground and bring the secular teaching closer to the readership, and
also to provide time to contemplate and digest the teaching. The storytelling technique is very simple, with rhyming couplets as an aid to
memory. This example illustrates the difference between prose and
verse (see above) and bears witness to the dissemination of knowledge
to illiterate masses in the Middle Ages:

> Now wolde I wite wheþer wore / Soule or body made bifore.
> The body is first made clere and fair / Of fire and watir, erthe and air;
> In man of þise iiij þei were.
> And whanne þe body was made also, /God of his grace come þerto
> And blewe in him a goost of lyf /And sithen made of him a wyf,
> And lord and sire made him to be / Of al þat he in erthe might se;
> But whan he þe appel ches, / Clothing of grace he forlees:
> And þat angrid him ful sore / As 3e haue herd bifore.
> (*Sidrak and Bokkus,* ed. Burton 1998: 498)

> 'Now I want to know whether the soul or the body was made first.
> The body was made first clear and fair, of fire and water, earth and air –
> man consists of these four.
> And when the body had been made, God in his mercy came to it and blew
> into man the spirit of life and then made of him a wife, and made him the
> lord and master of all that he could see on earth. But when he chose the
> apple, he lost the clothing of grace, which made him very angry, as you
> have heard before.'

Perhaps some clues for answering Fludernik's questions about general
versus genre-specific developments and the relations between prose and
verse can be found in these canonical narratives. They occur in various
versions modelled after the capacities and needs of their audiences. In
popular verse they occur in simplified forms, disseminating knowledge
to the widest possible audience, as in the above example.

12.5 Conclusion: At the crossroads

Narratives form one of the prototypical continua throughout the
history of English. The main narrative genres of the late medieval and
early modern periods fall into either fiction or non-fiction, but the distinction between the two modes of writing cannot be drawn in the same
way in the early periods as today; here again, as in so many other things
in the past, the borderlines are fuzzy. Another blurred line runs along

the axis of religious and secular writing, as biblical narratives influence all kinds of texts. The lives of saints are often modelled as secular
romances, and they share features with romantic literature. Chronicles
record events of the state and community in the order in which they
took place, but ecclesiastical matters are included and religion plays an
important role in historical writings in general. The early travelogues
often focus on pilgrimages and routes to the Holy City and other sacred
places, as do imaginative accounts. The wonders of the East belong to
fiction rather than factual writing, but late medieval and early modern
people were likely to take mythical animals, strange habits and events as
real. Biographies are generally non-literary but there is a considerable
overlap with saints' lives. Autobiographies are in principle non-literary
but they often acquire more meditative aspects and enter the realm of
literary writings.

   Literary and linguistic studies have several points in common, and
they can offer a great deal to one another. Literary texts offer exciting
testing grounds for linguistic theories and linguistic metalanguage 'can
account systematically for what the analyst feels as significant features
of language in a text' (Simpson 1993: 4). Pragmatic notions are analysed
with terminology derived from linguistics. By explaining the functions of linguistic features and analysing their use in detail we can gain
deeper insights both into literary and non-literary texts and into larger
issues of culture. Deictic elements, for instance, provide a new way of
probing into the text world of narratives, and there is plenty of room for
more research. Linguistics can add detailed evidence of the functions
of linguistic features and thus offer a more analytical basis to literary interpretations. In turn, literary research can provide insights into
meanings and larger contexts for linguists. Narratives are a central area
of research, cutting across historical, cultural and disciplinary boundaries, so that both literary and non-literary studies are involved. The two
disciplines interact in a fruitful way in this intersection. From the point
of view of historical pragmatics, paying attention to the communicative
functions and meaning-making potential of narratives is central.

Exercises

1. Prefaces
   Biblical echoes can be seen in several narratives; for example, in
   the following preface. The story is a commonplace, repeated and
   attached to various kinds of texts. In the following extract, what is the
   function of the biblical elements and what narrative clauses can you
   distinguish?

With þe my3t, wisdom, & grace of þe holy trynite, I write to 3ou a tretice in englisch breuely drawe out of þe book of quintis essencijs in latyn, þat hermys þe prophete and kyng of Egipt, after the flood of Noe, fadir of philosophris, hadde by reuelacioun of an aungil of god to him sende, þat þe wijsdom and þe science of þis book schulde not perische, but be kept and preserued vnto þe eende of þe world, of alle holy men from al wickid peple and tyrauntis, for greet perilis þat my3te falle þerof. (MEMT, *Quinte essence*)

'With the might, wisdom and grace of the Holy Trinity, I write to you a treatise briefly in English. It is taken from the book of quintessence in Latin that Hermes the Prophet and King of Egypt, after Noah's Flood, father of philosophers, had by revelation sent to him by God's angel, that the wisdom and science of this work should not perish but be kept and preserved until the end of the world, to all holy men from all wicked people and tyrants for fear of great perils that could fall.' (our translation)

2. Fiction

Caxton's text extract reproduced below relates to a long tradition of narratives in Western culture. Analyse the linguistic features that make this passage a narrative. How does the story line proceed? Is teaching involved? Do you recognise the intertextuality here?

It was aboute the tyme of penthecoste or whytsontyde / that #the wodes comynly be lusty and gladsom And the trees clad with leuys and blossoms and the ground with herbes and flowris swete smellyng and also the fowles and byrdes syngen melodyously in theyr armonye / That the lyon the noble kynge of all beestis # wolde in the holy dayes of thys feest holde on open Court at stade / whyche he dyde to knowe ouer alle in his lande / And commanded by strayte commyssyons and maundements that euery beest shold come thyder / in suche wyse that alle the beestis grete # and smale cam to the courte sauf reynard the fox / for he knewe hym self fawty and gylty in many thynges ayenst many beestis that thyder sholde comen that he durste not auenture to goo thyder /<P 7>whan the kynge of alle beestis had assemblid alle his court / # ther was none of them alle / but that he had complayned sore on #Reynart the foxe (HC M4 REYNARD 1420–1500)

3. Handbooks

A different use of narratives is found in texts where the medical treatise is embedded in the narrative, and not vice versa, as in the above examples. This is the case in several mimetic dialogues from the sixteenth century where a literary frame is provided and a didactic text in the dialogue form ensues. Some of these texts have even been recognised for their literary merits; for example, William Bullein's (c. 1515–76) works have been included in literary histories. Some of his medical works have narrative plots that run through the treatise. Analyse the beginning of the *Fever Pestilence* (...) as a narrative opening:

> Mendicus [begger]. God saue my gud Maister and maistresse, the Barnes [children], and all this halie househaulde, and shilde you from all doolle and shem, and sende you comfort of all thynges that you waulde haue gud of, and God and our dere Leddie shilde and defende you from this Pest. Our father whiche art in heauen, hallowed be your name; your kingdome come, your willes bee dooen in yearth as it is in heauen, &c.

> Ciuis [citizen]. Me thinke I doe heare a good mannerly Begger at the doore, and well brought up. How reuerently he saieth his Pater noster! . . .
> (EMEMT Bullein Dialogue)

4. Travelogue
   How would you describe the text strategy of the following passage from Celia Fiennes's travelogue:

> So I went to Ipswitch 9 mile more, this is a very clean town and much bigger than Colchester is now, Ipswitch has 12 Churches, their streetes of a good size well pitch'd with small stones, a good Market Cross railed in, I was there on Satturday which is their market day and saw they sold their butter by the pinte, 20 ounces for 6 pence, and often for 5d. or 4d. they make it up in a mold just in the shape of a pinte pot and so sell it;

> (Fiennes, Celia. *The Journeys Of Celia Fiennes*. Ed. C. Morris. London: The Cresset Press, 1947, pp. 141.1–154.29)

5. (Auto)biography
   Biographies and autobiographies are essentially narratives and exhibit an interesting mix of similarities and differences compared with narrative prose fiction and news narratives, and they constitute a non-fictional, prototypically non-literary genre with, in some cases, a near-literary status (Semino and Short 2004). Their function is both informative and aesthetic/entertaining (cf. fictional prose), and contain more dialogue than, for example, history books, and the narrative techniques are fairly similar to fiction. Autobiography deals with the crucial events of human life (cf. natural narratives). How does the story line proceed in the following narrative, and what is the function of direct speech quotations?

<P 199> Thys done, layed me downe apone my bed, and slepte untyl v a clocke yn the mornynge; and than my kepar came and opynyd the dore, bade me good morowe, and askyd me and I were redye. "Wherunto?" sayed I. "To suffer deathe," sayd the keapar. "Whate kyend of deathe?" sayed I, "and whan shall yt be." "Your tyme ys neare at hand, (sayed he,) and that ys to be hangyd and drawne as a trayetor, and burnde as an herytyke; and thys muste be done # even this foorenoone. Loke well to yourselve, therfore, and saye # that yow be frendly usyd." "Your frend-shyp, mr. Charlys, ys but hard and scares, yn gyvvynge me thys *Scharborowe warnynge*; but gyve # me
<P 200> leave, I praye yow frendly, to talke with you, and be not # offendyd [{with{] whate I shall saye unto yow. Thys tale that yow have # tolde me, ys yt trwe yn ded?" "Ye, (sayed he,) and that yow are lyke for to knowe. Dyspache therfor, I praye yow with speed." # "Contentyd I hame with all my harte so to doo. Where ys the wryte of execusyon? let me see yt, I praye yow." (HC EI MOWNTAYNE 1500–1570)

Further reading

There is a considerable body of literature at the interface between language and literature. From the narrative point of view, Michael Toolan's (2001) *Narrative: A Critical Linguistic Introduction* provides a good point of departure, and his books *Language in Literature: An Introduction to Stylistics* (1998) and *Narrative Progression in the Short Story: A Corpus Stylistic Approach* (2009) are helpful, too. Geoffrey N. Leech and Michael H. Short's (2007) *Style in Fiction. A Linguistic Introduction to English Fictional Prose* is a classic in the field. Catherine Emmot's (1997) *Narrative Comprehension: A Discourse Perspective* and Monika Fludernik's (1996) *Towards a 'Natural' Narratology* are also important. Fludernik's *Fictions of Language and Languages of Fiction* (1993) deals with speech and thought presentation, and the same topic is dealt with from a corpus linguistic perspective by Elena Semino and Mick Short (2004) *Corpus Stylistics: Speech, Writing and Thought Presentation in a Corpus of English Writing.* Other helpful books include Paul Simpson's (1993) *Language, Ideology and Point of View* and Tzvetan Todorov's (1990) *Genres in Discourse,* which is inspiring from the genre point of view.

Corpora and other electronic data sources

The following list contains short references to corpora that we find useful for retrieving material for historical pragmatic studies. Longer references and details of availability can be found in the Corpus Resource Database (CoRD) by the Research Unit for the Study of Variation, Contacts and Change in English, University of Helsinki. http://www.helsinki.fi/varieng/CoRD/index.html

British National Corpus (BNC) http://es-bncweb.uzh.ch/

British Newspapers 1680–1980 online. Seventeenth- and eighteenth-century Burnley Collection. Nineteenth-century British Library newspapers. John Johnson's *Ephmera*.

Corpus of Contemporary American English (COCA) http://corpus.byu.edu/coca/

Corpus of Historical American English (COHA) http://corpus.byu.edu/coha/

Corpus of Early English Correspondence (CEEC), with various compilations, some of which are publicly available. Compiled by Terttu Nevalainen, Helena Raumolin-Brunberg, Jukka Keränen, Minna Nevala, Arja Nurmi and Minna Palander-Collin.

Corpus of Early English Medical Writing, see EMEMT and MEMT below.

A Corpus of English Dialogues 1560–1760 (CED) (2006). Compiled under the supervision of Merja Kytö (Uppsala University) and Jonathan Culpeper (Lancaster University).

Corpus of Late Modern English Texts (CLMET) (2006). Compiled by Hendrik De Smet. Department of Linguistics, University of Leuven. Version 3.0 (2013) has been created by Hendrik De Smet, Hans-Jürgen Diller and Jukka Tyrkkö.

Corpus of Middle English Prose and Verse http://quod.lib.umich.edu/c/cme/

Dictionary of Old English Corpus, original release (1981) compiled by Angus Cameron, Ashley Crandell Amos, Sharon Butler, and Antonette di Paolo Healey (Toronto: DOE Project 1981); 2009 release compiled by Antonette di Paolo Healey, Joan Holland, Ian McDougall, and David McDougall, with TEI-P5 conformant-version by Xin Xiang (Toronto: DOE Project 2009).

Early English Books Online (EEBO). ProQuest LLC. http://eebo.chadwyck.com/home

Early English Prose Fiction, see LION.

Early Modern English Medical Texts (EMEMT) (2010). Compiled by Irma

218

Taavitsainen, Päivi Pahta, Turo Hiltunen, Ville Marttila, Martti Mäkinen, Maura Ratia, Carla Suhr and Jukka Tyrkkö, with software by Raymond Hickey. Amsterdam and Philadelphia: John Benjamins. CD-ROM with an accompanying book: Taavitsainen, Irma and Pahta, Päivi (eds) *Early Modern English Medical Text: Corpus Description and Studies.*

Eighteenth Century Collections Online (ECCO) ProQuest LLC.

English Drama, see LION.

English Short Title Catalogue (ESTC) British Library. Online: http://estc.bl.uk

Google Books Corpus http://googlebooks.byu.edu/

The Helsinki Corpus of English Texts (HC) (1991). Department of Modern Languages, University of Helsinki. Compiled by Matti Rissanen (Project leader); Merja Kytö (Project secretary); Leena Kahlas-Tarkka, Matti Kilpiö (Old English); Saara Nevanlinna, Irma Taavitsainen (Middle English); Terttu Nevalainen, Helena Raumolin-Brunberg (Early Modern English). In ICAME Collection of English Language Corpora (CD-ROM), 2nd edn.

Historical Thesaurus of English. Oxford: Oxford University Press. http://www.oed.com/thesaurus/ See also http://libra.englang.arts.gla.ac.uk/historicalthesaurus/

The Lampeter Corpus of Early Modern English Tracts (1999). Compiled by Josef Schmied, Claudia Claridge, and Rainer Siemund.

Literature Online (LION) http://lion.chadwyck.com/

Middle English Compendium http://quod.lib.umich.edu/m/mec/

Middle English Dictionary http://quod.lib.umich.edu/c/cme/

Middle English Medical Texts (MEMT) (2005). Compiled by Irma Taavitsainen, Päivi Pahta and Martti Mäkinen, with software by Raymond Hickey. Amsterdam and Philadelphia: John Benjamins. CD-ROM.

Oxford Dictionary of National Biography (2004). Oxford: Oxford University Press. Online edition: http://www.oxforddnb.com/public/index.html

Oxford English Dictionary (OED) (1989–2010). Oxford: Oxford University Press. Online edition: http://dictionary.oed.com/

Sociopragmatic Corpus. A Specialised Sub-section of A Corpus of English Dialogues 1560–1760 (SPC). Compiled by Jonathan Culpeper and Dawn Archer. Lancaster: Department of Linguistics and English Language, Lancaster University.

Time Magazine Corpus http://corpus.byu.edu/time/

The University of Virginia Electronic Text Center, Modern English Collection http://etext.lib.virginia.edu/modeng/modengS.browse.html

Variorum Chaucer (1979–). Provides a comprehensive overview of text and commentary of Chaucer's works. The University of Oklahoma Press. For the project and publications, see www.ou.edu/variorum/

ZEN, *Zurich English Newspaper* Corpus Version 1.0. English Department of the University of Zurich. http://es-zen.uzh.ch.

References

Alonso-Almeida, Francisco, and Mercedes Cabrera-Abreu (2002) 'The formulation of promise in Medieval English medical recipes: A relevance-theoretic approach', *Neophilologus* 86, 137–54.

Ameka, Felix (1992) 'Interjections: The universal yet neglected part of speech', *Journal of Pragmatics* 18, 101–18.

Archer, Dawn (2007) 'Developing a more detailed picture of the English courtroom (1640–1760): Data and methodological issues facing historical pragmatics', in Susan M. Fitzmaurice and Irma Taavitsainen (eds), *Methodological Issues in Historical Pragmatics*, Berlin: Mouton de Gruyter, 185–217.

Archer, Dawn, and Jonathan Culpeper (2009) 'Identifying "key" sociophilological usage in plays and trial proceedings (1640–1760): An empirical approach via corpus annotation', *Journal of Historical Pragmatics* 10.2, 286–309.

Arnovick, Leslie K. (1995) 'Sounding and flyting the English agonistic insult: Writing pragmatic history in a cross-cultural context', in Mava Jo Powell (ed.), *The Twenty-First LACUS Forum 1994*, Chapel Hill, NC: The Linguistic Association of Canada and the United States, 600–19.

Arnovick, Leslie K. (1999) *Diachronic Pragmatics. Seven Case Studies in English Illocutionary Development* (Pragmatics & Beyond New Series 68), Amsterdam/ Philadelphia: John Benjamins.

Austen, Jane ([1798/9] 1998) *Northhanger Abbey*, Oxford: Oxford University Press.

Austin, J. L. (1962) *How to Do Things With Words. The William James Lectures Delivered at Harvard University in 1955*, Oxford: Oxford University Press.

Baker, Paul (2006) *Using Corpora in Discourse Analysis*, London: Continuum.

Baker, Paul, and Tony McEnery (2005) 'A corpus-based approach to discourse of refugees and asylum seekers in UN and newspaper texts', *Journal of Language and Politics* 4.2, 197–226.

Bakhtin, M. M [1953] (1986) *Speech Genres and Other Late Essays*, Austin: University of Texas Press.

Bell, Allan (1998) 'The discourse structure of news stories', in Allan Bell and Peter Garrett (eds), *Approaches to Media Discourse*, Oxford: Blackwell, 64–104.

Benson, Larry D. (1987) *The Riverside Chaucer*, 3rd edn, Boston: Houghton Mifflin.

Biber, Douglas (1988) *Variation across Speech and Writing*, Cambridge: Cambridge University Press.

Biber, Douglas (1989) 'A typology of English texts', *Linguistics* 27, 3–43.

Biber, Douglas (2004) 'Historical patterns for the grammatical marking of stance: A cross-register comparison', *Journal of Historical Pragmatics* 5.1, 107–35.

Biber, Douglas, and Susan Conrad (2009) *Register, Genre, and Style*, Cambridge: Cambridge University Press.

Biber, Douglas, and Edward Finegan (1989) 'Drift and the evolution of English style: A history of three genres', *Language* 65.3, 487–517.

Biber, Douglas, Stig Johansson, Geoffrey Leech, Susan Conrad and Edward Finegan (1999) *Longman Grammar of Spoken and Written English*, London: Longman.

Blake, Norman F. (1996) *A History of the English Language*, London: Macmillan.

Bloomfield, Leonard (1933) *Language*, London: Allen & Unwin.

Blum-Kulka, Shoshana, Juliane House and Gabriele Kasper (eds) (1989) *Cross-Cultural Pragmatics: Requests and Apologies*, Norwood, NJ: Ablex.

Bousfield, Derek (2008) *Impoliteness in Interaction* (Pragmatics & Beyond New Series 167), Amsterdam/Philadelphia: John Benjamins.

Brinton, Laurel J. (1996) *Pragmatic Markers in English. Grammaticalization and Discourse Functions*, Berlin: Mouton de Gruyter.

Brinton, Laurel J. (2001) 'Historical discourse analysis', in Deborah Schiffrin, Deborah Tannen and Heidi E. Hamilton (eds), *The Handbook of Discourse Analysis*, Oxford: Blackwell, 138–60.

Brinton, Laurel J. (2008) *The Comment Clause in English: Syntactic Origins and Pragmatic Development*, Cambridge: Cambridge University Press.

Brinton, Laurel J. (2010) 'Discourse markers', in Andreas H. Jucker and Irma Taavitsainen (eds), *Historical Pragmatics* (Handbooks of Pragmatics 8), Berlin and New York: De Gruyter Mouton, 285–314.

Brown, Roger, and Albert Gilman (1960) 'The pronouns of power and solidarity', in Thomas A. Sebeok (ed.), *Style in Language*, Cambridge, MA: MIT Press, 253–76.

Brown, Roger, and Albert Gilman (1989) 'Politeness theory and Shakespeare's four major tragedies', *Language in Society* 18.2, 159–212.

Brown, Penelope, and Stephen C. Levinson (1978) 'Universals in language usage: Politeness phenomena', in Esther Goody (ed.), *Questions and Politeness: Strategies in Social Interaction*. Cambridge: Cambridge University Press, 56–310.

Brown, Penelope, and Stephen C. Levinson (1987) *Politeness. Some Universals in Language Usage* (Studies in Interactional Sociolinguistics 4), Cambridge: Cambridge University Press.

Brownlees, Nicholas (ed.) (2006) *News Discourse in Early Modern Britain. Selected Papers of CHINED 2004*, Bern: Peter Lang.

Brownlees, Nicholas (2011) *The Language of Periodical News in Seventeenth-Century England*, Newcastle upon Tyne: Cambridge Scholars.

Bublitz, Wolfram, Andreas H. Jucker and Klaus P. Schneider (eds) (2010–) *Handbooks of Pragmatics*, 9 vols, Berlin: De Gruyter Mouton.

Burnley, David (1983) *A Guide to Chaucer's Language*, London: Macmillan.

Burton, Tom L. (ed.) (1998) *Sidrak and Bokkus: A Parallel-text Edition from Bodl. Library Laud Misc. 559 and British Library, MS Lansdowne 793*, 2 vols. (Early English Text Society 312), Oxford: Oxford University Press.

Busse, Beatrix (2006) *Vocative Constructions in the Language of Shakespeare* (Pragmatics & Beyond New Series 150), Amsterdam/Philadelphia: John Benjamins.

Busse, Ulrich (1998) '"Stand, sir, and throw us that you have about ye." Zur Grammatik und Pragmatik des Anredepronomens *ye* in Shakespeares Dramen', in Eberhard Klein and Stefan J. Schierholz (eds), *Betrachtungen zum Wort. Lexik im Spannungsfeld von Syntax, Semantik und Pragmatik*, Tübingen: Stauffenburg Verlag, 85–115.

Busse, Ulrich (2002) *Linguistic Variation in the Shakespeare Corpus. Morpho-Syntactic Variability of Second Person Pronouns* (Pragmatics & Beyond New Series 106), Amsterdam/Philadelphia: John Benjamins.

Busse, Ulrich (2003) 'The co-occurrence of nominal and pronominal address forms in the Shakespeare Corpus: Who says thou or you to whom?', in Irma Taavitsainen and Andreas H. Jucker (eds), *Diachronic Perspectives on Address Term Systems* (Pragmatics & Beyond New Series 107), Amsterdam/Philadelphia: John Benjamins, 193–221.

Busse, Ulrich, and Beatrix Busse (2010) 'Shakespeare', in Andreas H. Jucker and Irma Taavitsainen (eds), *Historical Pragmatics* (Handbooks of Pragmatics 8), Berlin and New York: De Gruyter Mouton, 247–81.

Campbell, James (ed.) (1991) *The Anglo-Saxons*, London: Penguin Books.

Chapman, Siobhan (2011) *Pragmatics* (Palgrave Modern Linguistics), Basingstoke: Palgrave Macmillan.

Claridge, Claudia (2012) 'Linguistic levels: Styles, registers, genres, text types', in Alex Bergs and Laurel Brinton (eds), *Historical Linguistics of English* (HSK 34.1), Berlin: Mouton de Gruyter, pp. 237–53.

Claridge, Claudia, and Leslie Arnovick (2010) 'Pragmaticalisation and discursisation', in Andreas H. Jucker and Irma Taavitsainen (eds), *Historical Pragmatics* (Handbooks of Pragmatics 8), Berlin and New York: De Gruyter Mouton, 165–92.

Clover, Carol J. (1980) 'The Germanic context of the Unferð episode.' *Speculum* 55.3, 444–68. Reprinted in Peter S. Baker (ed.) (2000) *The Beowulf Reader*, New York: Garland, 127–54.

Conboy, Martin (2010) *The Language of Newspapers. Socio-Historical Perspectives*, London: Continuum.

Culpeper, Jonathan (1996) 'Towards an anatomy of impoliteness', *Journal of Pragmatics* 25, 349–67.

Culpeper, Jonathan (2005) 'Impoliteness and entertainment in the television quiz show: The Weakest Link', *Journal of Politeness Research* 1, 35–72.

Culpeper, Jonathan (2011) *Impoliteness. Using Language to Cause Offence*, Cambridge: Cambridge University Press.

Culpeper, Jonathan, and Merja Kytö (2000) 'Data in historical pragmatics:

Spoken discourse (re)cast as writing', *Journal of Historical Pragmatics* 1.2, 175–99.

Culpeper, Jonathan, and Merja Kytö (2010) *Early Modern English Dialogues. Spoken Interaction as Writing* (Studies in English Language), Cambridge: Cambridge University Press.

Cummings, Louise (ed.) (2010) *The Pragmatics Encyclopedia*, London: Routledge.

Cusack, Bridget (ed.) (1998) *Everyday English 1500–1700: A Reader*, Edinburgh: Edinburgh University Press.

Defour, Tine (2008) 'The speaker's voice. A diachronic study on the use of "well" and "now" as pragmatic markers', *English Text Construction* 1.1, 62–82.

Deutschmann, Mats (2003) *Apologising in British English* (Skrifter från moderna språk 10), Umeå: Institutionen för moderna språk, Umeå University.

Dickens, Charles [1857/8] *Little Dorrit*, http://www.gutenberg.org/ebooks/963

Dodiya, Jaydipsinh (2006) *Perspectives On Indian English Fiction*, New Delhi: Sarup & Sons.

Donne, John ([1621] 1957) *The Sermons*, 10 vols, ed. by George R. Potter and Evelyn M. Simpson, Berkeley and Los Angeles: University of California Press, Vol. III, pp. 241–55.

Eelen, Gino (2001) *A Critique of Politeness Theories* (Encounters 1), Manchester: St. Jerome.

Eggins, Suzanne, and J. R. Martin (1997) 'Genres and registers of discourse', in Teun A. van Dijk (ed.), *Discourse as Structure and Process*, London, New Delhi and Thousand Oaks, CA: Sage Publications, 230–56.

Emmott, Catherine (1997) *Narrative Comprehension: A Discourse Perspective*, Oxford: Clarendon Press.

Enkvist, Nils Erik (1987) 'Text strategies: Single, dual, multiple', in R. Steele and T. Threadgold (eds) *Language Topics. Essays in Honour of Michael Halliday*, Vol. II, Amsterdam: John Benjamins, 203–11.

Erman, Britt, and Ulla-Britt Kotsinas (1993) 'Pragmaticalization: The case of *ba'* and *you know*', *Studier i modern språkvetenskap* 10, 76–93.

Evans, G. Blakemore (ed.) (1974) *The Riverside Shakespeare*, Boston: Houghton Mifflin.

Evans, G. Blakemore (ed.) (2003) *Romeo and Juliet*, updated edition, Cambridge: Cambridge University Press.

Facchinetti, Roberta, Nicholas Brownlees, Birte Bös and Udo Fries (2012) *News as Changing Texts. Corpora, Methodologies and Analysis*, Newcastle upon Tyne: Cambridge Scholars.

Finkenstaedt, Thomas (1963) *You and thou: Studien zur Anrede im Englischen*, Berlin: Walter de Gruyter.

Fludernik, Monika (1993) *The Fictions of Language and the Languages of Fiction*, London and New York: Routledge.

Fludernik, Monika (1996) *Towards a 'Natural' Narratology*, London: Routledge.

Fludernik, Monika (2000) 'Narrative discourse markers in Malory's *Morte d'Arthur'*, *Journal of Historical Pragmatics* 1.2, 231–62.

Fludernik, Monika (2007) 'Letters as narrative: Narrative patterns and episode structure in early letters', in Susan M. Fitzmaurice and Irma Taavitsainen (eds), *Methodological Issues in Historical Pragmatics*, Berlin: Mouton de Gruyter, 241–66.

Fludernik, Monika and Greta Olson (2011) 'Introduction', in Greta Olson (ed.), *Current Trends in Narratology*, Berlin: Walter de Gruyter, 1–33.

Forster, E. M. (1927/1974) *Aspects of the Novel, and Related Writings*, The Provost and Scholars of King's College, Cambridge.

Fowler, Alastair (1982) *Kinds of Literature. An Introduction to the Theory of Genre and Modes*, Oxford: Clarendon Press.

Fox, Kate (2004) *Watching the English. The Hidden Rules of English Behaviour*, London: Hodder & Stoughton.

Frye, Northrop (1982) *The Great Code: The Bible and Literature*, London and New York: Routledge.

Gehweiler, Elke (2008) 'From proper name to primary interjections: The case of *gee!*, *Journal of Historical Pragmatics* 9.1, 71–93.

Gehweiler, Elke (2010) 'Interjections and expletives', in Andreas H. Jucker and Irma Taavitsainen (eds), *Historical Pragmatics* (Handbooks of Pragmatics 8), Berlin and New York: De Gruyter Mouton, 315–49.

Ghadessy, Mohsen (ed.) (1988) *Registers of Written English. Situational Factors and Linguistic Features*, London: Frances Pinter.

Gotti, Maurizio (2001) 'The experimental essay in Early Modern English', *European Journal of English Studies*. Special Issue: *Early Modern English Text Types* 5.2, 221–40.

Grafton, Anthony, April Shelford and Nancy Siraisi (1992) *New Worlds, Ancient Texts: The Power of Tradition and the Shock of Discovery*, Cambridge, MA and London: The Belknap Press of Harvard University Press.

Griffiths, Dennis (2006) *Fleet Street. Five Hundred Years of the Press*, London: The British Library.

Hiltunen, Risto (2006) '"Eala, geferan and gode wyrhtan": On interjections in Old English', in John Walmsley (ed.), *Inside Old English: Essays in Honour of Bruce Mitchell*, Oxford: Blackwell, 91–116.

Honegger, Thomas (2003) '"And if ye wol nat so, my lady sweete, thanne preye I thee, [...].": Forms of address in Chaucer's Knight's Tale', in Irma Taavitsainen and Andreas H. Jucker (eds), *Diachronic Perspectives on Address Term Systems* (Pragmatics & Beyond New Series 107), Amsterdam and Philadelphia: John Benjamins, 61–84.

Hope, Jonathan (1994) 'The use of *thou* and *you* in Early Modern spoken English: Evidence from depositions in the Durham ecclesiastical court records', in Dieter Kastovsky (ed.), *Studies in Early Modern English*, Berlin: Mouton de Gruyter, 141–52.

Hope, Jonathan (2003) *Shakespeare's Grammar*, London: The Arden Shakespeare.

Hopper, Paul J., and Elizabeth Closs Traugott (2003) *Grammaticalization*, 2nd edn, Cambridge: Cambridge University Press.

Horn, Laurence R., and Gregory Ward (eds) (2004) *The Handbook of Pragmatics*, Oxford: Blackwell.

Huang, Yan (2007) *Pragmatics*, Oxford: Oxford University Press.

Huang, Yan (2012) *The Oxford Dictionary of Pragmatics*, Oxford: Oxford University Press.

Huddleston, Rodney, and Geoffrey K. Pullum (2002) *The Cambridge Grammar of the English Language*, Cambridge: Cambridge University Press.

Jacobs, Andreas, and Andreas H. Jucker (1995) 'The historical perspective in pragmatics', in Andreas H. Jucker (ed.), *Historical Pragmatics. Pragmatic Developments in the History of English* (Pragmatics & Beyond New Series 35), Amsterdam and Philadelphia: John Benjamins, 3–33.

Jauss, Hans Robert (1979) 'The alterity and modernity of medieval literature', in Hans Robert Jauss and Timothy Bahti (eds), *New Literary History* 10.2, *Medieval Literature and Contemporary Theory*, 181–229.

Jenner, Mark S. R., and Patrick Wallis (2007) 'The medical marketplace', in Mark S. R. Jenner and Patrick Wallis (eds), *Medicine and the Market in England and its Colonies, c. 1450–1850*, Basingstoke and New York: Palgrave Macmillan.

Jones, Claire (2004) 'Discourse communities and medical texts', in Irma Taavitsainen and Päivi Pahta (eds), *Medical and Scientific Writing in English 1375–1500*, Cambridge: Cambridge University Press, 23–36.

Jones, Peter Murray (2011) 'Medical literacies and medical culture', in Irma Taavitsainen and Päivi Pahta (eds), *Medical Writing in Early Modern English* (Studies in English Language), Cambridge: Cambridge University Press, 30–43.

Jucker, Andreas H. (1997) 'The discourse marker *well* in the history of English', *English Language and Linguistics* 1.1, 91–110.

Jucker, Andreas H. (1998) 'Historical pragmatics: An interdisciplinary approach', in Borgmeier, Raimund, Herbert Grabes and Andreas H. Jucker (eds), *Anglistentag 1997 Giessen. Proceedings*, Trier: Wissenschaftlicher Verlag, 3–7.

Jucker, Andreas H. (2000) 'English historical pragmatics: Problems of data and methodology', in Gabriella di Martino and Maria Lima (eds), *English Diachronic Pragmatics*, Napoli: CUEN, 17–55.

Jucker, Andreas H. (2002) 'Discourse markers in Early Modern English', in Richard Watts and Peter Trudgill (eds), *Alternative Histories of English*, London and New York: Routledge, 210–30.

Jucker, Andreas H. (2006a) 'Historical pragmatics', in Keith Brown (ed.), *Encyclopedia of Language and Linguistics*, 2nd edn, Oxford: Elsevier, 329–32.

Jucker, Andreas H. (2006b) '"Thou art so loothly and so oold also": The use of *ye* and *thou* in Chaucer's *Canterbury Tales*', *Anglistik* 17.2, 57–72.

Jucker, Andreas H. (2008a) 'Historical pragmatics', *Language and Linguistics Compass* 2.5, 894–906.

Jucker, Andreas H. (2008b) 'Politeness in the history of English', in Richard Dury, Maurizio Gotti and Marina Dossena (eds), *English Historical Linguistics 2006. Volume II: Lexical and Semantic Change. Selected Papers from the Fourteenth International Conference on English Historical Linguistics (ICEHL 14), Bergamo, 21–25 August 2006*. Amsterdam and Philadelphia: John Benjamins, 3–29.

Jucker, Andreas H. (2009a) 'Historical pragmatics', in Jacob L. Mey (ed.) *Concise*

Encyclopedia of Pragmatics, 2nd edn, Amsterdam: Elsevier. Reprint of Jucker (2006a).

Jucker, Andreas H. (2009b) 'Newspapers, pamphlets and scientific news discourse in Early Modern Britain', in Andreas H. Jucker (ed.), *Early Modern English News Discourse. Newspapers, Pamphlets and Scientific News Discourse* (Pragmatics & Beyond New Series 187), Amsterdam and Philadelphia: John Benjamins, 1–9.

Jucker, Andreas H. (2012a) '"What's in a name?": Names and terms of address in Shakespeare's *Romeo and Juliet*', in Sarah Chevalier and Thomas Honegger (eds), *Words, Words, Words: Philology and Beyond. Festschrift for Andreas Fischer on the Occasion of his 65th Birthday*, Tübingen: Narr Francke Attempto, 77–97.

Jucker, Andreas H. (2012b) 'Changes in politeness cultures', in Terttu Nevalainen and Elizabeth Traugott (eds), *The Oxford Handbook of the History of English*, New York: Oxford University Press, 422–33.

Jucker, Andreas H., and Irma Taavitsainen (2000) 'Diachronic speech act analysis: Insults from flyting to flaming', *Journal of Historical Pragmatics* 1.1, 67–95.

Jucker, Andreas H., and Irma Taavitsainen (eds) (2008) *Speech Acts in the History of English* (Pragmatics & Beyond New Series 176), Amsterdam and Philadelphia: John Benjamins.

Jucker, Andreas H., and Irma Taavitsainen (eds) (2010) *Historical Pragmatics* (Handbooks of Pragmatics 8), Berlin and New York: De Gruyter Mouton.

Jucker, Andreas H., and Irma Taavitsainen (2012) 'Pragmatic variables', in Juan Manuel Hernández-Campoy (ed.), *The Handbook of Historical Sociolinguistics*, Oxford: Wiley-Blackwell, 303-17.

Jucker, Andreas H., and Irma Taavitsainen (forthcoming) 'Complimenting in the history of American English: A metacommunicative expression analysis', in Irma Taavitsainen and Andreas H. Jucker (eds), *Diachronic Corpus Pragmatics*.

Jucker, Andreas H., Gerold Schneider, Irma Taavitsainen and Barb Breustedt (2008) 'Fishing for compliments: Precision and recall in corpus-linguistic compliment research', in Andreas H. Jucker and Irma Taavitsainen (eds), *Speech Acts in the History of English* (Pragmatics & Beyond New Series 176), Amsterdam and Philadelphia: John Benjamins, 273–94.

Kahlas-Tarkka, Leena, and Matti Rissanen (2007) 'The sullen and the talkative: Discourse strategies in the Salem examinations', *Journal of Historical Pragmatics* 8.1, 1–24.

King, James, and Charles Ryskamp (ed.) (1986) *William Cowper. The Letters and Prose Writings of William Cowper V*, Oxford: Clarendon Press.

Knappe, Gabriele, and Michael Schümann (2006) '*Thou* and *ye*. A collocational-phraseological approach to pronoun change in Chaucer's *Canterbury Tales*', *Studia Anglica Posnaniensia* 42, 213–38.

Koch, Peter (1999) 'Court records and cartoons: Reflections of spontaneous dialogue in Early Romance texts', in Andreas H. Jucker, Gerd Fritz, and Franz Lebsanft (eds), *Historical Dialogue Analysis* (Pragmatics & Beyond New Series 66), Amsterdam and Philadelphia: John Benjamins, 399–429.

Koch, Peter, and Wulf Oesterreicher (1985) *Sprache der Nähe — Sprache der Distanz: Mündlichkeit und Schriftlichkeit im Spannungsfeld von Sprachtheorie und Sprachgeschichte*, Romanistisches Jahrbuch 36, 15–43.

Kohnen, Thomas (2008a) 'Directives in Old English: Beyond politeness?', in Andreas H. Jucker and Irma Taavitsainen (eds), *Speech Acts in the History of English* (Pragmatics & Beyond New Series 176), Amsterdam and Philadelphia: John Benjamins, 27–44.

Kohnen, Thomas (2008b) 'Tracing directives through text and time: Towards a methodology of a corpus-based diachronic speech-act analysis', in Andreas H. Jucker and Irma Taavitsainen (eds), *Speech Acts in the History of English* (Pragmatics & Beyond New Series 176), Amsterdam and Philadelphia: John Benjamins, 295–310.

Kohnen, Thomas (2008c) 'Linguistic politeness in Anglo-Saxon England? A study of Old English address terms', *Journal of Historical Pragmatics* 9.1, 140–58.

Kohnen, Thomas (2011) 'Understanding Anglo-Saxon "politeness": Directive constructions with *ic wille / ic wolde*', *Journal of Historical Pragmatics* 12.1–2, 230–54.

Kopytko, Roman (1995) 'Linguistic politeness strategies in Shakespeare's plays', in Andreas H. Jucker (ed.), *Historical Pragmatics. Pragmatic Developments in the History of English* (Pragmatics & Beyond New Series 35), Amsterdam and Philadelphia: John Benjamins, 515–40.

Kytö, Merja (2010) 'Data in historical pragmatics', in Andreas H. Jucker and Irma Taavitsainen (eds), *Historical Pragmatics* (Handbooks of Pragmatics 8), Berlin and New York: De Gruyter Mouton, 33–67.

Labov, William (1994) *Principles of Linguistic Change*, Volume 1: *Internal Factors*, Oxford: Blackwell.

Labov, William, and Joshua Waletzky (1967) 'Narrative analysis: oral versions of personal experience', in June Helm (ed.), *Essays on the Verbal and Visual Arts. Proceedings of the 1966 Annual Spring Meeting of the American Ethnological Society*, Seattle: American Ethnological Society, 12–44. Reprinted in *Journal of Narrative and Life History* 7.1–4 (1997), 3–38.

Lakoff, George (1987) *Women, Fire and Dangerous Things. What Categories Reveal about the Mind*, Chicago and London: The University of Chicago Press.

Leech, Geoffrey, Marianne Hundt, Christian Mair and Nicholas Smith (2009) *Change in Contemporary English. A Grammatical Study* (Studies in English Language), Cambridge: Cambridge University Press.

Leech, Geoffrey N. and Michael H. Short (2007) *Style in Fiction. A Linguistic Introduction to English Fictional Prose*, 2nd edn, London: Longman.

López-Couso, María José (2010) 'Subjectification and intersubjectification', in Andreas H. Jucker and Irma Taavitsainen (eds), *Historical Pragmatics* (Handbooks of Pragmatics 8), Berlin and New York: De Gruyter Mouton, 127–63.

Mäkinen, Martti (2002) 'Henry Daniel's Rosemary in MS X.90 of the Royal Library, Stockholm', *Neuphilologische Mitteilungen* 103:3, 305–27.

Manes, Joan, and Nessa Wolfson (1981) 'The compliment formula', in Florian
Coulmas (ed.), *Conversational Routine. Explorations in Standardized Communication
Situations and Prepatterned Speech*, The Hague: Mouton, 115–32.

Mazzon, Gabriella (2000) 'Social relations and form of address in the *Canterbury
Tales*', in Dieter Kastovsky and Arthur Mettinger (eds), *The History of English
in a Social Context. A Contribution to Historical Sociolinguistics*, Berlin: Mouton de
Gruyter, 135–68.

Mazzon, Gabriella (2003) 'Pronouns and nominal address in Shakespearean
English: A socio-affective marking system in transition', in Irma Taavitsainen
and Andreas H. Jucker (eds), *Diachronic Perspectives on Address Term Systems*
(Pragmatics & Beyond New Series 107), Amsterdam and Philadelphia: John
Benjamins, 223–49.

Mazzon, Gabriella (2010) 'Terms of address', in Andreas H. Jucker and Irma
Taavitsainen (eds), *Historical Pragmatics* (Handbooks of Pragmatics 8), Berlin
and New York: De Gruyter Mouton, 351–76.

McArthur, Tom (2002) *The Oxford Guide to World English*, Oxford: Oxford
University Press.

McConchie, R. W. (1997) *Lexicography and Physicke: The Record of Sixteenth-
Century English Terminology*, Oxford: Clarendon Press.

McEnery, Tony (2006) 'The moral panic about bad language in England,
1691–1745', *Journal of Historical Pragmatics* 7.1, 89–113.

McEnery, Tony, and Andrew Wilson (2001) *Corpus Linguistics*, 2nd edn
(Edinburgh Textbooks in Empirical Linguistics), Edinburgh: Edinburgh
University Press.

Mey, Jacob L. (2001) *Pragmatics. An Introduction*, 2nd edn, Oxford: Blackwell.

Mey, Jacob L. (2009) *Concise Encyclopedia of Pragmatics*, 2nd edn, Amsterdam:
Elsevier.

Mikkeli, Heikki and Ville Marttila (2010) 'Change and continuity in early
modern medicine (1500–1700)', in Irma Taavitsainen and Päivi Pahta (eds),
Early Modern English Medical Texts: Corpus Description and Studies, Amsterdam:
John Benjamins, 13–27.

Moessner, Lilo (2001) 'Genre, text type, style, register: A terminological maze?'
European Journal of English Studies. Special Issue: *Early Modern English Text
Types* 5.2, 131–8.

Narrog, Heiko, and Bernd Heine (eds) (2011) *The Oxford Handbook of
Grammaticalization* (Oxford Handbooks in Linguistics), Oxford: Oxford
University Press.

Nevala, Minna (2004) *Address in Early English Correspondence. Its Forms and Sociopragmatic Functions* (Mémoires de la Société Néophilologique de Helsinki 64),
Helsinki: Société Néophilologique.

Nevalainen, Terttu, and Helena Raumolin-Brunberg (1995) 'Constraints on
politeness: The pragmatics of address formulae in Early English correspondence', in Andreas H. Jucker (ed.), *Historical Pragmatics. Pragmatic Developments
in the History of English* (Pragmatics & Beyond New Series 35), Amsterdam and
Philadelphia: John Benjamins, 541–601.

Nevalainen, Terttu, and Helena Raumolin-Brunberg (2003) *Historical Sociolinguistics: Language Change in Tudor and Stuart England*, London: Pearson Education.

Nevanlinna, Saara and Irma Taavitsainen (eds) (1993) *St. Katherine of Alexandria. The Late Middle English Prose Legend of St. Katherine of Alexandria* in Southwell Minster MS 7, Cambridge and Helsinki: Boydell & Brewer and the Finnish Academy of Science and Letters.

Opie, Iona, and Peter Opie (1974) *The Classic Fairy Tales*, London, Toronto, Sydney and New York: Granada.

Östman, Jan-Ola (1995) 'Pragmatic particles twenty years after', in Brita Wårvik, Sanna-Kaisa Tanskanen and Risto Hiltunen (eds), *Organization in Discourse. Proceedings from the Turku Conference* (Anglicana Turkuensia 14), Turku: University of Turku, 95–108.

Page, Ruth (2010) 'Narrative Discourse', in Louise Cummings (ed.), *The Pragmatics Encyclopaedia*, London and New York: Routledge, 283–5.

Pahta, Päivi, and Irma Taavitsainen (2010) 'Scientific discourse', in Andreas H. Jucker and Irma Taavitsainen (eds), *Historical Pragmatics* (Handbooks of Pragmatics 8), Berlin and New York: De Gruyter Mouton, 549–86.

Pahta, Päivi, and Irma Taavitsainen (2011) 'An interdisciplinary approach to medical writing in Early Modern English', in Irma Taavitsainen and Päivi Pahta (eds), *Medical Writing in Early Modern English* (Studies in English Language), Cambridge: Cambridge University Press, 1–8.

Pakkala-Weckström, Mari (2005) *The Dialogue of Love, Marriage and Maistrie in Chaucer's* Canterbury Tales (Mémoires de la Société Néophilologique de Helsinki 67), Helsinki: Société Néophilologique.

Palander-Collin, Minna (2009) 'Variation and change in patterns of self-reference in early English correspondence', *Journal of Historical Pragmatics* 10.2, 260–85.

Paltridge, Brian (1997) *Genre, Frames and Writing in Research Settings* (Pragmatics & Beyond New Series 45), Amsterdam: John Benjamins.

Person, Raymond R., Jr (2009) '"Oh" in Shakespeare: A conversation analytic approach', *Journal of Historical Pragmatics* 10.1, 84–107.

Prentice, Sheryl, and Andrew Hardie (2009) 'Empowerment and disempowerment in the Glencairn Uprising: A corpus-based critical analysis of Early Modern English news discourse', *Journal of Historical Pragmatics* 10.1, 23–55.

Porter, Roy (1985) 'Lay medical knowledge in the Eighteenth century: The evidence of the *Gentleman's Magazine*', *Medical History* 29, 138–68.

Power, Henry (1664) *Experimental Philosophy in Three Books: Containing New Experiments Microscopical, Mercurial, Magnetical*, London: T. Roycroft.

Propp, Vladimir (1968/1928) *The Morphology of the Folktale*, Austin: University of Texas Press.

Raumolin-Brunberg, Helena (1996) 'Forms of address in early English correspondence', in Terttu Nevalainen and Helena Raumolin-Brunberg (eds), *Sociolinguistics and Language History. Studies based on the Corpus of Early English Correspondence*, Amsterdam: Rodopi, 167–81.

Raymond, Joad (2003) *Pamphlets and Pamphleteering in Early Modern Britain*, Cambridge: Cambridge University Press.

Rosch, Elinor, and Carolyn B. Mervis (1975) 'Family resemblances: Studies in the internal structure of categories', *Cognitive Psychology* 7, 573–605.

Salmon, Vivian (1965) 'Sentence structures in colloquial Shakespearian English', *Transactions of the Philological Society*, 105–40. Reprinted in Salmon and Burness (1987).

Salmon, Vivian, and Edwina Burness (compilers) (1987) *A Reader in the Language of Shakespearean Drama*, Amsterdam and Philadelphia: John Benjamins.

Sauer, Hans (2009) 'How the Anglo-Saxons expressed their emotions with the help of interjections', *Brno Studies in English* 35.2, 167–83.

Schwenter, Scott A., and Elizabeth Closs Traugott (2000) 'Invoking scalarity: The development of *in fact*', *Journal of Historical Pragmatics* 1.1, 7–25.

Searle, John R. (1969) *Speech Acts. An Essay in the Philosophy of Language*, Cambridge: Cambridge University Press.

Searle, John R. (1979) *Expression and Meaning. Studies in the Theory of Speech Acts*, Cambridge: Cambridge University Press.

Semino, Elena, and Mick Short (2004) *Corpus Stylistics: Speech, Writing and Thought Presentation in a Corpus of English Writing*, London, New York: Routledge.

Simpson, Paul (1993) *Language, Ideology and Point of View*, London: Routledge.

Slack, Paul (1979) 'Mirrors of health and treasures of poor men: The uses of the vernacular medical literature of Tudor England', in Charles Webster (ed.), *Health, Medicine and Mortality in the Sixteenth Century*, Cambridge: Cambridge University Press, 237–73.

Stein, Dieter (2003) 'Pronominal usage in Shakespeare: Between sociolinguistics and conversational analysis', in Irma Taavitsainen and Andreas H. Jucker (eds), *Diachronic Perspectives on Address Term Systems* (Pragmatics & Beyond New Series 107), Amsterdam and Philadelphia: John Benjamins, 251–307.

Stein, Dieter, and Susan Wright (eds) (1995) *Subjectivity and Subjectivisation. Linguistic Perspectives*, Cambridge: Cambridge University Press.

Studer, Patrick (2003) 'Textual structures in eighteenth-century newspapers: A corpus-based study of headlines', *Journal of Historical Pragmatics* 4.1, *Special Issue on Media and Language Change*, ed. Susan C. Herring, 19–43.

Suhr, Carla (2011) *Publishing for the Masses. Early Modern English Witchcraft Pamphlets* (Mémoires de la Société Néophilologique de Helsinki 83), Helsinki: Société Néophilologique.

Swales, John M. (1990) *Genre Analysis. English in Academic and Research Settings*, Cambridge: Cambridge University Press.

Taavitsainen, Irma (1987) 'Storia Lune and Its Paraphrase in Prose. Two Versions of a Middle English Lunary', in Leena Kahlas-Tarkka (ed.), *Neophilologica fennica* (Mémoires de la Société Néophilologique de Helsinki 45), Helsinki: Société Néophilologique de Helsinki, 521–55.

Taavitsainen, Irma (ed.) (1988) *Middle English Lunaries: A Study of the Genre*, Helsinki: Société Néophilologique.

Taavitsainen, Irma (1994) 'A Zodiacal Lunary for Medical Professionals', in

Lister M. Matheson (ed.), *Popular and Practical Science of Medieval England*, East Lansing, MI and Cambridge: Colleagues Press / Boydell & Brewer, 283–98.

Taavitsainen, Irma (1995) 'Interjections in Early Modern English: From imitation of spoken to conventions of written language', in Andreas H. Jucker (ed.), *Historical Pragmatics. Pragmatic Developments in the History of English*, Amsterdam: John Benjamins, 439–65.

Taavitsainen, Irma (1997) '"By Saint Tanne": Pious oaths or swearing in Middle English? An assessment of genres', in Raymond Hickey and Stanislaw Puppel (eds), *Language History and Linguistics Modelling. A Festschrift for Jacek Fisiak on his 60th Birthday*, Berlin: Mouton de Gruyter, 815–26.

Taavitsainen, Irma (1998) 'Emphatic language and Romantic prose: Changing Functions of interjections in a sociocultural perspective', *European Journal of English Studies* 2.2, 195–214.

Taavitsainen, Irma (2000) 'Science', in Peter Brown (ed.), *The Chaucer Companion*, Oxford: Blackwells, 378–96.

Taavitsainen, Irma (2001) 'Changing conventions of writing: The dynamics of genres, text types, and text traditions', *European Journal of English Studies. Special Issue: Early Modern English Text Types*. 5.2, 139–50.

Taavitsainen, Irma (2005) 'Genres and the appropriation of science', in Janne Skaffari et al. (eds), *Opening Windows on Texts and Discourses of the Past*, Amsterdam and Philadelphia: John Benjamins, 179–96.

Taavitsainen, Irma (2006) '*Lingua francas* of medical communication', *The Encyclopedia of Language and Linguistics*, 2nd edn, Oxford: Elsevier, 642–3.

Taavitsainen, Irma (2009a) 'Authority and instruction in two sixteenth-century medical dialogues', in Matti Peikola, Janne Skaffari and Sanna-Kaisa Tanskanen (eds), *Instructional Writing in English: Studies in Honour of Risto Hiltunen*, Amsterdam and Philadelphia: John Benjamins, 105–24.

Taavitsainen, Irma (2009b) 'The pragmatics of knowledge and meaning: Corpus linguistic approaches to changing thought-styles in early modern medical discourse', in Andreas H. Jucker, Daniel Schreier and Marianne Hundt (eds), *Corpora: Pragmatics and Discourse*, Amsterdam: Rodopi, 37–62.

Taavitsainen, Irma (2010) 'Discourse and genre dynamics in Early Modern English medical writing', in Irma Taavitsainen and Päivi Pahta (eds), *Early Modern English Medical Texts: Corpus Description and Studies*, Amsterdam: John Benjamins, 29–53.

Taavitsainen, Irma (2012) 'Historical pragmatics', in Alex Bergs and Laurel Brinton (eds), *Handbook of Historical Linguistics*, Berlin and New York: Mouton de Gruyter, 1457–74.

Taavitsainen, Irma, and Susan Fitzmaurice (2007) 'Historical pragmatics: What it is and how to do it', in Susan M. Fitzmaurice and Irma Taavitsainen (eds), *Methodological Issues in Historical Pragmatics*, Berlin: Mouton de Gruyter, 11–36.

Taavitsainen, Irma, and Andreas H. Jucker (2007) 'Speech act verbs and speech acts in the history of English', in Susan M. Fitzmaurice and Irma Taavitsainen (eds), *Methods in Historical Pragmatics*, Berlin: Mouton de Gruyter, 107–38.

Taavitsainen, Irma, and Andreas H. Jucker (2008) '"Methinks you seem more beautiful than ever": Compliments and gender in the history of English', in Andreas H. Jucker, and Irma Taavitsainen (eds), *Speech Acts in the History of English* (Pragmatics & Beyond New Series 176), Amsterdam and Philadelphia: John Benjamins, 195–228.

Taavitsainen, Irma, and Andreas H. Jucker (2010) 'Expressive speech acts and politeness in eighteenth-century English', in Raymond Hickey (ed.), *Eighteenth-Century English: Ideology and Change* (Studies in English Language), Cambridge: Cambridge University Press, 159–81.

Taavitsainen, Irma, and Päivi Pahta (2000) 'Conventions of professional writing: The modern medical case report in a historical perspective', *Journal of English Linguistics* 28.1, 60–76.

Taavitsainen, Irma, and Päivi Pahta (eds) (2004) *Medical and Scientific Writing in English 1375–1500*, Cambridge: Cambridge University Press.

Taavitsainen, Irma and Pahta, Päivi (eds) (2010) *Early Modern English Medical Texts: Corpus Description and Studies.* Compiled by Irma Taavitsainen, Päivi Pahta, Turo Hiltunen, Ville Marttila, Martti Mäkinen, Maura Ratia, Carla Suhr and Jukka Tyrkkö, with software by Raymond Hickey. Amsterdam and Philadelphia: John Benjamins. CD-ROM with an accompanying book.

Taavitsainen, Irma, and Päivi Pahta (eds) (2011) *Medical Writing in Early Modern English*, Cambridge: Cambridge University Press.

Taavitsainen, Irma, Turo Hiltunen, Anu Lehto, Ville Marttila, Martti Mäkinen, Raisa Oinonen, Päivi Pahta, Maura Ratia, Carla Suhr and Jukka Tyrkkö (compilers) (forthcoming) *Late Modern English Medical Texts 1700–1800* (LMEMT).

Todorov, Tzvetan (1990) *Genres in Discourse*, Cambridge: Cambridge University Press.

Toolan, Michael (1998) *Language in Literature: An Introduction to Stylistics*, London: Hodder.

Toolan, Michael (2001) *Narrative: A Critical Linguistic Introduction*, 2nd edn, London and New York: Routledge.

Toolan, Michael (2009) *Narrative Progression in the Short Story: A Corpus Stylistic Approach*, Amsterdam: John Bejamins.

Traugott, Elizabeth Closs (1995) 'Subjectification in grammaticalisation', in Dieter Stein and Susan Wright (eds), *Subjectivity and Subjectivisation. Linguistic Perspectives*, Cambridge: Cambridge University Press, 31–54.

Traugott, Elizabeth Closs (2004) 'Historical pragmatics', in Laurence R. Horn and Gregory Ward (eds), *The Handbook of Pragmatics*, Oxford: Blackwell, 538–61.

Traugott, Elizabeth Closs (2008) 'The state of English language studies: A linguistic perspective', in Marainne Thormählen (ed.), *English Now. Selected Papers from the 20th IAUPE Conference in Lund 2007*, Lund: Lund Studies in English, 199–225.

Traugott, Elizabeth Closs (2010) 'Grammaticalization', in Andreas H. Jucker and Irma Taavitsainen (eds), *Historical Pragmatics* (Handbooks of Pragmatics 8), Berlin and New York: De Gruyter Mouton, 97–126.

Traugott, Elizabeth Closs, and Richard B. Dasher (2005) *Regularity in Semantic Change*, Cambridge: Cambridge University Press.

Trevisa, John (1975) *John Trevisa's* Translation of Bartholomaeus Anglicus de Propietatibus Rerum. Vol. 1: *A Critical Text.* M. C. Seymour (Gen. Ed.), Oxford: Clarendon Press.

Trosborg, Anna (1995) *Interlanguage Pragmatics. Requests, Complaints and Apologies*, Berlin: Mouton de Gruyter.

Truss, Lynne (2003) *Eats, Shoots & Leaves: The Zero Tolerance Approach to Punctuation*, London: Profile Books.

Ungerer, Friedrich (2002) 'When news stories are not longer just stories: The emergence of the top-down structure in news reports in English newspapers', in Andreas Fischer, Gunnel Tottie and Hans Martin Lehmann (eds), *Text Types and Corpora. Studies in Honour of Udo Fries*, Tübingen: Gunter Narr, 91–104.

Valkonen, Petteri (2008) 'Showing a little promise: Identifying and retrieving explicit illocutionary acts from a corpus of written prose', in Andreas H. Jucker, and Irma Taavitsainen (eds), *Speech Acts in the History of English* (Pragmatics & Beyond New Series 176), Amsterdam and Philadelphia: John Benjamins, 247–72.

Vasko, Anna-Liisa (2010) *Cambridgeshire Dialect Grammar* (Studies in Variation, Contacts and Change in English 4), Helsinki: Research Unit for Variation, Contact and Change in English. http://www.helsinki.fi/varieng/journal/volumes/04/

Verschueren, Jef (1999) *Understanding Pragmatics* (Understanding Language Series), London: Arnold.

Verschueren, Jef, Jan-Ola Östman, Jan Blommaert and Chris Bulcaen (eds) (2003) *Handbook of Pragmatics Online*, Amsterdam: John Benjamins.

Walker, Terry (2007) Thou *and* You *in Early Modern English Dialogues. Trials, Depositions, and Drama Comedy* (Pragmatics & Beyond New Series 158), Amsterdam and Philadelphia: John Benjamins.

Watts, Richard J. (1999) 'Language and politeness in early eighteenth century Britain', in Manfred Kienpointer (ed.), *Ideologies of Politeness*. Special issue of *Pragmatics* 9.1, 5–20.

Watts, Richard J. (2003) *Politeness* (Key Topics in Sociolinguistics), Cambridge: Cambridge University Press.

Werlich, Egon (1982) *A Text Grammar of English* (UTB 597), 2nd edn (1st edn 1974), Heidelberg: Quelle & Meyer.

Wierzbicka, Anna (2006) 'Anglo scripts against "putting pressure" on other people and their linguistic manifestations', in Cliff Goddard (ed.), *Ethnopragmatics. Understanding Discourse in Cultural Context*, Berlin: Mouton de Gruyter, 31–64.

Williams, Graham (2010) '"trobled wth a tedious discours": Sincerity, sarcasm and seriousness in the letters of Maria Thynne, c. 1601–1610', *Journal of Historical Pragmatics* 11.2, 169–93.

Würzbach, Natascha (1990) *The Rise of the English Street Ballad, 1550–1650*, Cambridge: Cambridge University Press.

Index